HOSPITALITY 2010
The Future of Hospitality and Travel

HOSPITALITY 2010
The Future of Hospitality and Travel

Marvin Cetron
Fred DeMicco
Owen Davies

PEARSON

Prentice
Hall

Upper Saddle River, NJ 07458

Library of Congress Cataloging-in-Publication Data

Cetron, Marvin J.
  Hospitality 2010: the future of hospitality and travel / Marvin Cetron, Fred
DeMicco, Owen Davies.—1st ed.
    p. cm.
  Includes bibliographical references.
  ISBN 0-13-147579-7
  1. Hospitality industry. 2. Tourism. I. DeMicco, Fred. II. Davies, Owen.
III. Title.

  TX911.C42 2006
  647.94--dc22

2004028354

Executive Editor: Vernon R. Anthony
Editorial Assistant: Beth Dyke
Senior Marketing Manager: Ryan DeGrote
Senior Marketing Coordinator: Elizabeth
  Farrell
Marketing Assistant: Les Roberts
Director of Manufacturing and Production:
  Bruce Johnson
Managing Editor: Mary Carnis
Production Liaison: Jane Bonnell
Production Editor: Mike Remillard, Pine Tree
  Composition

Manufacturing Manager: Ilene Sanford
Manufacturing Buyer: Cathleen Petersen
Creative Director: Cheryl Asherman
Senior Design Coordinator: Miguel Ortiz
Cover Design: Joseph DePinho, dePINHO
  DESIGN
Cover Image: Patricia De La Rosa, Getty
  Images/Stone
Composition: Pine Tree Composition
Printer/Binder: Phoenix Book Tech Park
Cover Printer: Phoenix Book Tech Park

Pearson Education LTD.
Pearson Education Australia PTY, Limited
Pearson Education Singapore, Pte. Ltd.
Pearson Education North Asia Ltd.
Pearson Education Canada, Ltd.
Pearson Educación de Mexico, S.A. de C.V.
Pearson Education–Japan
Pearson Education Malaysia, Pte. Ltd.

10 9 8 7 6 5 4 3 2 1
ISBN 0-13-147579-7

To our families.

We hope it will be a very hospitable future for them.

Contents

Foreword

In a fast-changing world, there are a few enduring issues that people in any business must focus on if they are to be successful. This book deals with one of them. Here I want to consider another.

The first issue, and the subject of this volume, is change itself. When today's senior executives were beginning their careers, we were just starting to understand that something new was abroad in the world, a process of transformation that our parents had not recognized and our grandparents had not faced. After World War II, most people had expected things to go "back to normal." Twenty-five years later, many of us were still adapting to the idea that it was not to be.

The process of constant change began earlier—arguably much earlier—but it became a way of life in the 1950s, when American executives fanned out across the world, spreading the gospel of capitalism; their students built Germany, Japan, and other countries into mighty international competitors. People whose grandparents had been born, lived, and died on the family farm began following their jobs from Nebraska to Texas to New York and Oregon. Tiny restaurants specializing in hamburgers and fried chicken spawned vast chains that transformed the world's eating habits. Hotels proliferated to meet the growing demand for accommodations. First airlines and then telecommunications knitted the world together into one global economy. Hospitality companies were born, grew, shrank, merged, and grew some more.

Somewhere along the way, we came to understand that change is now a permanent part of our lives, and one that is moving faster every day. No one can manage a business or plan a career without being able to anticipate where technology, demographics, and other transforming forces will lead us. Unfortunately, making successful forecasts has been a difficult skill to learn, not only because forecasting itself is challenging, but because few specific resources have been available to help with the task.

This is where *Hospitality 2010* shines. Marvin Cetron is a pioneer of forecasting, with a remarkable record of successful predictions in business, technology, politics, and lifestyles; he has been working with hospitality executives to project the course of our industry for some 30 years. Fred DeMicco is one of the leading educators specializing in the hospitality industry, and he too has demonstrated a consistent ability to anticipate our needs. If anyone can teach practical forecasting for hospitality and show us what lies ahead, these authors are the obvious choices.

In fact, they have managed this task remarkably well. In the pages ahead, the authors explain the basics of forecasting as it is done by one of the art's most capable practitioners. Then they examine specific areas of hospitality—airlines, hotels, restaurants, and others—and spell out where current trends are leading our industry. By the time you are done reading, you should have a much better sense of what lies ahead and be ready to begin making sound forecasts of your own.

However, change is not the only critical issue in hospitality. It is not even the most important, as the authors themselves clearly recognize. More than any other, the hospitality industry exists to provide service to its customers. The quality of our service is the issue that dominates my work day, and the one that I want to consider here. It is the issue that should most concern you.

There was a time when hospitality providers could compete effectively on the basis of location and price. Today, multiple hotels are available almost anywhere people want to stay, and the Internet enables consumers to find the lowest price for everything they buy or do. Much of the same trend is seen in other branches of the hospitality industry.

This competitive pressure has begun to remove the traditional selling points from the customer's decision making. For repeat guests, the most important issue is how satisfied they were on their last visit. For new patrons, one of the most important is the reputation we have built among other consumers. That is where service comes in. It is the one area left in which we can distinguish ourselves from everyone else who wants the customer's business.

When we look at trends in the hospitality industry, we are trying to anticipate, more than anything else, what services our guests will value in the future. Then we must figure out how best to meet those changing needs. This is a constant challenge.

There are eight insights that can help companies improve their performance. They form a "how-to" for better customer service that everyone in the hospitality industry should keep in mind.

1. Build a strong foundation.

Service does not happen in a vacuum; it grows out of a complete mastery of the basics. Just for a start, you need to know the strengths and weaknesses of your own business, understanding what is necessary and doing it well. For a restaurant, this can mean anything from providing quick and accurate service at the drive-through to visiting the docks as the fishing boats arrive to select the absolute best of the day's catch. The details vary with the business; only the mandate is constant.

If there are problems, they need to be caught and fixed quickly. Left unattended, they will alienate customers and harm your reputation.

Finally, get to know your guests personally. Customers always come back to a restaurant whose maitre d' addresses them by name and recalls what they enjoyed a year earlier. Fortunately, computers now can bring this kind of personalized service within reach of hotel and restaurant staff even if they lack such a remarkable memory themselves.

All this boils down to a single piece of advice: Be brilliant on the basics. It requires no more than constant, almost obsessive, attention to detail from every member of your staff.

2. Make every customer feel special.

Customers are individuals, and they should be treated as such. This means giving them choices wherever possible, making them feel important, and building personal relationships with them. (See the previous rule.) Treat customers like family, and they will keep coming back.

3. Have the courage to set bold goals.

It is no longer enough to be good at what you do. Continued success requires constant improvement, and often the development of entirely new abilities to meet your customers' changing needs.

This is a mandate for setting long-term goals. Make broad plans to meet your customers' needs. Then choose concrete targets, begin work immediately to achieve them, and make sure that your people have the tools they need to get the job done.

It often helps to bring in someone from outside to provide a fresh perspective or to aid in accomplishing your objectives. Talk to people from other departments. Recruit suppliers and vendors to help. Even work with competitors when it will bring mutual benefit.

4. Simplify, simplify, simplify.

This is a powerful idea, and it reaches into all aspects of your business. Think of the craftsmen of an earlier era. Their priorities were clear and few: Deal with people plainly and honestly, and give customers what they want without needless complications. And if some other rule or procedure gets in the way, bend it, break it, or get rid of it entirely. Those priorities made things simple for the craftsman and easy for his customer. They can do the same for your company today.

Make each decision pass a litmus test. Is this good for our people, customers, and profits? If it's good for all three, then do it. If it's good for two, talk about it. If it's good for one, you should probably skip it. And if it doesn't add value, eliminate it.

That kind of simplicity will make your company more efficient and your customers happier.

5. Make technology your servant.

In the 1980s and early 1990s, many executives seemed to think of technology as a kind of magic: Buy some computers, and your business would suddenly be more profitable. It did not work out that way.

Technology adds value only when it helps you meet the customer's needs. It does so by gathering useful information—for example, customer feedback, which should be collected and acted on within 24 hours—and routing it to the people who can apply it. Make sure that technology is easy for your staff to use—the people who will have to work with your IT system should help design it—and transparent for your customers.

Used properly, technology can be a powerful ally in giving each customer a highly personalized experience, and this can be one of your most valuable tools in cultivating repeat business. This is one place where the authors' forecasts directly advance the quest for better service. Several of the chapters ahead offer concrete suggestions for using technology to individualize your dealings with customers.

6. Measure well, act fast.

One purpose of technology is to measure things so that you can act on them. How close are you to meeting your goals? How satisfied are your customers? What are their most important needs? If you don't know—and by that I mean if you do not have sound quantitative data for analysis—you have little hope of doing better. But with the data that technology provides, you can focus your efforts on the areas that will do you and your customers the most good.

One critical area for measurement is customer *dis*satisfaction. Only about 5 percent of dissatisfied customers will actually complain about what bothers them. However, seven out of ten will tell their friends what a bad job you did. (Contrast that with the number who will tell their friends what a *good* job you did: only 30 percent!) In the age of the Internet, those "friends" may be thousands of people all over the world, and a single negative report on the right Web site can deter motivated consumers for years.

Fortunately, measuring results quickly and accurately also makes it easier to deal with complaints fast, and to build personal relationships with your customers. And their emotional response to that kind of service can turn them into loyal visitors for years to come.

7. Unleash the power of people.

This process begins when you first think about recruiting a new worker. Begin by analyzing your best performers and figuring out what makes them special. Then you can hire people like them. You will look for basic skills, but chances are that you will wind up hiring for passion and personality.

Once on staff, your people deserve your trust, respect, and support. They require recognition when they do well, training when it is needed (and not when it isn't, or they will lose interest), and the authority to work like they own the place.

That last requirement is becoming more important every day. As the authors point out later in this book, today's younger workers have a powerful need to do things their own way. So long as they accomplish the company's goals, how they do it must increasingly be up to them. Loyalty to employers is foreign to under-40 employees; you will have to give them all the leeway you can to keep them working efficiently.

8. Lead with care.

Leaders create an environment in which people make an effort because they want to do their job, rather than because they must. The leader's role is to provide inspiration, integrity, and vision. There are two keys here: how you treat employees and how you treat yourself.

This late in our discussion, it should be clear how successful leaders deal with employees. They give workers the power to make decisions and trust them to make good ones. They pare away needless rules that can leave workers feeling harried, underappreciated, and stifled in their jobs. They live up to their commitments. In short, they treat workers like family. Do this consistently, and workers will consistently give you their best.

How successful leaders treat themselves is less obvious. A good place to start is by seeking out a mentor who has already mastered the art of firing his own enthusiasm. Take time off from work to recharge by spending time with friends, family, and hobbies. Then go back to work refreshed and ready. A leader's passion for the job is one of his company's most precious assets. It deserves the same care that he gives the firm's property, personnel, and customers.

The future is about quality and service. Exactly what that means depends on your business. For a hotel or resort, it can be developing the friendliest, most informative data systems so that guests can make reservations effortlessly over the Internet and your staff will "remember" their preferences from previous visits. For a quick-service restaurant, it can be providing an extra drive-through lane to speed traffic and installing better loudspeakers so that customers and staff can understand each other. For full-service restaurants, it might be improving the menu, listing calories and carb counts not only for the entrees but for salad dressings and other options. New possibilities will arise daily, as your customers' needs change and technology brings new ways to meet them.

The ideas above provide a framework for your efforts, and the chapters ahead can help you to anticipate future needs. Yet in the end, your own attention to detail will be the most important factor in your company's success.

Marv Cetron tells of staying at a top-of-the-line hotel, part of a chain that is well known for its devotion to quality and customer service. One of the chain's customer-pleasing efforts was a money-back guarantee that room service would deliver breakfast in ten minutes. While waiting for his breakfast one morning, Marv happened to open the door to the hall—and there was the waiter, looking at his watch and carefully counting down so that he could deliver the rapidly cooling meal in exactly ten minutes, just as the company had promised!

No matter how hard you try, there is always some way to make your service just a little bit better. Identifying that opportunity can be a challenge, but your customers will appreciate the results. So will your bottom line.

Roger Dow
President and Chief Executive Officer
Travel Industry Association of America (T.I.A.A.)

Acknowledgments

That only the authors get to put their names on a book's cover is one of life's great inequities. Invariably, there are many others whose contributions deserve equally public acclaim. Yet it falls to us to recognize their efforts here, on an unjustly inconspicuous inner page. So be it. In no particular order, we wish to thank:

Vernon R. Anthony, our skilled and patient editor at Prentice Hall, whose guidance and encouragement were critical factors in bringing this effort to fruition.

Beth Dyke, editorial assistant at Prentice Hall, without whose diligent efforts *Hospitality 2010* would still be in preparation.

Roger Dow, president and CEO of the Travel Industry Association of America. His generosity in sharing his unique insights into the hospitality industry, and in contributing a sterling Foreword, made this a far better and more useful book.

Ilsa Whittemore, executive editor of *HSMAI Marketing Review*, for encouraging us to write the columns on which this work was based, and too often for her patience while those columns were in the works.

Justin Cetron and Wayne Jackson, undergraduate and master's students, respectively, with the University of Delaware hospitality program. Their long hours of research provided most of Appendices C, D, and E and useful data for other portions of the book.

And Mike Remillard and his colleagues at Pine Tree Composition, who converted our manuscript to the printed page quickly, efficiently, and without so much as a typo that we were able to find—an amazing performance!

No doubt many others should have been included here, and we apologize for their omission. Our thanks to them all. They deserve much of the credit for all that is good about *Hospitality 2010*.

Of course, the blame for any mistakes of fact or interpretation rests solely with the authors.

HOSPITALITY 2010
The Future of Hospitality and Travel

Part I

Common Concerns
for the Hospitality Industry

Chapter 1

Practical Prophecy
for Beginners

Do you worry when attending meetings off the beaten path? Imagine being taken hostage by terrorists while vacationing in the Middle East or visiting a supplier in South America? Limit your options to jobs or investments in the United States, because you never know what's going to happen in foreign lands, even when they appear to be stable?

Who could blame you? Whether you are a student thinking about graduate school abroad or a business executive scoping out foreign competition, national stability is one of the most important factors to consider in making plans that involve other countries. It also can be one of the most difficult. After all, stability is not a single factor, but a complicated vector sum of economic conditions, demographic trends, political forces, religion, technology, personalities—an endless list of factors. If revolutions, coups, wars, and weapons tests regularly take the CIA by surprise, how can you be expected to know what's brewing in far-away places with strange-sounding names?

That reasoning applies just as well to a host of other problems you will inevitably face in a career in the hospitality industry. How will demographic changes affect the food preferences of diners at mid-priced restaurants? How will technology continue to change hotel management? What can you expect from the economy over the next one, five, or ten years? You will encounter these and many similar issues in the years ahead. And despite the CIA's problems, you will be expected to assess them correctly.

We can help. In fact, that is the whole purpose of this book.

Over some five decades of work, Forecasting International (FI)—the firm founded by one of the authors and long employing another—has spent much of its time evaluating the stability of nations for clients ranging from the Department of Defense to *Fortune* 500 companies to foreign governments. In the process, we have managed to anticipate calamities that took many onlookers by surprise, from the fundamentalist revolution in Iran to the Los Angeles riots in the wake of the Rodney King beating.

The credit goes to a series of tools and techniques that make it possible to evaluate the vital signs of the future, much as a doctor takes your temperature and blood pressure to evaluate your health. They can ease your worries—or steer you out of potential trouble.

CONSULTING THE ORACLE

One common forecasting technique is the Delphi survey or poll. In a Delphi poll, a panel of experts fills out a questionnaire designed to elicit their views about the issues under study. The answers from this first survey are then circulated among participants, and the poll is repeated. In the second round of questioning, participants reconsider their original views in light of the opinions of their peers. This usually results in a narrower range of replies and a more "solid" consensus, as the extreme views are mitigated by further thought, and perhaps a bit of peer pressure. The Delphi technique has been used in several thousand studies and is generally held to produce the most reliable analyses and forecasts available.

Forecasting International has used Delphi studies with considerable success in a wide variety of fields. However, we often modify the basic method by including a number of participants who are professional forecasters, rather than subject specialists. This change frequently produces useful results that a more narrowly focused study might overlook. The forecasters tend to consider data from other fields that the specialists would not, and their insights trigger new ideas from the specialists in the second round of questioning.

For example, we consulted both forecasters and subject specialists for a study of future terrorism carried out for the Department of Defense in 1994. Nearly seven years before the September 11 attacks, we were able to predict virtually the entire course of terrorism as it has developed since then. Specific predictions included the rise of international terrorism based in the Muslim extremist movement; a second, much more successful attack on the World Trade Center; a terrorist incident in the Midwest by an American-born extremist connected to the militia movement; and even the deliberate crash of an airplane into the Pentagon. (The State Department made us omit that last item for fear of giving someone ideas.) In reviewing this study, we concluded that it would not have been nearly so wide-ranging and accurate if it had been limited to terrorism specialists. This experience has led us to adopt this more inclusive kind of study panel whenever we use the Delphi technique.

FICTIONAL FUTURES

Another useful tool is the scenario. *Webster's* first definition of the word *scenario* is "an outline or synopsis of a play." As descriptions borrowed from other fields go, this one is not bad. Scenarios are portraits of alternative futures that might conceivably develop from today's world. They are not forecasts in that we do not expect tomorrow's reality to resemble them, save in limited and unpredictable ways. A good scenario can make us see the evolution of a future we would scarcely recognize if we were magically transported into the middle of it.

That is very much their purpose. Scenarios often are used in developing forecasts, to help identify issues that need further research. They also can broaden our imaginations, allowing us to envision a wider range of possible futures. Sometimes we use them to broaden the imaginations of our clients, enabling them to consider forecasts that they otherwise might find too "far out" to be taken seriously.

Scenarios begin with drivers, a defined set of forces that we choose to examine. Will new technologies dominate future society? Will the capitalist economic model continue to spread throughout the world? Will a sudden change of heart sweep across the globe, so that environmentalism guides our decisions? Scenarios can spin out any combination of postulates, each one leading to a different, yet convincing, future. The only limitation is that scenarios must be internally consistent. A scenario of economic decline, for example, is unlikely to include full employment or a wealthy middle class; joblessness and privation are the order of that future day.

One of the most commonly used scenarios, and one that has had a powerful influence on the work of Forecasting International, is the 2050 Global Normative Scenario, evolved by the United Nations Millennium Project. It represents a consensus vision of the future compiled from the ideas of over 1,000 participants in a continuing attempt to anticipate what is to come. In the Millennium Project's scenario, the world of 2050 has changed in many ways. Predictably, it is driven and dominated by science and technology. The Internet, biotechnology, nanomachines, and space all have contributed to this prosperous new world. In all, technology, global communications, human development, and enlightened economic policies have worked together to make the world a better place than seemed possible at the end of the 20th century.

Another tool uses three scenarios: one optimistic, one pessimistic, and one that deliberately parts company with most of the trends we see around us today. These scenarios grew from the work of the Global Scenario Group of the Stockholm Environmental Institute. Over the last few years, the Brookings Institute, the Santa Fe Initiative, and FI all have employed them in a wide variety of contexts. They are commonly known as "Market World," "Fortress World," and "Transformed World."

"Market World" projects a glowing capitalist vision of economic reform and technological innovation. In this scenario, developing regions are quickly integrated into the global economy. Countries privatize government-run industries, cut through tangled regulations, trim public spending, and let the market have its way. In the real world, this formula has turned many backward Asian lands into industrial powers.

"Fortress World" represents the dark side of capitalism. Economies grow rapidly, but the boom leaves whole regions of the world untouched. The poor become poorer. The environment suffers. Terrorism grows. By 2050, all we can see ahead is growing desperation and violence as what little remains of the social contract continues to disintegrate.

"Transformed World" steps outside the either/or of capitalist vision and nightmare. In this scenario, a pragmatic idealism replaces consumer society's will to get and spend with an altruistic desire to provide for basic human needs and the shared vision of a better life for all. Environmentalism prospers. Urban crime, drug use, and poverty decline as education, employment, and the city environment improve. By 2050 democracy has become almost universal. With many shared values and general tolerance for what differences remain, the world has all but achieved a single global civilization. It is a stable and happy place at last.

These three scenarios are largely generic, and that is much of their value. In the process of adapting them for each study, we often learn things that would not turn up in a more straightforward examination of the future. Dozens of forecasts have been performed for the hospitality industry. So far as we know, none of them anticipated the sudden collapse of travel that followed the September 11 terrorist attacks, nor the effect of SARS on Asia. These are insights that could have been derived only by asking "What if?" And that is the realm of the scenario.

IF THIS GOES ON . . .

One of the most valuable forecasting techniques is trend analysis. It comes in two forms: trend extrapolation and trend correlation. The basic idea of trend extrapolation is that the changes we see happening around us are likely to continue, and the future will grow out of them. Any reasonable forecast has to assume that technology will continue to deliver new miracles, that countries where birthrates are out of control are likely to have much larger populations in the years ahead, and so on. We need good reasons to deviate from those straight-line projections, and those reasons can be among the most useful insights derived from a study.

Trend correlation is even simpler in principle. Some trends follow others. Thus, when you know where one trend is headed, you can be reasonably sure about the other. For example, a rise in the number of construction permits issued in a community reliably foretells an increase in the number of buildings built. A rise in birthrates presages a long-term increase in the demand for housing, schools, and eventually hotels, restaurants, and other aspects of the hospitality industry.

About fifteen years ago, we developed a unique tool to help with trend analysis. You will find it in Appendix A. After nearly thirty years in forecasting, we reviewed what we knew about the future and condensed our knowledge into a list of trends that we could see changing the world. We have updated that list frequently over the years. The number of entries varies from time to time as trends mature and die and new forces arise to shift the course of events. At the moment, FI is tracking 52 major trends in world politics, technology, national and international economies, and other important aspects of global society. These are the broad forces that will help to shape the future, and they give us a necessary context in which to consider any specific subject.

Since developing our list of trends, we have used them to predict the future of companies, industries, and entire countries. In each study, we look at the specific circumstances of the subject—say, the hospitality industry—and try to figure out how they will interact with the broader trends. How will the economy affect them? What about demographics, technology, and changing societal values?

Trend extrapolation does have its limitations. Unlike scenarios, this is not a technique for "thinking the unthinkable," as the pioneering forecaster Herman Kahn wrote in a book about nuclear war. Over time, surprises occur that cumulatively change the course of events. Barring a surprise on the scale of September 11, forecasts are likely to be very accurate over the next year or two, slightly less accurate over five years, significantly off course after ten years, and seriously wrong twenty years ahead. However, extrapolating trends can be useful even for long-range forecasts, because the process itself helps us to identify the areas in which surprises are most likely to occur and will have the greatest impact. In this way, it provides a basic framework for understanding the future.

Trend analysis is the most valuable tool we have for charting the most likely path of future events. The chapters ahead all grew out of this process.

NATIONAL STABILITY

In an age of terrorism, and for an industry that is exposed to risks all over the world, one of the most important issues is the stability of foreign lands. Do we dare to put a new hotel, resort, or restaurant in a given country? Should we consider moving out of existing operations there? Can airlines and cruise ships safely stop at its air and sea ports? We have seen all too often that a country that appears stable today can erupt into violence almost without warning.

And yet, there invariably are subtle warnings, if only we recognize them. Identifying them, and figuring out what they mean, is one more job for forecasting.

For this purpose, we supplement our trends with a series of indicators that we collect for each country under study. These include a wide range of economic, demographic, technological, and military data. Virtually all of them are readily available. After half a century of working with classified information under government contracts, we have found that at least 95 percent—and probably closer to 98 percent—of what you need to know comes from unclassified sources.

Whenever possible, we like to find the same information from two or more independent authorities, just for confirmation. We use the Bureau of Labor Statistics and the U.S. Census for economic and demographic data, Jane's for military data, the Worldwatch Institute for environmental data, and *The Economist* and *Christian Science Monitor* for a wide variety of information. Other useful sources include Web sites operated by the United Nations, the World Bank, and the International Monetary Fund. We read *The Futurist* as well, for invaluable background in thinking of things to come.

The indicators in Appendix B: Vital Signs for National Security have proved to be extraordinarily useful and versatile. Not all indicators are important for every nation. Each must be weighted according to the conditions in the country at hand, and thus far that is largely a task for experience and human judgment.

FI tracks more than forty indicators that can be valuable in evaluating the stability of a nation, and for a definitive analysis we wish to include as many of them as possible. Yet for a quicker, and still very good, investigation, the list can be pared significantly. The accompanying tables give basic data for a number of important countries.

As they stand, these tables have important limitations. For a practical study, we would have to fill in some gaps.

Only the most prominent countries in each category are included in each table. The United States is listed in the tables for GDP and nuclear warheads, for example, but its oil reserves and number of environmental treaties are omitted, while Indonesia appears only in the tables of the opacity index and number of trouble-prone young men. For a real-world study, the missing data would have to be added. Fortunately, nearly all these figures can be found readily on the Internet.

In these tables, the countries are simply rank-ordered. The land with the greatest supply of water per person, the largest GDP, or whatever stands in first position, with the remainder trailing down the table. For practical work, we would need to weight each indicator to reflect its significance to the country. For example, the United States does not appear on the list of nations with the largest oil reserves, yet that very lack of supply is extremely important to the economy. Iceland has more fresh water per person than any other country on the planet, but this asset has not given it prominence on the global stage.

Weighting these factors correctly sometimes requires practice, but simple logic will carry us through most studies. It helps not to view the data as a mass of discrete facts but as elements in a complex network of mutual influences. You will get the hang of it.

Most importantly, the data presented here are single points. They present a snapshot of each country, when a video would tell us much more. For any study we carried out at FI, we would look not at GDP or military spending, but at trends in those data. The whole point of forecasting is not to find out where the subject stands, but where it is going.

For a better idea of how this works, let us take a country and see what we can find out about it. We will look at Britain, which is globally significant and is represented in many of the tables. On the way by, we will supplement the tables with data that is readily available online, and perhaps with some of our own background information.

For a start, the United Kingdom has a GDP of $1.52 billion, making it the seventh largest in the world. A quick look at the online edition of the *CIA World FactBook* shows that this translates to a comfortable $25,500 per capita, which places Britain at roughly the same level as France and Germany, a bit behind Japan, and significantly behind the United States.

Britain is a major exporting country, sixth in the world, and ranks sixth in the World Economic Forum's index of business competitiveness. When you think about it, that is a remarkably good performance. Britain exports over 39 percent as much goods, in dollar terms, as the United States with less than 21 percent of the population. Of course, the other way to look at it is that the United States is so large and prosperous that it can use most of its products at home.

One other economic factor seems interesting. Britain still has not adopted the euro, the currency of nearly all its partners in the European Union. This means that its companies may face some risks from currency exchange even when they trade within the EU. It also suggests that some people visiting the continent from abroad may decide to stay there, rather than going through the hassle of converting their money to pounds Sterling in order to see England, while those who visit Britain may not travel further. This is not likely to be more than a small handicap for the British hospitality industry, but it could be worth looking into in a more thorough study.

In resources, the United Kingdom does not have enough oil or fresh water to rank among the top ten in either table, and it is not among the ten largest exporters of farm products. However, it does rank as the *eleventh* largest agricultural exporter. This is an interesting accomplishment for a few small islands, and for some studies we might want to look into that further. In addition, we remember that Britain once pumped quite a bit of oil from the North Sea, and another check with the *CIA World FactBook* reveals that there are large reserves of coal and natural gas as well as oil, so that primary energy production contributes no less than 10 percent to the nation's GDP; this is one of the highest shares among the industrialized nations. It would be nice to know how long that oil can be expected to last, but we will ignore that issue for now.

The United Kingdom has a solid base in technology. Its scientists have won 47 Nobel prizes, compared with 137 for the United States and 49 for Germany. It ranks eighth in the number of Internet users, despite a relative shortage of personal computers. There have been news stories, too, in the last few years that some American scientists are emigrating to Britain, where they can experiment with cloning and perform stem-cell research without the restrictions placed on them in the United States. However, according to the table, in the number of patents granted it falls somewhere behind Luxembourg and Finland. This seems odd, and it might have something to do with patent law rather than inventiveness. It might also be that whoever compiled the table just skipped over the United Kingdom. Then again, it might not. Depending on the purpose of our study, this could be worth more research.

Britain also may have the kind of social base that contributes to a stable, economically successful society. With roughly two rooms per person, it ranks in fourth place for its housing supply. However, the U.N. Human Development Index does not seem to rate its quality of life among the top ten, and it lags in the number of university students per 100,000 population. This data category also may justify more study.

Militarily, the United Kingdom is the world's third-largest spender; yet the budget for its armed forces is barely more than one-tenth that of the United States. It is the sixth-largest weapons exporter, though only 18 percent as large in this market as the United States and 12 percent as large as Russia. And with 200 warheads, it owns a significant nuclear deterrent.

Diplomatically, Britain is a permanent member of the United Nations Security Council, which gives it much more power than mere size would suggest. It also ranks fifth among the world's donors of foreign aid, which confers some status of its own. It does not rank in the top nine signatories of environmental treaties, but what that indicates will not be clear without further study.

Britain's opacity index is only 38, signifying that its business and political operations are relatively open to public scrutiny. This tends to be a sign of basic stability, as the governments of unstable countries seldom want anyone watching their actions too closely.

The table of young-male populations does not include the United Kingdom. (It is not a top-ten list, but a group of countries that interested us when it was compiled.) However, the UN's World Population Prospects database (http://esa.un.org/unpp/index.asp?panel=2) reports that in 2000 there were 5.5 million males in the violence-prone ages between 15 and 29, or about 9.3 percent of the total population. This is roughly the same as Egypt and India, which are not the world's most stable places. This may be one country where the indicator should be weighted less heavily than in other lands.

Culturally, data from the movie industry suggest that Britain consumes the good-life fantasies of Hollywood more than it exports its own. It ranks seventh in the number of movie tickets sold each year, third in the motion-picture industry. However, it is not among the top ten producers of feature films.

Without going into depth, the data we have collected thus far paints a picture of the United Kingdom as a significant economic, military, and diplomatic power in the world. It also suggests that we can expect Britain to remain economically comfortable, stable, and influential for some time to come. In a formal research project, we would collect much more data and try to fill in the details of this quick impression.

However, even this brief—extremely brief—study raises some interesting questions:

How long will that North Sea oil last? And how will the economy react when it runs out? Will Britain's environment suffer if the country reverts to burning coal? Will the United Kingdom become as dependent as the United States on oil from the Middle East? We clearly have more work to do in this area.

How long can Britain remain a global economic leader? The world increasingly depends on technology, and the United Kingdom does not seem to be producing all that many college graduates. Can it maintain a strong technology base without them? Does Britain have some alternative way of training engineers and technicians that does not show up on college data? Perhaps a system of technical schools, possibly supplemented by on-the-job training? Or does it rely on technologically sophisticated immigrants from India and other lands? For a serious study, we would have to know.

And what does that large population of young males indicate? The well-educated industrialized lands almost all have low birthrates. Does Britain have an unusually large, fertile immigrant population? If so, where are they from? Recent news reports have said that militant religious leaders in Britain may be attracting young Muslims to the *jihad* against the West, and even against their adopted homeland. How many of Britain's young men are potential converts to Muslim extremism? Flag this area for much more research! It could be critical to the economic and political stability of the United Kingdom, and to the safety of the hospitality industry there.

We see in these questions the power of trend data. Some of them would be answered if we were working with trends, rather than looking at single data points. That issue of how long the North Sea oil will last is an obvious example.

We see also the value offered by even a cursory look ahead. In a few minutes of thinking about the most basic data, we have identified several important issues that must be examined further before we can feel confident that our image of Britain will not change abruptly within just a few years. Forecasters often carry out such preliminary studies to learn whether a subject merits greater effort.

Most of us learn best by doing something, not by reading about it. So for a more valuable introduction to forecasting, why not try this on your own? Pick a country, and make your own forecast. Gather the necessary data, see what the trends and indicators imply for it, and evaluate that nation's stability and future. Then see how things are likely to evolve over the next ten years or so, and try to figure out the merits of siting a new hotel or resort there. This exercise will give you a far better sense of how much can be accomplished using publicly available data and relatively simple methods of analysis.

If you want a really interesting challenge, try looking at India. It is a huge country, with an extraordinarily varied population and culture, and it is changing rapidly in ways that are likely to be felt around the world. Compare India with China, and you will have seen the future of one of the world's most important bilateral relationships, two of its largest and fastest growing markets, and 40 percent of its population.

LOOKING AHEAD

In a fast-changing world, the cost of being unprepared seems to grow every day. A glance at eight-track tapes or a beta-format VCR moldering in the attic, or the memory of buying tech stocks just before the NASDAQ crash, should be enough to convince anyone that we all need better information about the future.

It is available. With a little effort, we can diagnose the future as a doctor diagnoses a patient. The vital signs are there to be read.

This chapter can provide only a brief sample of the ways in which forecasting methods such as our trends and indicators can be used to anticipate developments affecting the hospitality industry, and in turn many aspects of our own lives and careers. It should be a good place to start your own study of the subjects that concern you, and a guide to the kind of reasoning that can give you a leg up in many other fields as well.

"If only I had known then what I know today. . . ." How often have you heard that said? How often have you said it yourself? Learn to look ahead as forecasters do, and you may never say it again.

MILITARY INDICATORS

Table 1–1 Military Spending

Rank	Country	In billions
1	United States	$335.7
2	Japan	40.7
3	United Kingdom	36.0
4	France	33.6
5	China	31.1
6	Germany	27.7
7	Saudi Arabia	21.6
8	Italy	21.1
9	Iran	17.5
10	South Korea	13.5

Table 1–2 Nuclear Warheads

Rank	Country	Total
1	United States	10,640
2	Russia	8,600
3	China	400
4	France	350
5	United Kingdom	200
6	Israel	100–200 (est.)
7	India	30–35 (est.)
8	Pakistan	24–48 (est.)
9	North Korea	20–40 (est.)
10	Iran	?

Table 1–3 Weapons Exports

Rank	Country	In billions
1	Russia	$5.9
2	United States	3.9
3	France	1.6
4	China	0.8
5	Germany	0.7
6	United Kingdom	0.7
7	Italy	0.5
8	Canada	0.3
9	Ukraine	0.3
10	Netherlands	0.3

ECONOMIC INDICATORS

Table 1–4   Total GDP

Rank	Country	In billions
1	United States	$10,082
2	China	6,000
3	Japan	3,550
4	India	2,660
5	Germany	2,184
6	France	1,540
7	United Kingdom	1,520
8	Italy	1,438
9	Brazil	1,340
10	Russia	1,270

Table 1–5   Competitiveness*

Rank	Country	2002–03 rank
1	Finland	2
2	United States	1
3	Sweden	6
4	Denmark	8
5	Germany	4
6	United Kingdom	3
7	Switzerland	5
8	Singapore	9
9	Netherlands	7
10	France	15

*World Economic Forum Ranking of Business Competitiveness 2003–04

Table 1–6   Exports

Rank	Country	In billions
1	United States	$731
2	Germany	608
3	Japan	384
4	China	313
5	France	308
6	United Kingdom	286
7	Canada	261
8	Italy	259
9	Netherlands	222
10	Hong Kong	191

RESOURCE INDICATORS

Table 1–7   Oil Reserves

Rank	Country	Billions of barrels
1	Saudi Arabia	261.8
2	Canada	180.0
3	Iraq	112.5
4	UAE	97.8
5	Kuwait	96.5
6	Iran	89.7
7	Venezuela	77.8
8	Russia	60.0
9	Libya	29.5
10	Nigeria	24.0

Table 1–8   Freshwater Supplies

Rank	Country	Cubic meters per capita
1	Iceland	294.34
2	Gabon	176.37
3	Papua New Guinea	154.61
4	Canada	84.51
5	New Zealand	79.81
6	Liberia	58.85
7	Norway	57.71
8	Congo	53.89
9	Bolivia	51.39
10	Peru	47.55

Table 1–9   Agricultural Exports

Rank	Country	In billions
1	United States	$55.6
2	France	34.5
3	Netherlands	32.5
4	Germany	26.6
5	Belgium	18.6
6	Italy	17.5
7	Brazil	16.7
8	Canada	16.5
9	Spain	16.4
10	Australia	15.4

TECHNOLOGY INDICATORS

Table 1–10   Nobel Prizes in Science

Rank	Country	Total*
1	United States	137
2	Germany	49
3	United Kingdom	47
4	France	18
5	Netherlands	11
5	Russia/USSR	11
6	Switzerland	10
7	Japan	8
7	Sweden	8
8	Canada	6

* 1901–2003

Table 1–11   Patents Granted

Rank	Country	Per million people
1	Japan	994
2	South Korea	779
3	United States	289
4	Sweden	271
5	Germany	235
6	France	205
7	Luxembourg	202
8	Netherlands	189
9	Finland	187
10	Switzerland	183

Table 1–12   Internet Users

Rank	Country	Percent
1	Iceland	76
2	Sweden	68
3	Denmark	63
4	Netherlands	61
5	Hong Kong	60
6	Norway	59
7	United States	59
8	United Kingdom	57
9	Australia	54
10	South Korea	53

Table 1–13   Personal Computers

Rank	Country	Per 1,000 people
1	San Marino	738
2	United States	574
3	Sweden	507
4	Denmark	503
5	Switzerland	493
6	Norway	486
7	Bermuda	469
8	Australia	460
9	Luxembourg	446
10	Singapore	436

DIPLOMACY INDICATORS

Table 1–14 Donors of Foreign Aid

Rank	Country	In billions
1	United States	$12.9
2	Japan	9.2
3	Germany	5.4
4	France	5.2
5	United Kingdom	4.8
6	Netherlands	3.4
7	Italy	2.3
8	Canada	2.0
9	Sweden	1.8
10	Norway	1.8

Table 1–15 U.N. Security Council

Rank	Country	Membership ends
1	China	Permanent
1	France	Permanent
1	Russia	Permanent
1	United Kingdom	Permanent
1	United States	Permanent
2	Angola	2004
2	Chile	2004
2	Germany	2004
2	Pakistan	2004
2	Spain	2004

Table 1–16 Environmental Treaties

Rank	Country	Number
1	Norway	26
2	Netherlands	25
3	Sweden	24
4	Denmark	23
5	Switzerland	22
6	Canada	21
7	Austria	20
8	Bulgaria	19
9	Luxembourg	19
10	Czech Republic	18

SOCIAL INDICATORS

Table 1–17   Housing—People Per Room

Rank	Country	No. of people
1	Norway	0.5
2	Sweden	0.5
3	Canada	0.5
4	Belgium	0.5
5	Australia	0.5
6	United States	0.5
7	Iceland	0.6
8	Netherlands	0.6
9	Japan	0.6
10	Finland	0.6

Table 1–18   Quality of Life[*]

Rank	Country
1	Norway
2	Sweden
3	Canada
4	Belgium
5	Australia
6	United States
7	Iceland
8	Netherlands
9	Japan
10	Finland

[*]UN Human Development Index

Table 1–19   University Students

Rank	Country	Per 100,000 adults
1	Canada	5,997
2	South Korea	5,609
3	Australia	5,552
4	United States	5,339
5	New Zealand	4,508
6	Finland	4,190
7	Norway	4,164
8	Spain	4,017
9	Ireland	3,618
10	France	3,600

CULTURAL INDICATORS

Table 1–20   Feature Film Production

Rank	Country	Films per year
1	India	1,200
2	United States	543
3	Japan	293
4	France	200
5	Spain	137
6	Italy	130
7	Germany	116
8	China	100
9	Philippines	97
10	Hong Kong	92

Table 1–21   Film Investment

Rank	Country	In millions
1	United States	$14,461
2	Japan	1,292
3	United Kingdom	852
4	France	813
5	Germany	687
6	Spain	304
7	Italy	247
8	India	192
9	South Korea	134
10	Canada	133

Table 1–22   Movie Tickets Sold/Year

Rank	Country	In millions
1	India	2,860
2	United States	1,421
3	Indonesia	190
4	France	155
5	Germany	149
6	Japan	145
7	United Kingdom	139
8	Spain	131
9	Mexico	120
10	Canada	113

SECURITY INDICATORS

Table 1–23   Opacity Index

Country	Index
Singapore	29
Chile	36
United States	36
United Kingdom	38
Hong Kong	45
Italy	48
Mexico	48
Israel	53
Egypt	58
Peru	58
Colombia	60
Japan	60
South Africa	60
Argentina	61
Brazil	61
Taiwan	61
Pakistan	62
Venezuela	63
India	64
Thailand	67
South Korea	73
Turkey	74
Indonesia	75
Russia	84
China	87

Table 1–24   Trouble-Prone Young Men

Country	Males, Age 15–29	
	Number (thousands) in 2000	Percent of population
Iraq	3,335	28.3%
Iran	10,645	21.6
Algeria	4,681	15.5
Turkey	9,946	14.6
Indonesia	30,800	14.6
South Africa	6,416	14.6
Mexico	14,366	14.5
Brazil	24,490	14.3
India	142,384	14.0
Egypt	9,436	13.9
Afghanistan	2,974	13.9
Pakistan	19,337	13.6
Gaza and West Bank	431	13.5
China	165,111	12.9
Kazakhstan	2,011	12.9
Argentina	4,785	12.9
Israel	774	12.8
Cuba	1,307	11.7
Greece	1,193	10.6
Japan	13,294	10.5
United States	29,951	10.5

Chapter 2

Coming Global Growth
Is Hospitable for Hospitality

In September 2004, nearly three years after the recent recession officially ended, many Americans are still acting like bears waking from hibernation after a long, cold winter. They are looking around, sniffing the air, and hoping that the worst is finally over. Yet it seems that many are not yet convinced. And as we will see, they have reasons for concern. So does the rest of the world, because the United States plays such an enormous role in global trade. When America gets a cold, the rest of the world gets pneumonia.

Nonetheless, at Forecasting International (FI) we believe that any risk of a "double-dip" recession is long past. That unfamiliar perfume on the nation's atmosphere is the scent of new growth, and most economists and business leaders are convinced that it represents sustainably better economic times, not just a temporary recovery in a protracted slump.

The United States is not alone in its recovery. In Europe, several key economies are growing after long stagnation. Even Japan seems to have emerged at last from a decade of recession.

Why we believe that global prosperity is at hand, what this means for the hospitality industry, and how things still might go wrong are the subjects of this chapter. Unfortunately, the explanation will require spending more time poring over dry economic statistics than most of us would prefer.

For the hospitality industry, the arrival of a solid worldwide economic recovery is the best possible news. People seldom take expensive vacations when they feel poor or fear for their jobs, and in bad times companies cut back on meetings and business trips. When prosperity returns, travel and tourism recover as well.

It can't happen too soon. Over the last few years, American economic problems have been felt throughout the world. According to the Italian National Tourist Office, the number of Americans visiting Italy declined by 15 percent between 2000 and 2002—before the dollar lost much of its value in international currency markets—and by 25 percent in 2003. With the dollar so weak and travel to other lands comparatively expensive for Americans in 2004, they expect that when the numbers are all in tourism will turn out to have been down throughout Europe by 20 to 30 percent. Early in the year, business at restaurants in major European tourist destinations was off by 40 to 50 percent. And when Americans do travel, they have been staying at cheap hotels near the bus station, rather than pricey ones in the scenic districts, and going to cafeterias instead of more expensive restaurants. Economic recovery in the United States should help to bring the tourists back. Prosperity in other lands could turn the coming good years into an all-out boom for the global hospitality industry.

LOOKING UP

In fact, the American recovery started quite a while ago. According to the Bureau of Economic Analysis, the U.S. economy has been expanding continuously since the fourth quarter of 2001. In 2003, it grew by 3.1 percent for the year, peaking at a spectacular rate of 8.2 percent annually in the third quarter. In the first three months of 2004, the GDP grew at an average annual rate of 3.9 percent. For the year, growth is expected to come in at 4 percent or so, a level that most economists believe can be sustained for several years.

Economic data through late spring and early summer confirmed that a strong recovery is well under way in the United States:

- By early February 2004, the Standard & Poors Index was up 43 percent in eleven months. By August, despite several down months in response to the threat of higher interest rates, it retained more than three-fourths of its gains. Investors, at least, expected the current economic growth to continue for the next six months or more.
- Retail sales were up 0.7 percent in July 2004, a bit less than expected, but marking 19 months of almost continuous growth since January 2003.
- Durable goods orders rose 1.7 percent in July, the best gain in four months. This is strong evidence that the current economic expansion can be expected to continue.
- The Institute for Supply Management Index, another respected measure of manufacturing strength, came in at 62.0 in July 2004, slightly higher than expected. Any reading over 50 signals growth in this crucial sector.
- Unemployment seems to have stabilized at 5.4 to 5.6 percent in the first eight months of 2004—not the 4 percent seen at the height of the boom in the 1990s, but typical of a healthy American economy.

- Job growth, long lagging the rest of the economy, finally broke out in March 2004, with a spectacular increase of 308,000 in nonfarm employment. Job growth has lagged since then, but remained positive through August.

- Inflation, however, is beginning to cause concern. The Consumer Price Index was up 0.5 percent in March 2004, for an annual inflation rate of 6 percent. Virtually all of this and later increases have come from the energy sector, owing to the Iraq war, OPEC policy decisions, and the Yukos dispute in Russia. In response, the Federal Open Market Committee has been gradually raising interest rates.

- The Conference Board's Index of Leading Indicators, which foretells future economic growth, rose 0.3 percent in March 2004, its seventh increase in six months. However, slight declines in June and July—the first since March 2003—despite a spike in oil prices suggests that no major inflation is news.

All this speaks of economic strength, both present and future. The consensus among economists is that the recession of 2001 was the briefest, shallowest on record, with just three quarters of consecutive decline, and that it is unlikely to return. In this, the economists are clearly correct.

American consumers seem to agree, at least if we look at their behavior. With the exception of the first three months of 2000, when the economy was still growing, and September 2001, when the country was reeling from the terrorist attack on the World Trade Center and Pentagon, they have continued to spend freely, a little more each month. Between April 2003 and July 2004, the most recent data yet available, only September 2003 showed a decline in personal consumption spending, and the dip was more than made up by November. After a flat month in April 2004, consumer spending grew at a rate of about 4 percent in May and June, twice as fast as it had a year earlier. This is important, because consumer spending makes up about two-thirds of the American economy. It was consumers, not business, whose spending carried the country through the recent recession.

When American consumers are asked how they feel about the economy, the picture also was brighter in mid-2004 than it had been a year earlier. With interruptions of no more than a month or two, the Conference Board's Consumer Confidence Index declined from 120 in June 2001 to just over 60 in March 2003. By July 2004, it was back to 105.7. The University of Michigan's Index of Consumer Sentiment declined steadily from mid-1999 through early 2003 and then began to rise. In July 2004, it stood at 96.7, up nearly 25 points from its low some 18 months earlier.

So happy days are here again. American tourists will hurry back to European hotels and restaurants, executives will make more business trips, and cruise passengers will finally be willing to pay full fare for their sea-going vacations. Right?

CONSUMERS INVITE CAUTION

Not necessarily. Consumer confidence took a hit in August 2004, with the Consumer Confidence Index down to 98.2 and the Index of Consumer Sentiment off to 95.9. And anything that threatens consumer confidence invites concern about the future of the hospitality markets.

One problem is the situation in Iraq. In September 2004, the number of American deaths since the war began topped 1,000, and more than 7,500 have been injured. Despite many optimistic forecasts from Washington, the death rate for Americans in Iraq remained high even after the Iraqi interim government assumed something resembling sovereignty at the end of June 2004. And when Americans worry about anything, it colors their feelings about the economy.

The other problem is jobs. According to most estimates, there were about 1 million fewer of them in the United States in August 2004 than there were in 2000. This represents the first sustained decline in employment since the Great Depression of 1929. In fact, from one point of view the situation may be worse than it appears. According to several estimates, if the current recovery had followed the track of previous upturns, the economy would not have lost jobs but instead would be something more than 3 million jobs to the good. Some economists therefore argue that the U.S. is suffering a jobs deficit, not of 2 million jobs at its low point but more like 5.3 million. According to the Economic Policy Institute, if we include laid-off workers who want jobs but have become too discouraged to look for them, and therefore are not included in the official numbers, the unemployment rate would not be 5.7 percent, but more like 7.5 percent. That is bad, even for the middle of a recession.

The job picture has improved in late spring and early summer, and we will get to that in a moment. For now, however, we will continue to examine why employment statistics have weighed so heavily on consumer confidence and sentiment. This process will provide a useful context for interpreting the latest job figures.

It takes around 150,000 new hires each month just to absorb the extra workers being added to the labor pool. At this point in the recovery from a recession, new jobs are usually appearing at a rate of 200,000 to 300,000 per month. Yet this time new jobs remained scarce for a long time. Government forecasters predicted that 150,000 jobs would be created last December; only 8,000 were. They said that 175,000 jobs would appear in January 2004; 97,000 did. In February, the number was back down to 21,000. It has remained erratic, but generally lower than expected, ever since.

These hard, well-publicized numbers contrasted unfavorably with the annual *Economic Report of the President,* which forecast that average payrolls in 2004 would be 2.6 million jobs larger than in 2003. Administration officials quickly backed away from that prediction when skeptics pointed out that meeting the target would require creating about 320,000 jobs per month for the rest of the year.

In an election year, all this is big political news, and it has many working-class Americans worried. What if the economy is not as strong as those GDP numbers suggest? What if companies just don't need well-paid American workers anymore to produce their goods? What if the government hasn't a clue how to fix the situation? Hence February's decline in consumer confidence.

A FEW CHALLENGES

There are several issues to look at here, and we will take them in turn.

One is labor productivity. During the recession, companies maintained profits by cutting payrolls, learning better ways to use all those computers they bought in the 1990s, and pushing their remaining employees to turn out more work per hour. Now that the recession is over, they are still pushing. Labor productivity has risen almost uninterruptedly since 1990, and it rose almost twice as fast between January 2000 and mid-2004 as it did in between 1992 (the baseline year) and 1999. At the end of 2003, American workers turned out nearly 30 percent more goods and services per hour than they did in 1992. That means companies need fewer employees to get their work done.

When economists know how fast the economy and productivity are growing, they can get a fairly good idea of how many new jobs the economy will create. With GDP growth of 4.5 percent per year, cutting productivity growth to 1.5 percent per year would create 320,000 jobs per month and lead most consumers to start thinking about their next vacation. Productivity growth of 2.7 percent would force employers to create 150,000 new jobs per month, or enough to absorb the new workers coming into the labor market. In 2003, labor productivity actually rose by 4.1 percent, and that allows room for hardly any new hires at all. Productivity growth in 2004 seems likely to average about 3 percent–it was 2.9 percent in the second quarter–leaving job creation to limp along much as it did in December 2003 and January 2004.

Another issue is outsourcing. Increasingly, companies are cutting costs by shipping jobs to low-wage countries like China, Russia, and especially India, where universities graduate more English-speaking scientists, engineers, and technicians than the rest of the world combined. Outsourcing is where many of those lost factory jobs, the ones not displaced by computer-aided design and manufacturing, have been going since the 1980s. Today the trend is being felt in computers and information technology, telephone customer support, many services, and even some professions. No fewer than one-third of American programmers and software engineers are expected to lose their jobs to outsourcing in the next six years; in the most vulnerable segments of the industry, salaries for the survivors have already fallen by nearly 10 percent.

There are few industries where outsourcing will not make itself felt. Architects and consultants are safe; their customers like to be able to talk with them in person. So are construction workers and auto mechanics. Relatively few jobs will be lost from the hospitality industry; no one in Bangalore can clean a hotel room in New York or cook a restaurant meal in Chicago. But not all physicians have to see their patients, so a few hospitals already are e-mailing X-rays to be read by Indian doctors. And a growing cadre of accountants is preparing U.S. tax returns in India. Of the top 1,000 American companies, more than 400 will have at least pilot projects offshore before 2006 is over. A recent study at the University of California at Berkeley found that 14 percent of all American jobs could eventually migrate overseas.

This trend is spreading around the world. Germany and Britain have well-established outsourcing movements, and the process is getting under way in the Netherlands, Belgium, Sweden, and Switzerland. Even France is beginning to experience outsourcing, despite some of the world's most restrictive labor laws and powerful unions. In the future, India will begin outsourcing its labor to former British colonies in Africa, where English is spoken and labor costs will remain low. Ghana, South Africa, and Zimbabwe all are beginning to profit from outsourcing. As outsourcing spreads in Europe, French-speaking Africa will benefit from this trend as well.

A few economists deny that outsourcing has really cost significant numbers of American jobs. Some say it actually creates new employment. In February, Gregory Mankiw, chairman of the President's Council of Economic Advisors, found himself in hot water for publicly applauding the process. Outsourcing, he said, cuts costs, and that will make the economy stronger and Americans more prosperous. In the long run, he was probably right, but it was not what increasingly skittish consumers wanted to hear.

Finally, a few economists doubt that the country really is short of jobs at all. The federal Bureau of Labor Statistics performs two different surveys in an effort to track the nation's employment status. The one we all hear about each month comes from payroll records at 400,000 companies, and it shows that the country has lost 716,000 jobs since the bottom of the recession in November 2001. The other survey, much less publicized, asks 60,000 households about their employment. This study says that the economy has not lost jobs after all; it actually has created 2.2 million jobs since the end of 2001, 496,000 in January alone! This obvious conflict puzzles many economists.

AS WE SEE IT

Here is how Forecasting International makes sense of all this:

The American economy really is growing at a rate that should average about 4 percent in 2004. That represents a solid, sustainable expansion that should continue for several years.

In any previous recovery, it would have resulted in the rehiring of laid-off workers and the creation of more than enough jobs to employ all the new workers who enter the labor force each month. New hiring was delayed because services are now automating their processes, much as manufacturing has been doing for 20 years, and because outsourcing truly is draining jobs from the United States.

We do not fully understand why official unemployment rates have remained so much lower than many economists would have expected. In part, it is because people who lost their jobs in the last few years eventually gave up looking for work and are no longer counted in the official government figures. However, the Bureau of Labor Statistics puts the number of "discouraged workers" at only 514,000, compared with 8.4 million unemployed persons in March 2004. This is not enough to raise the unemployment figure significantly.

Some of the unemployed have found work of sorts—there really are more jobs than the payroll survey shows—but it is not always the kind of work anyone can be happy about. Perhaps one-third of displaced manufacturing workers and engineers have had to settle for service jobs that pay much less than they were accustomed to and provide no health insurance or other benefits. Many of those jobs are part time, and many are off the books. Increasingly, workers get paid in cash and employers bury the cost in other parts of the balance sheet. These jobs are uncounted and untaxed. They explain much of the difference, between the BLS payroll survey and the household survey. In fact, BLS reports that fully 97 percent of the jobs added to the household survey between March and June 2004 were part-time. This does not qualify as a major recovery in employment.

It also is true that outsourcing will strengthen the American economy, and the economies of many European nations as well. Cutting costs makes business more efficient and reduces the price that consumers pay for goods and services, and the money saved is eventually reinvested, creating new jobs. However, that is a process for the long run. At the moment, there simply aren't enough white-collar and factory jobs to go around. That means the retraining programs some politicians have suggested will not work; there is no point in training the unemployed for jobs that do not, and will not, exist. Many displaced workers have had their lives permanently changed for the worse. Until job creation catches up with labor supply, many workers will have to settle for jobs far below their talent, skill, and ambition.

And yet, in the long run outsourcing may not be quite as disruptive as it now seems. Many employers have found that moving their operations offshore does not work out as well as they once hoped. Dell, for example, found so many customers were dissatisfied by the support work done at a Bangalore call center that it shifted the operation back to Texas and Tennessee. Others have found that offshore support costs were more than they expected, and their numbers are likely to grow quickly. Salaries for Indian programmers already are beginning to rise, even as American wages decline. In five years, IT workers in Bangalore and Hyderabad will receive not 10 percent of American salaries, but 40 percent, and that will remove much of the incentive to send jobs there. China, however, will remain an extremely low-cost alternative to American workers. Current estimates say that outsourcing will leach 3 to 10 million jobs from the American economy over the next ten years. At FI, we believe the number will be near the lower end of that range. This will be painful for the individuals whose jobs move overseas, but the dislocation will not be as severe as many now fear.

In September 2004, the economy seems to be at a turning point. The healthy employment growth seen from March through May suddenly dipped to only 78,000 new jobs in June and 32,000 in July. Until June's employment numbers came in, it appeared that the expansion had finally become self-sustaining–at least until the next downturn. August's preliminary figure of 144,000 new jobs is not really enough to confirm that better times are ahead. Yet on balance the outlook still seems positive. If this proves correct, we can expect to see continuing expansion in jobs, improved consumer confidence, and better times ahead for the hospitality industry.

As the economy labors to put the finishing touches on its somewhat flawed recovery, both the U.S. and the world's hospitality industry are receiving valuable help from around the globe. Japan, China, India, and significant parts of Europe all are enjoying prosperity of their own, which in some cases has been a long time coming. Its arrival just when America can most benefit from vital trading partners promises widespread economic growth that should continue at least for several years. Current estimates put world GDP growth in 2004 and 2005 at about 4 percent, a bit better than average, and we expect this expansion to continue for some time. This means that travel and tourism, and all the industries that depend on them, should enjoy good times through 2008 and perhaps beyond.

WORLD TOUR

Let us look at some of the major contributors to the coming global wave of well-being.

China The world's largest country also is one of the fastest growing. Over the last twenty years, this largely rural nation has transformed itself into the fourth-biggest industrial producer, after the U.S., Japan, and Germany. It manufactures more than half of the world's cameras, 20 to 25 percent of its major kitchen appliances, and about 37 percent of its hard drives. As a competitor, China has a big advantage over other nations: Wages there still average just $0.40 an hour, one-sixth the price of labor in Mexico. It also has a government that is solidly behind capitalism. The National People's Congress, once devoted to Mao's austere brand of communism, now has many members who formerly headed private companies, rather than government departments.

All this has turned China into a trading powerhouse. Chinese exports grew no less than 50 percent in the five years ending in 2002 and are continuing to expand by an amazing 20 percent per year; in the United States, they are credited with knocking several percent off the price of consumer goods. In return, the cheap dollar helped U.S. exports to China grow by some $6 billion in 2003, to a total of $28.4 billion. Even with the SARS epidemic to slow it down, the Chinese economy grew by no less than 9.1 percent in 2003, rising to 9.9 percent in the fourth quarter and a torrid 10.7 percent in the first quarter of 2004. After that performance, a dip to 9.6 percent growth in the second quarter actually came as good news: It seems that China may be achieving a "soft landing," at a growth rate it can sustain, rather than collapsing into a recession as some economists had feared.

The future is looking even better. Demand for raw materials such as steel scrap is credited as a major cause for the faint stirrings of price inflation now being seen in the United States. China's extraordinary growth could slow a bit in the next couple of years, as Beijing—under heavy pressure from its trading partners—finally allows the undervalued *yuan* to rise in the world's currency markets. Yet that increase and the resulting slowdown both will be limited. At the same time, Citigroup, along with the Hongkong Shanghai Bank Corporation, recently received approval to issue credit cards on the mainland. Allowing foreign banks to operate in its territory no later than 2006 is one requirement that China accepted when it joined the World Trade Organization in late 2001. Living up to that commitment nearly two years before the deadline should reassure outside investors that China means to bring its policies in line with those expected of capitalist nations. At the same time, Beijing has committed to developing a host of new tourist destinations in the next few years and training 100,000 hospitality professionals by 2010. And all this can only be good for China's economic prospects.

India   The world's second most populous country once was viewed as a perpetual beggar-land. Today, it fairly radiates economic health. India's GDP in 2003 expanded by about 8 percent, after years of growth in the range of 4 to 6 percent; not even the so-called "Asian flu" that decimated economies throughout the region in the late 1990s did much to slow India's economy. Goldman Sachs, a leading American investment bank with a good record of prescience, forecasts that India's GDP will continue to grow by an average of 5 percent annually *for the next half century.* According to the report, the Indian economy will be bigger than Japan's by 2032. By 2050, the country's per capita income will grow by 3500 percent!

To achieve this fantastic success, India needs to meet several challenges. It must continue to strip away the protectionist trade barriers and bureaucratic red tape that long stifled its economy, eliminate the corruption traditionally endemic in both industry and government, diversify the economy, slow its population growth, bring its massive government debt under control, clean up the environment, and provide education for its young people, nearly 20 percent of whom receive no schooling at all. It also needs to make peace in Kashmir.

For a day or two, that process seemed endangered by the stunning upset that returned the Congress Party to power in the 2004 general election. After all, the Congress Party, under the Nehru family's leadership, created the socialist system that stifled India's economic growth for decades. However, the appointment of Manmohan Singh as the new prime minister went a long way to relieve those worries; it was Dr. Singh, an Oxford-trained economist, who formulated the economic reform plan responsible for India's current prosperity. Thus far, he has made no significant changes in the economic policies he established in the early 1990s and the former BJP government followed later on.

None of India's problems will be easy to solve, but after carrying out a year-long study of India recently we believe that India will succeed. The government's Central Vigilance Commission already has cleaned up most of the country's banking system, a good start on a long and difficult process. Wireless Internet is bringing classes to rural areas and beginning to cut the rate of illiteracy, which is estimated at 35 percent. And because education gives women more control over their reproductive lives, the birthrate is beginning to fall. With these issues in hand, it becomes possible to conquer the rest.

With 4,000 years of civilization behind it, India is a paradise of exotic travel destinations. The holy Ganges, the Taj Mahal, and the old city of Bombay hardly begin the list of cultural attractions now being developed and promoted for tourism. Even Kashmir, one of the most beautiful parts of the subcontinent, is beginning to draw visitors now that peace with Pakistan seems to be a realistic possibility.

As the Indian economy expands, the country's middle class—now estimated at about 300 million people—is growing even larger and more prosperous. Thus, India also will become one of the largest sources of tourists to Europe and America. For the world's hospitality industry, the rise of India will be one of the most important trends of the next 30 years.

Japan   After a dozen years of stagnation, and sometimes outright recession, it looks like this one-time powerhouse may finally be back on track. Japan's economy grew at a yearly rate of 7.3 percent in the fourth quarter of 2003 and 6.1 percent in the first quarter of 2004. (This compares to an average of only 0.4 percent per year from 1998 through 2002!) Exports surged by 17.9 percent annualized in 2003, yet foreign demand added only 1.6 percentage points to fourth-quarter growth. The remainder came from domestic consumption and corporate capital spending, a strong hint that both consumers and companies are beginning to anticipate a brighter future. The Conference Board's leading index for the country suggests that they may be right; by August 2004 it had been rising almost continuously for 16 months and was headed up at a rate of 3 to 5 percent annually.

Europe   The entire region did poorly throughout 2002, with just 0.9 percent GDP growth for the year, and 2003, which came in at only 0.4 percent. Business and consumer confidence for most of the period were weak, thanks largely to the Iraq war and to the cheap dollar, which has cut demand for relatively expensive European exports throughout much of the world. Germany, Italy, and the Netherlands were officially in recession in the first half of 2003, while the French economy shrank owing to widespread strikes. The region actually lost jobs for the first time since 1994, which also hurt consumer spending.

In 2004, those problems are largely past. The decline in Europe bottomed out in the second half of 2003, sentiment indicators improved, and retail sales began to pick up throughout most of Europe in August and September. Even manufacturing, which had lagged other segments of the continental economy, began to pick up toward the end of the year.

Several policy changes should keep the recovery going. Toward the end of 2004, the United States has begun to raise its interest rates, and while German economics minister Wolfgang Clement is pushing the European central bank to bring theirs down, from 2 percent to 1 percent. This will raise the price of the dollar on currency markets, while lowering the value of the euro. These changes will effectively reduce the cost of European exports and of foreign travel to the continent, improving the balance of trade and bringing a lot more American tourists back to Europe. It helps also that the European Union has already decided to suspend limits on budget deficits in member countries, allowing national governments to spend more on stimulating their economies. All these developments point to a slow but steady recovery, which now seems well under way.

In the long run, one more change should help the EU. This is the addition of ten new member states in April 2004. Those countries, most of them formerly belonging to the Warsaw Pact, are much less prosperous than existing members. Yet they still represent the markets and productive capacity of 75 million people. Over the next ten years, those new resources will make themselves felt.

France   Economic growth was weak or nonexistent through most of 2002 and the beginning of 2003, thanks in part to the Iraq war, oil worries, and labor unrest. Things turned up in the fourth quarter, which delivered 2.5 percent growth, and another 3.1 percent in the first quarter of 2004. Yet consumer spending remains weak, thanks to unemployment of over 9 percent.

Nonetheless, by January 2004 the Conference Board's leading index for France had been rising solidly for five straight months; it did not show an actual decline until May–even then the decrease was a mere 0.1 percent–and it began to rise again almost immediately. In 2004 the second-largest economy in the "euro zone" is projecting GDP growth of 2 to 3 percent in anticipation of more business investment and a bit of new hiring in the second half of the year. A rise in tourism as the American economy continues to rebound should go a long way toward restoring prosperity to France. A general recovery in Europe will help as well; 60 percent of French foreign trade is within the continent. And perhaps best of all, in these relatively promising times France is dusting off its dormant plans to privatize some government holdings. Air France and at least some of the state's 97-percent holding in Aerospatiale are slated to go on the auction block. This can only make the French economy more efficient and improve the nation's chances of achieving sustained growth.

Germany   Europe's largest economy, and the world's fifth-largest, has been sluggish since 2002, with little or no growth last year and unemployment hovering around 10 percent. Blame this on a combination of high taxes, high-priced labor, copious red tape, the continuing cost of absorbing the former East Germany (about $70 billion per year), and—again—the weakness of the dollar, which here as elsewhere discourages both exports and tourism.

However, since mid-2003, both consumer and industrial demand have been improving gradually. Growth in 2004 now is expected to come in at a modest 1.6 percent, and 1.75 percent in 2005. Again, that could be improved by a stronger dollar, but any significant benefit is unlikely to be felt before the second quarter of 2005.

United Kingdom   Britain has outperformed both the United States and the rest of Europe since the high-tech bubble burst at the end of the 1990s: It barely avoided recession. Yet the slowdown in global financial services has hurt. Finance is a major part of London's economy, and that accounts for 17.5 percent of the nation's GDP. Productivity growth is declining as well, and it seems that the economy—like that of the United States in 2002 and 2003—has been held up only by consumer spending.

However, it appears that things are looking up. The index of leading indicators was rising at 3 to 5 percent annually as of May, held even in June, and dipped only slightly in July. Corporate investment and net exports are beginning to quicken, and household spending is still rising gradually. Unemployment has hovered in the neighborhood of 5 percent, and inflation has remained under control. All these point to future GDP growth, most likely close to 3 percent in 2004 and 2005.

Russia Three weeks before his expected coronation in the election of March 14, 2004, Vladimir Putin fired his prime minister and the entire cabinet. At the time, it seemed little more than a Soviet-style power grab, intended primarily to get rid of Prime Minister Mikhail Kasayanov, a Yeltsin holdover. Kasayanov's replacement turned out to be the relatively little-known Mikhail Fradkov, a Soviet-era trade minister and later chief of the tax police who had been serving as Russia's minister to the European Union. In addition to taking the blame for future cuts in subsidies for housing, education, and healthcare, Fradkov is expected to build closer ties between Russia and Western Europe, particularly in the areas of trade and tourism.

Economically, Russia has been doing pretty well of late. Since the collapse in 1998, the country's GDP has grown rapidly—more than 6 percent per year in 1999, 2000, and 2001; 4.2 percent in 2002; a claim of 7 percent in 2003; and an expected 4.5 percent in 2004 and 4.2 percent in 2005.

That is not good enough, however. Much of that growth comes from the strength of the world's oil and gas markets; Russia owes roughly one-fourth of its GDP to petroleum. And the unstable price of a commodity, even oil, is a fragile basis for the prosperity of one of the world's largest countries. (It has been made even less stable by Putin's war on Yukos, the country's second largest oil producer, but in late September it appears that this long-running conflict is at last being settled.) Add in metals and timber, and raw materials account for 80 percent of Russian exports. Even in these relatively comfortable times, 25 percent of the nation's population live below the local poverty line; 53 percent earn less than $4 per day. In a general downturn, the economic situation would be grim indeed; in 1999, 40 percent of the population was considered impoverished.

Putin's cure for instability is to diversify the economy, and his chosen tool is tourism. Most tourists visit only St. Petersburg and Moscow. In the future, he hopes foreign visitors will fan out across the country, taking trains and river barges, and visiting less well-known destinations. In the process, those tourists will employ Russian citizens and earn foreign currency in a field not directly dependent on the price of oil and gas. At the same time, the new attractions will provide investment and marketing opportunities for hospitality concerns throughout the world.

A BENEVOLENT CYCLE

In all these countries, we see the results of a cycle that has existed since World War II. When the American economy declines, economies around the world follow; when it recovers, the rest have at least the chance to grow. In the next few years, prosperity in each country will create new affluence for all its trading partners, which will generate still more wealth at home. Though some displaced white-collar workers will miss out on the coming good times, as laid-off manufacturing workers did in the boom of the 1990s, we are entering a period of growing affluence that should last for at least four or five years. It could endure longer than that.

This promises new prosperity for the hospitality industry around the world. Wealthy people have continued to travel throughout the recession; the slowdown had little effect on their disposable income. This is why the most expensive resorts remained full and Cunard had so little trouble marketing rooms on the *Queen Mary 2*. It was the middle class that had to cut back during the recent downturn. As the nascent expansion continues to develop, those vacationers, probably feeling a bit deprived, will loosen their purse strings. Americans who now visit Orlando will return to Europe, and those who have still been traveling abroad will find their way back to city-center hotels and restaurants with better food and more pleasant surroundings than cafeterias can offer. European tourists, though, may stay closer to home as the dollar gains in value and American vacations again become more costly.

The new prosperity is likely to have one more effect as well. Global economic expansion has brought new wealth to many developing countries whose economies depend heavily on mining and trade in raw materials. Some of the profits will be invested to develop new tourist destinations, which serve as more stable sources of foreign currency. Expect to see new resorts and exotic-tour possibilities opening up throughout Asia and sub-Saharan Africa.

Although we at FI are optimistic about the course of economic events in the next few years, it is important to note that at least three factors could derail this optimistic scenario.

In early May 2004, China experienced its first death from SARS since the epidemic of 2002 ended. Another outbreak of SARS, an epidemic of bird flu among humans, or some other contagion in Asia would trigger a rerun of the chaos in 2003. This would hit the region's hospitality sector hard and cause milder damage to other industries. Yet it is difficult to see this having a major impact outside Asia. It might even help some regions in the United States and Europe if international meetings scheduled for Asia had to be hastily relocated.

In the long run, failure to control growing deficits in the United States could have a greater impact. Eventually, America's creditors abroad will grow tired of buying U.S. debt and defending their export markets; Japan spent an estimated $80 billion to prop up the dollar in January 2004 alone! When that happens, the Federal Reserve Board will have to raise interest rates significantly to attract overseas bond buyers. That in turn will raise the rate of inflation, rein in the stock market, and reduce the capital available for future growth. Further cuts in federal spending will do relatively little good; there just isn't that much left to cut, with defense, Social Security, and interest payments essentially off limits. That leaves raising taxes to bring down the deficit, and this again could slow the nation's economic growth.

Finally, and most threateningly, another major terrorist incident could be catastrophic, particularly if it caused another round of American retrenchment. The September 11 attack cost the U.S. economy an estimated $100 billion in immediate property losses, repairs, and lost productivity. Add in the loss of stock-market wealth, and the cost of the event was probably closer to $2 trillion—and this does not include the ancillary costs of the war in Afghanistan. Before September 11, no one was quite certain the United States had entered a recession; after September 11, no one doubted it. Another such attack could easily trigger a major downturn and eat up much of the capital that otherwise would power the next expansion.

However, these potential disasters are significant only because their impact would be so bad, not because they are at all likely. The most probable scenario is the one we have described above. For the next few years, global prosperity should ensure growth of travel and tourism. The good times should last at least through 2008, and very possibly into the years beyond.

KEY TRENDS FOR THE ECONOMY

(Trend numbers below and in the following chapters correspond to the list in Appendix A.)

1. The economy of the developed world will continue to grow for at least the next five years. Any interruptions will be relatively short-lived.

Summary: After a brief but painful recession, the U.S. economy has been growing steadily for nearly three years, through the first quarter of 2004. Job creation lagged far behind GDP growth, but it too appears to have begun a substantial recovery.

Similar improvements are being seen around the world. Many of the European economies are emerging from years of stagnation, while Japan is seeing its first significant expansion in a decade. India and China are achieving GDP growth that averages 6 percent or better each year.

Barring another terrorist incident on the scale of 9/11, or some equivalent shock, this widespread prosperity should feed upon itself, with each trading nation helping to generate the continued well-being of its partners. It can be sustained for some years to come.

Implications for the Economy: This widespread prosperity should feed upon itself, with each trading nation helping to generate the continued well-being of its partners.

Labor markets will remain tight, particularly in skilled fields. This calls for new creativity in recruiting, benefits, and perks, especially profit sharing. This hypercompetitive business environment demands new emphasis on rewarding speed, creativity, and innovation within the workforce.

In the United States, the growing concentration of wealth among the elderly, who as a group already are comparatively well off, creates an equal deprivation among the young and the poorer old. This implies a loss of purchasing power among much of the population; in time, it could partially offset the forces promoting economic growth.

2. The world's population will grow to 9 billion by 2050.

Summary: The greatest fertility is found in those countries least able to support their existing populations. Populations in many developing countries will double between 2000 and 2050; in the Palestinian Territories, they will rise by 217%. In contrast, the developed nations will fall from 23% of the total world population in 1950 and about 14% in 2000 to only 10% in 2050. In 10 years or so, the workforce in Japan and much of Europe will be shrinking by 1% per year.

Implications for the Economy: Rapid population growth will reinforce American domination of the global economy, as the European Union falls to third place behind the United States and China.

To meet human nutritional needs over the next 40 years, global agriculture will have to supply as much food as has been produced during all of human history.

Unless fertility in the developed lands climbs dramatically, either would-be retirees will have to remain on the job, or the industrialized nations will have to encourage even more immigration from the developing world. The third alternative is a sharp economic contraction and loss of living standards.

Barring enactment of strict immigration controls, rapid migration will continue from the Southern Hemisphere to the North, and especially from former colonies to Europe. A growing percentage of job applicants in the United States and Europe will be recent immigrants from developing countries.

3. The growth of the information industries is creating a knowledge-dependent global society.

Summary: Information is the primary commodity of more and more industries. As a result, 80% of companies worldwide expect to have employees who work at home by 2005, up from 54% in 2003. By 2007, 83% of American management personnel will be knowledge workers, and Europe and Japan are not far behind. Computer competence is rapidly approaching 100% in these countries. The Internet makes it possible for small businesses throughout the world to compete for market share on an even footing with industry leaders.

Implications for the Economy: Knowledge workers are generally better paid than less-skilled workers, and their proliferation is raising overall prosperity.

Even entry-level workers and those in formerly unskilled positions require a growing level of education. For a good career in almost any field, computer competence is mandatory. This is one major trend raising the level of education required for a productive role in today's workforce. For many workers, the opportunity for training is becoming one of the most desirable benefits any job can offer.

New technologies create new industries, jobs, and career paths, which can bring new income to developing countries. An example is the transfer of functions such as technical support in the computer industry to Asian divisions and service firms.

For some developing countries, computer skills are making it faster and easier to create wealth than a traditional manufacturing economy ever could. India, for example, is rapidly growing a middle class, largely on the strength of its computer and telecom industries. Many other lands will follow its example.

4. The global economy is growing more integrated.

Summary: The Internet is reshaping sourcing and distribution networks in many industries by making it practical for companies to farm out secondary functions to suppliers, service firms, and consultants, which increasingly are located in other countries. At the same time, relaxation of border and capital controls in the European Union, and the use of a common currency and uniform products standards there, are making it still easier for companies to distribute products and support functions throughout the continent. NAFTA has had a similar, but much less sweeping, effect in the Americas.

Implications for the Economy: The growth of commerce on the Internet makes it possible to shop globally for raw materials and supplies, thus reducing the cost of doing business. In niche markets, the Internet also makes it possible for small companies to compete with giants worldwide with relatively little investment.

Demand for personnel in distant countries will increase the need for foreign-language training, employee incentives suited to other cultures, aid to executives going overseas, and the many other aspects of doing business in other countries. As eastern Europe integrates more fully with the European Union, a major investment in personnel development will be needed over the next few years.

In the wake of the "Asian flu," Western companies may have to accept that proprietary information will be shared, not just with their immediate partners in Asian joint ventures, but with other members of the partners' trading conglomerates. In high technology and aerospace, that may expose companies to extra scrutiny due to national-security concerns.

5. Societal values are changing rapidly.

Summary: Industrialization raises educational levels, changes attitudes toward authority, reduces fertility, alters gender roles, and encourages broader political participation. This process is just beginning throughout the developing world. The future will be dominated by the materialistic values of Generations X and Dot-com.

Implications for the Economy: Narrow, extremist views of the left and right will slowly lose their popularity in the developed lands. This should bring more pragmatic government that will bring consumers greater security, and thereby promote economic growth.

Growing demand for quality and convenience is creating many new niche markets. This will be a prime field for entrepreneurs over the next ten years, in hospitality and many other industries.

The demand for greater accountability and transparency in business will be crucial, not only in the United States business community, but also for countries that wish to attract international investors.

Reaction against changing values is one of the prime motives of cultural extremism, particularly in the Muslim world and in parts of India. As values change in those lands, terrorism is likely to proliferate, slowing economic growth and raising the cost of doing business.

6. Young people place increasing importance on economic success, which they have come to expect.

Summary: This is characteristic of Generations X and Dot-com throughout the world. These are the most entrepreneurial generations in history, preferring to found their own business rather than to become a political leader or high-level executive at a major corporation. In the United States especially, most young people have high aspirations, but many lack the education to achieve them.

Implications for the Economy: Gen-X and dot-com entrepreneurs are largely responsible for the current economic growth in India and China, where they are becoming a major force in the Communist party. In India, the younger generations dress and think like their American counterparts, not their parents.

If younger-generation workers find their ambitions thwarted, they will create growing pressure for economic reform and deregulation. If reforms do not come fast enough in the developing world, disappointed expectations will raise the number of young people who emigrate to the developed lands.

Disappointment also will drive underemployed young men in the developing world into fringe political and religious movements. This could cause a new wave of terrorism and instability in the years after 2005 or so, with profound effects on the economies of the United States and other target countries.

7. Tourism, vacationing, and travel (especially international) will continue to grow in the next decade, as they did throughout the 1990s.

Summary: Once current worries over the threat of terrorism recede, American tourism will resume its traditional 5% annual growth. Other countries—particularly China and India—are contributing to this demand, as their economies grow and their citizens become more free to travel. Tourism will benefit as

Internet "virtual" tours replace printed brochures in promoting vacation destinations and provide current, detailed information on travel conditions.

Implications for the Economy: The hospitality industry will grow at a rate of at least 5% per year for the foreseeable future, and perhaps a bit more.

Tourism offers growing opportunities for out-of-the-way destinations that have not yet cashed in on the boom. This will make it an important industry for still more developing countries.

The number of people whose jobs depend on tourism will approach 14 percent of the global workforce.

8. Consumerism is still growing rapidly.

Summary: A networked society facilitates a consumerist society. Shoppers increasingly have access to information about pricing, services, delivery time, and customer reviews on the Internet. In most industrialized countries, their needs are increasingly being written into laws and regulations, which are generally enforced.

Implications for the Economy: This is a mandate for quality. Brands with good reputations will have a strong market advantage over lesser competitors and unknowns.

A second-rate or poor reputation will be even harder to overcome than it is today.

It will take very few mistakes to undermine a reputation for quality.

9. Oil prices are stable at $25 to $28 per barrel; they rise above that level only in times of trouble.

Summary: In Autumn 2004, OPEC's aim was to hold the price of oil at relatively high levels, and the instability in the Middle East is making this relatively easy. However, keeping prices high requires a unity of purpose that member countries have never been able to sustain for very long. The cost of raising a barrel of oil from the ground in this region is around one-tenth the wholesale price. New oil supplies coming on line in the former Soviet Union, China, and other parts of the world will make it even more difficult to sustain prices at artificially high levels. Prices above $28 per barrel are simply unsustainable.

Implications for the Economy: One of the major costs of doing business should remain under control. This will make it possible for companies to earn acceptable profits while keeping prices relatively affordable.

Inflation also should remain under control, with benefits for disposable income and consumer confidence.

10. People around the world are becoming increasingly sensitive to environmental issues such as air pollution, as the consequences of neglect, indifference, and ignorance become ever more apparent.

Summary: Soot and other particulates are coming under greater scrutiny as threats more dangerous to human health than sulfur dioxide and other gaseous pollutants. In the United States alone, medical researchers estimate that some 64,000 people each year die from cardiopulmonary disease as a result of breathing particulates. In sub-Saharan Africa, the toll is between 300,000 and 500,000 deaths per year, and in Asia, between 500,000 and 1 million people annually die of particulate exposure. Though government policies in some developing countries—and the United States, at the moment—rate industrial development more important, the trend is clearly toward a cleaner, healthier environment.

Implications for the Economy: Demands for still more environmental controls are inevitable, especially in relatively pristine regions. This will limit industrial development in these areas, but will leave them open to controlled tourism.

Manufacturers throughout the developed lands will have to spend more on pollution controls and recycling. This will eat into their net profits in the short run, but eventually will make them more efficient and more profitable.

The developed countries will have to subsidize antipollution efforts in many of the developing lands, which view the environmental movement as a devious way for the industrialized countries to deprive them of their fair share of the world's resources.

11. Industrial development trumps environmental concerns in many parts of the world.

Summary: Studies in India, South Africa, and other countries show that few citizens are concerned with environmental decay, but are very eager for the wealth that comes from industrialization. China, India, and other developing lands are generating increasing quantities of the pollutants that most of the industrialized world now seeks to eliminate.

Implications for the Economy: Broad regions of the planet will be subject to pollution, deforestation, and other environmental ills in the coming decades.

Diseases related to air and water pollution will spread dramatically in the years ahead. Already, chronic obstructive pulmonary disease is five times more common in China than in the United States. As citizens of the developing countries grow to expect modern health care, this will create a growing burden on their economies.

This is just a taste of future problems, and perhaps not the most troublesome. Even the U.S. government now admits that global warming is a result of human activities that produce greenhouse gases. It now seems that China and India soon will produce even more of them than the major industrialized nations. Helping the developing lands to raise their standards of living without causing wholesale pollution will require much more aid and diplomacy than the developed world has ever been willing to devote to this cause.

12. Technology increasingly dominates both the economy and society.

Summary: In all fields, the previous state of the art is being replaced by new high-tech developments at an ever faster rate. Computers and telecommunications have become an ordinary part of our environment, rather than just tools we use for specific tasks. Biotechnology, and eventually nanotechnology, may do so as well. These developments provide dozens of new opportunities to create businesses and jobs, but they often require a higher level of education and training to use them effectively.

Implications for the Economy: New technologies should continue to improve efficiency in many industries, helping to keep costs under control. However, this increased productivity retarded U.S. job creation from 2002 through early 2004. Other developed countries are likely to feel the same effect in the future.

New technologies often require a higher level of education and training to use them effectively. They also provide dozens of new opportunities to create businesses and jobs.

Automation will continue to cut the cost of many services and products, making it possible to reduce prices while still improving profits. This will be critical to business survival as the Internet continues to push the price of many products to the commodity level.

New technology also will make it easier for industry to minimize and capture its effluent. This will be a crucial ability in the environmentally conscious future.

Consumers are increasingly shopping on the Internet, and posting their reactions there. One dissatisfied customer's negative report on the Internet can influence the buying decisions of potential customers for years.

13. Research and development plays a growing role in the economy.

Summary: R&D spending is growing most quickly in the fields of information technology, electronics, biotechnology, aerospace, pharmaceuticals, and chemistry. In the developed countries, high-tech jobs are slowly replacing those lost in low-tech manufacturing industries. R&D outlays have risen almost continuously in Japan but have declined in Britain and Russia. In the United States, federal funding for basic research has almost disappeared, as Washington focuses on military research and engineering.

Implications for the Economy: The demand for scientists, engineers, and technicians will continue to grow, particularly in fields where research promises an immediate business payoff.

Low-wage countries such as China will continue to take low-wage jobs from advanced industrialized countries such as the United States, but those jobs will be replaced by higher-paid jobs in technology and service industries.

Countries like India, China, and Russia may continue to suffer a "brain drain" as those with high-tech skills emigrate to high-demand, high-wage destinations. However, there is some evidence that growing numbers of technology students and professionals are spending time in the West to learn cutting-edge skills, and then returning to their native lands to work, start companies, and teach. This trend may promote the growth of some developing countries while reducing the competitive advantages of the developed world.

By inhibiting stem-cell research, the United States has made itself a less attractive place for cutting-edge biomedical scientists. The United Kingdom is capitalizing on this to become the world's leader in stem-cell research. In the process, it is reversing the brain drain that once deprived it of top scientists.

Washington's neglect of basic science is being felt in the declining fraction of patents, Nobel prizes, and other awards going to American scientists. As other countries become more skilled in critical high-tech fields, the United States is fast losing its edge. If this trend is not reversed, it will begin to undermine the American economy and shift both economic and political power to other lands.

14. The Internet is growing logarithmically and globally.

Summary: In spring 2004, Net users number around 945 million worldwide. This population is expected to reach 1.1 billion by 2005, 1.28 billion by 2006, and 1.46 billion by 2007. One reason for this is the rapid expansion of Net connectivity in some developing lands. India had only 170,000 Net subscribers in 1998; by 2004, it had 39 million. In early 2004, China's population of Net users amounted to 96 million. Americans had declined from 42 percent of Net users in 2000 to under 20 percent in 2004.

Implications for the Economy: Internet-based commerce is growing rapidly. Total e-commerce revenue is expected to be about $2.7 trillion in 2004, $1 trillion in the United States alone. Business-to-business sales passed $1 trillion by the end of 2003.

B2B sales on the Internet are dramatically reducing business expenses throughout the Net-connected world, while giving suppliers access to customers they could never have reached by traditional means.

Internet-based operations require more sophisticated, knowledgeable workers. People with the right technical training will find a ready market for their services for at least the next fifteen years, as major businesses compete to hire them. However, the specialties required in any given country will change as some skills are outsourced abroad.

15. The service industry is the fastest-growing sector of the global economy.

Summary: Data processing, health care, transportation, and other services are expanding rapidly, even as manufacturing and resource industries decline in the developed world. Service jobs have replaced many of the well-paid positions lost in the developed countries, especially the United States, but many are relatively unskilled and poorly paid, and often part time.

Implications for the Economy: Services are now beginning to compete globally, just as manufacturing industries have done over the last twenty years. By creating competitive pressure on wages in the industrialized lands, this trend will help to keep inflation in check.

The growth of international business will act as a stabilizing force in world affairs, as most countries find that conflict is unacceptably hard on the bottom line.

16. Generations X and Dot-com will have major effects on the future.

Summary: Members of generation X—roughly, the 30-plus cohort—and especially of generation Dot-com, now in their 20s, have more in common with their peers throughout the world than with their parents' generation. They are entrepreneurial, well educated, and predominately English-speaking. Virtually all are materialistic, many are economically conservative, and they care for little but the bottom line—their own bottom line. Independent to a fault, they have no loyalty to employers at all.

Implications for the Economy: Younger consumers tend to be extremely well informed about their product choices, thanks in large part to their comfort with the Internet. Net-savvy travel marketers have a strong advantage in reaching this market.

Marketing to generations X and Dot-com requires a light hand, with strong emphasis on information and quality. Brands credibly positioned as "affordable luxury" will prosper.

Any perceived inadequacy of service will send them to a competitor. Under-40 customers make few allowances for other people's problems.

However, they are relatively tolerant of impersonal service. What they care most about is efficiency.

These generations also will be industry's future employees. The good news is that they are well equipped to work in an increasingly high-tech world. The bad is that they have little interest in their employer's needs and no job loyalty at all. They also have a powerful urge to do things their own way.

17. Time is becoming the world's most precious commodity.

Summary: Computers and other technologies are making national and international economies much more competitive. As a result, Americans have lost an average of 140 hours per year of leisure time. European executives and nonunionized workers face the same trend. In Britain, workers have lost an average of 100 hours per year of nonworking time.

Implications for the Economy: Stress-related problems affecting employee morale and wellness will continue to grow. Companies must help employees balance their time at work with their family lives and need for leisure. This may reduce short-term profits but will aid profitability in the long run.

As time for shopping continues to evaporate, Internet and mail-order marketers will have a growing advantage over traditional stores.

18. More entrepreneurs start new businesses every year.

Summary: Workers under age 30 would prefer to start their own company, rather than advance through the corporate ranks. Some 10 percent are actively trying to start their own businesses, three times as many as in previous generations. Like other Gen-X and Dot-com values, this preference is shared more or less universally throughout the world. A large majority simply distrust large institutions. Most believe that jobs cannot provide a secure economic future in a time of rapid technological change. By 2006, the number of self-employed people in the United States will be close to 12 million, FI believes.

Implications for the Economy: This is a self-perpetuating trend, as all those new service firms need other companies to handle chores outside their core business.

Specialty boutiques will continue to spring up on the Internet for at least the next twenty years.

This trend will help to ease the poverty of many developing countries, as it already is doing in India and China. In turn, this will add to the demand for goods and services, further accelerating economic growth.

19. International exposure includes a greater risk of terrorist attack.

Summary: State-sponsored terrorism appears to be on the decline, as tougher sanctions make it more trouble than it is worth. However, nothing will prevent small, local political organizations and special-interest groups from using terror to promote their causes. And as the United States learned on September 11, the most dangerous terrorist groups are no longer motivated by specific political goals, but by generalized, virulent hatred based on religion and culture. On balance, the amount of terrorist activity in the world is likely to go up, not down, in the next ten years.

Implications for the Economy: Until the terrorist problem is brought under control—probably not soon—the more volatile parts of the world will find it difficult to attract outside investment capital. The exceptions will be developing oil states, such as Kazakhstan.

American-owned facilities, and those where Americans congregate, will have to devote more of their budgets to security. This is rapidly becoming true for companies from other Western lands as well.

Some of the most important security measures will be invisible to customers, but highly intrusive for staff. These may include comprehensive background checks for new hires, much as airports need to screen such behind-the-scenes personnel as baggage handlers and fuel-truck drivers.

The economies of the industrialized nations could be thrown into recession at any time by another terrorist event on the scale of September 11. This is particularly true of the United States. The impact would be greatest if the attack discouraged travel, as the hijacking of airliners to attack the World Trade Center and Pentagon did in 2001 and 2002.

The U.S. economy is being affected already by American antiterrorism measures. Since Washington began to photograph incoming travelers and required more extensive identification from them, tourism to America is off by some 30 percent. The number of foreign students coming to American universities has declined by a similar amount.

20. Institutions are undergoing a bimodal distribution: The big get bigger, the small survive, and the midsized are squeezed out.

Summary: For at least 20 years, economies of scale have allowed the largest companies to buy their smaller competitors or drive them out of business. At the same time, thousands of tiny, agile companies are prospering in niche markets. We see this pattern among automakers, computer companies, airlines, banks, and many other industries.

Implications for the Economy: Thus far, industries dominated by small, regional, often family-owned companies have been relatively exempt from the consolidation now transforming many other businesses. Takeovers are likely even in these industries in the next decade.

This consolidation will extend increasingly to Internet-based businesses, where well-financed companies are trying to absorb or outcompete tiny online startups, much as they have done in the brick-and-mortar world.

No company is too large to be a takeover target if it dominates a profitable market or has other features attractive to profit-hungry investors.

Chapter 3

"Bang! You're Dead!" Hospitality in the Age of Terror

The world has lived with terrorism for decades, but in recent years things have changed. Attacks now often are carried out by international groups with sweeping cultural agendas, rather than national organizations with local goals. They are bloodier, intended more to cause mass casualties than to win support for a political cause. And it seems that the number of major attacks has grown since the Iraq war began. These are worrisome trends, and they threaten the hospitality industry more than any other sector of society.

Although the best known terrorist attacks are those with the highest death tolls—the September 11 assault on the World Trade Center and the slaughter of school children in Beslon, Russia, in September 2004—many of the most destructive incidents have struck at hospitality, tourism, and travel. Just since the invasion of Iraq, these have included:

- the car bombing of the Mount Lebanon Hotel in Baghdad, with at least seven dead—estimates ran as high as 28—and more than 40 injured;
- the bombing of the Marriott Hotel in Jakarta, where at least 13 people died and 149 were injured;
- a series of bombings in Morocco, with targets that included the Safir Hotel and the Casa de Espana restaurant, where 15 people died;
- the bombing of the Moscow subway by Chechnyan separatists, which killed 39 people and wounded more than 130;
- and, of course, the railway bombings in Spain, with 202 fatalities.

These attacks are part of a continuing wave of violence that began with Al Qaeda but is now being carried on independently by sympathizers around the world. They differ from the terrorism of the 1970s and 1980s in a number of key ways: They aim less to promote specific political goals than to wage a cultural war of Muslim extremists against, well, anyone who attracts their attention, but especially the United States and its allies. They no longer aim for limited destruction that makes a point and allows the terrorists to fight another day; instead, they are designed for mass blood-letting, to intimidate and destroy the terrorists' chosen enemies, even when that means "martyrdom" for the perpetrators. And, government targets being increasingly well defended, they very often aim at places where civilians congregate.

This is important for hospitality providers, not just because of the threat itself, but because of the effect it has had on many of the industry's customers. In late 2003, a poll asked more than 2,300 tourists in Southern California what factors were most important in planning a vacation or convention. On a scale of 1 to 10, with 10 being the most significant, domestic visitors gave safety an average rating of 8.9. No fewer than two-thirds of international visitors said that safety was their single most important concern. In choosing a hotel, 62 percent of domestic visitors and two-thirds of international travelers put safety and security at the head of the list.

Under the circumstances, it seems necessary to weigh the industry's vulnerabilities and figure out what can be done about them.

IN THE CROSSHAIRS

Terrorists are targeting the hospitality industry for sound tactical reasons. People gather with their guard down at hotels and restaurants in every city in the world. They pack into trains and planes. Often, they segregate themselves into convenient groups, American military personnel in this restaurant, Western tourists in that hotel, and no devout Muslims at all in the local bars and night clubs. And with the exception of airlines, and to some extent cruise ships, security measures at potential targets tends to be lax or nonexistent. No other sector of business offers more easy and conspicuous victims than hospitality.

Here are some of the more obvious vulnerabilities:

- **Hotels are popular targets, for good reason.**

There are just so many points of access, and each one offers opportunities for attack. Their lobbies are large, open spaces with multiple entrances and hundreds of people moving through them every day. Driveways make it easy to bring a car bomb right up to the door. Loading docks, garages, delivery vehicles, and luggage storage areas all present risks of their own. Ventilation systems and water supply also are vulnerable. And few hotel operators really want to provide effective security, for fear that airport-style lines and metal detectors will put off customers even more than the fear of terrorism does.

• **Transportation is a prime target for terrorists.**

And attacks on the transportation system can be devastating for the hospitality industry, as we know all too well. The bombing of Pan Am Flight 103 over Lockerbie, Scotland, in 1988 and the 1995 Sarin gas attack on the Tokyo subway system rattled nerves around the world. The hijacking of four airliners for use in the September 11 attacks all but put an end to elective travel for months. By September 21, hotels in New York City that are accustomed to being fully booked were running at 40 percent occupancy. Restaurants in European tourist centers quickly saw their business drop off by 40 percent or more. And over the next year, eight airlines either went out of business or filed for bankruptcy protection. So did eight cruise lines.

Since then, security has been tightened dramatically for airlines and cruise ships. Airline passengers and their carry-on luggage are routinely searched. Airport personnel must survive rigorous background checks and soon will be required to carry biometric ID cards. Cruise lines now forbid anyone but passengers to board their vessels. Cruise ships now pick up half a dozen sea marshals along with the harbor pilot to protect the bridge and engine room and patrol the rest of the ship for signs of trouble. In the port of Miami, divers even meticulously scan the hull for attached mines before the vessel is allowed to enter the harbor, and a Coast Guard cutter accompanies the ship to the dock.

Yet more travel-related attacks clearly are to come. Spanish authorities recently found a partially completed bomb under railroad tracks running between Madrid and Seville. A week later, a French railroad worker discovered a bomb under the line from Paris to Basel. It seems only a matter of time before another railroad bombing is successful.

Travel in the United States may be even more vulnerable than it is in Europe. New York City alone has no fewer than 468 subway stations, all of them inviting targets for a terrorist bomb. Much of the transportation on the East Coast is routed through tunnels into New York City, Baltimore, Norfolk, VA, and other cities. Much of the rest travels over major bridges. Al Qaeda leader Khalid Sheik Mohammed reportedly instructed a subordinate in the United States to look into blowing up the Brooklyn Bridge. On the West Coast, bridges form a series of choke points for most of the highway traffic from Seattle to San Diego. A single bus full of explosives could disrupt or block traffic for months. And, of course, Al Qaeda has long been rumored to be planning another spectacular attack using hijacked planes to destroy American targets. That could cause an all-out depression in the hospitality industry for years to come. No less than $11 billion had been spent on air security in the United States by early 2004, only $110 million on security for subways and commuter rail.

- **Major sports events are terrorist magnets.**

The assassination of 11 Israeli athletes at the Munich Olympics in 1972 set a precedent that today's extremists must long to follow. Over the next 29 years, until the September 11 attacks, no such assault ever garnered so much publicity for the terrorists' cause.

The Olympic Games in Athens in August 2004 were a rare opportunity for mass slaughter, with thousands of visitors packed onto cruise ships that served as hotels. Greece devoted a bit more than $1.2 billion to security for the Olympics; it even installed sonar to scan the harbors for underwater threats. Yet these events were extraordinarily difficult to protect against terrorists willing to sacrifice their lives for the cause of wholesale killing. The Atlanta Olympics in 1996 had the tightest security the organizers and city could provide for them. Yet someone managed to plant a bomb that killed one passing visitor. The Athens games could have seen far worse.

This seemed particularly likely in light of the Athens bombings of May 5, 2004. In this incident, 100 days before the start of the Olympics, three bombs severely damaged a police station in the densely populated Kalithea district near hotels soon to be used by Olympic officials. Officials said the bombing appeared to have been intended to cause as many casualties as possible. The fact that no major terrorist incident marred the games, stands as an anti-terrorist triumph. However, it does not make attacks any less likely at future sports events.

- **Reporters follow the money; terrorists could keep it from going anywhere.**

An attack on the financial infrastructure could cripple the hospitality industry, at least temporarily. About 80 percent of bills in this sector are paid by credit card. And in a recent study of terrorist risks to credit-card issuers, FI found some methods of attack that could be orders of magnitude more destructive than the worst case of credit-card fraud ever recorded.

In the United States, just ten data-processing centers transmit everything from huge corporate transfers to Social Security deposits to personal utility payments—more than $3.5 trillion per day in all. The equivalent systems in Europe and Asia also are highly concentrated. An assault on those centers—by destroying their telephone lines; detonating cheap, readily available (or easily made) electromagnetic-pulse bombs to wipe the memories of their computers; or simply applying for janitorial jobs and carrying pipe bombs to work—could create a liquidity crisis that would disrupt the global economy for weeks or months.

- **Destroying data could be safe, easy, and disastrous.**

Thus far, cyberterrorism has been more fantasy than reality; most terrorists probably find it easier to build bombs than to learn about computers and networks. Yet the risk is real. A virus that destroyed reservations or billing records could cost a company millions of dollars immediately, and the inconvenience to thousands of customers might ruin existing relationships and future sales. And we know of at least one case where a malicious hacker encrypted a company's data and offered to sell them the key for a hefty price. At this point, most firms have installed at least rudimentary firewalls and antivirus software, but we doubt that many could withstand the attention of a skilled and determined cyberterrorist. The situation would be even worse if the hacker were an employee or disgruntled former employee familiar with the company's security systems.

WEIGHING THE RISK

Anyone with a morbid imagination can spin this kind of scare scenario almost from thin air, and that can be a worthwhile exercise for hospitality executives trying to identify their own facility's risks. And if amateurs can recognize a few of their own vulnerabilities, terrorists can probably find a dozen more.

Nonetheless, it is important to keep the threat in perspective. The whole point of terrorism is to create a maximum of fear with a minimum of resources, so that small and weak forces can win out over an enemy they could not hope to defeat in a heads-up battle. By definition, only a few of the potential targets will ever be attacked.

In creating fear, terrorism clearly succeeds. Late in 2003, polls found that 70 percent of people in Italy and Germany were "somewhat worried" or "very worried" about terrorism. In Spain, where a native Basque terrorist movement is blamed for killing more than 1,000 people over a period of four decades, no fewer than 85 percent of respondents were similarly concerned, months before the train bombings in Madrid.

Yet consider these numbers: In an average year, roughly one in 4 million Americans dies after being struck by lightning. According to David Ropeik of the Harvard Center for Risk Analysis, the average American's chance of being killed by a terrorist in any given year is just 1 in 9.3 million. Not many Americans worry about being struck by lightning.

Even in the obvious hotspots, the fear of terrorism is much greater than the actual threat. In Israel, 174 people died in terrorist incidents in 2003. (This number excludes the terrorists themselves.) This is fewer than three for every 100,000 people, or about half the death rate from homicide in the United States.

However, the impact of a terrorist attack can be all out of proportion to the event itself. As horrifying as the September 11 attacks were, they killed only 7 percent as many people as traffic accidents did in the United States that year. Yet before it was all over, the world's airlines lost an estimated $25 billion and cut some 100,000 jobs. Eventually, eight airlines either went out of business or filed for bankruptcy protection. So did eight cruise lines.

In forecasting, we often distinguish among several different categories of events. There are high-probability, high-impact events, for which we all must plan. There are low-probability, low-impact events that can safely be ignored. The remainder fall somewhere along the spectra of probability and impact.

Even for the hospitality industry, terrorist attacks in almost any individual location are very low-probability events. Yet their impact is so high that we must plan for the possibility and avoid it as best we can, just as we avoid standing under trees during a lightning storm.

DANGEROUS GROUND

The Motel 6 on the outskirts of Rock Springs, Wyoming, is probably safer from terrorist attacks than the Marriott in Islamabad, Pakistan—but you probably had figured that out already. Fortunately, there are more useful things to be said about where terrorists are likely to strike.

As we have seen in the United States, Spain, France, and too many other countries, nowhere in the world is entirely safe from terrorism. Nonetheless, there are some characteristics that the most unstable, terror-prone lands have in common. We can avoid vacationing in places rife with terrorism *today* simply by watching the evening news. For investment and other longer-term planning, three factors are worth considering:

- **How rich are the very rich? How poor are the very poor?**

A wide gap between the richest and the poorest members of a society is one of the most reliable warnings of the social and political instability that can inspire terrorism.

To measure this gap, compare the share of total household income received by the richest tenth of a country's population with the share received by the poorest tenth. For example, in Brazil, the richest tenth of the population receives 48 percent of the nation's total household income, while the poorest tenth receives only 0.7 percent. That is, the rich receive about 68.6 times as much income as the poor. Countries with an index over 45 are likely to be highly unstable.

FI developed this indicator many years ago. It is the most valuable clue we have that a country may be on the brink of chaos. Several years ago, the CIA began to publish it in the *CIA World Factbook*, available online at http://www.odci.gov/cia/publications/factbook/index.html. Unfortunately, figures are available only for a limited number of countries. For the rest, you will have to dig out the data yourself.

- **How many young men are there?**

Throughout the world, the people most prone to violence, whether political or otherwise, are males from 15 to 30 years old. It is this group that provides the majority of terrorists, rioters, and mujahideen.

This indicator clearly differs between the prosperous industrialized countries, where birthrates are low and young men are a relatively small part of society, and the developing lands, where birthrates are high and this troublesome group is larger. In the United States and Japan, men of this age make up about 10.5 percent of the population. In contrast, 14.5 percent of the population in Mexico consists of men in their prime troublemaking years. In Iraq, the figure is 28.3 percent.

This information is readily available from the U.N. Population Division's World Population Prospects database, at http://esa.un.org/unpp/index.asp ?panel=2; only a little arithmetic is required to combine several five-year age cohorts and convert the result to a percentage of population. The table contains 2002 data for 20 countries with large populations in this group, plus the United States for comparison.

Males, Age 15–29

Country	Number (thousands) in 2000	Percent of population
Iraq	3,335	28.3%
Iran	10,645	21.6
Algeria	4,681	15.5
Turkey	9,946	14.6
Indonesia	30,800	14.6
South Africa	6,416	14.6
Mexico	14,366	14.5
Brazil	24,490	14.3
India	142,384	14.0
Egypt	9,436	13.9
Afghanistan	2,974	13.9
Pakistan	19,337	13.6
Gaza and West Bank	431	13.5
China	165,111	12.9
Kazakhstan	2,011	12.9
Argentina	4,785	12.9
Israel	774	12.8
Cuba	1,307	11.7
Greece	1,193	10.6
Japan	13,294	10.5
United States	29,951	10.5

Of course, there is more to it than statistics. In almost any society where there are enough young men, a few will commit political violence. Witness the bombing of the federal office building in Oklahoma City.

However, two factors can dramatically aggravate the risk of terrorism. These are employment and education. Where most young men have jobs, they have a stake in "the system" and are much less likely to become terrorists. There also is a good chance that they will be too tired after work to bother with activism in any form. But high levels of unemployment among young men create a reservoir of potential troublemakers ready to be exploited by unscrupulous leaders.

The situation is even more volatile where those young men have a good education. The poor and illiterate know they are likely to remain poor; they may consider this unjust, but they have grown up with limited expectations and generally have come to accept them. But throughout the Middle East, and in some other areas, there are hundreds of thousands of young men who were educated for a middle-class life that is no longer available to them. Without prospects and deeply embittered, they are the most ready of all to take up arms against a world they feel has closed them out. In the most terror-prone countries, large numbers of literate, unemployed young men face a life of poverty.

- **How large and influential is the Muslim community?**

It goes against the grain to single out any religion as a source of trouble. Yet it has been clear for years that the Muslim lands face major problems with religious extremists who are dedicated to advancing their political, social, and doctrinal views by any means necessary. In our 1994 study of terrorism, the spread of militant Islam was the single most obvious factor we found that would increase both the frequency and the intensity of terrorist violence in the years ahead. With deep reluctance, we gave in and added this to FI's list of major trends shortly before the September 11 attacks.

Islam has never undergone the equivalent of the Protestant Reformation or the Jewish Reform movement; thus the clergy remains the ultimate authority in all matters, civil as well as religious. Thanks to the apparently liberal tenet that Muslims can disagree in matters of dogma, yet remain true to the faith so long as they subscribe to a few core tenets, there is no religious doctrine or authority to weed out leaders whom other faiths would reject as vicious lunatics. And the idea of *jihad*—religious war against "enemies of Islam"—remains strong in the Muslim world.

This combination of factors—the availability of young men to act as foot soldiers, the disappointed expectations of a middle class that has lost its future, an untempered tradition of zealotry and religious war, and unscrupulous leaders willing to exploit them—is the primary source of terrorism in the world today. The most unstable, and often dangerous, countries in the years ahead will combine all these factors. They are easy to identify, and steer clear of, for anyone willing to do a little research when making long-term plans.

FUTURE SHOCKS

Terrorism is evolving in at least three ways: It is gaining a wider base of support, it is becoming decentralized, and it is aiming increasingly at civilian targets. In the years ahead, these trends will increase the terrorist threat to the hospitality industry throughout the world.

Whatever else the Iraq war has accomplished, it has been a godsend for the cause of terrorism. Iraq today is playing much the same role that Afghanistan did in the 1980s. It is an inspiration, a recruiting tool, and a training ground for the terrorists of the future.

The occupation of Afghanistan by the Soviet Union was a cause that radical Islamists could rally around. All over the Muslim world, extremists picked themselves up and hurried to the front, where fellow Islamists trained them in the ways of terrorism and the CIA provided weapons and supplies that are being used against the West to this day. This is where both Osama bin Laden and the Taliban's Mullah Omar got their start.

Afghanistan gave terrorists another useful tool as well, a global population of sympathizers willing to look the other way as they go about spreading fear and death. For every Muslim who went to Afghanistan, many others could not make that commitment, yet were sufficiently radicalized to view the terrorists as heroes, even when they continued bombing after the original cause was won.

Post-Afghanistan, bin Laden concerned himself with three issues: the presence of "infidel" troops in the religiously important Arab land of Saudi Arabia; the West's failure to deal effectively with the ethnic cleansing of Muslims in Bosnia, Croatia, and Kosovo; and the bombing of Iraq by the United States and its allies in the original Gulf War. These grievances resonated widely enough to bring Al Qaeda an estimated 5,000 members worldwide.

A dozen years later, American troops remain in Saudi Arabia, the United States has occupied Iraq, and in April 2004 American forces attacked a mosque in Fallujah, which the Shia consider a holy city. This second Iraq war is inspiring a new generation of terrorists, just as Afghanistan and the Gulf War did. It may be training and equipping them as well, given reports that foreign fighters are entering Iraq through Iran and Syria and that resistance fighters are using weapons the Americans supplied to the Iraqi police. We saw the result in the Madrid bombing, even before the Sadrist uprising. Terrorists inspired and trained by the American presence in Iraq will be responsible for many of the attacks that afflict the world in the next ten years.

Those incidents will be harder to prevent, because the structure of the terrorist community is changing. When Al Qaeda and its associated groups were still largely unchallenged, there was at least some recognizable organization to it. The 1998 attack by American cruise missiles on an al Qaeda compound in Afghanistan may have failed, but at least it had an identifiable target. Security officials still monitor 30 to 40 groups affiliated with Al Qaeda in Southeast and Central Asia, the Caucasus, North Africa, and Europe. Yet those groups are losing their significance. More and more, terrorists take inspiration from bin Laden, but specific incidents are carried out more or less spontaneously by small groups of like-minded individuals, who may have known each other for years. These cells are difficult to detect before it is too late, and virtually impossible to infiltrate.

In addition, terrorist groups that once focused on local goals, such as undermining the stability of oppressive governments, are heeding the call to *jihad.* The Pakistan-based Lashkar-e-Taiba used to concern itself only with "liberating" Muslim Kashmir from India. Late in 2003, Australian authorities arrested a member of the group believed to have been scouting out targets for attacks down under. And since the Iraq war began, the radical Ansar al-Islam has spread out from its base in the northern part of that country into parts of Europe, where members are believed to be recruiting suicide bombers for attacks not only in Iraq but on the continent. The group's founder, Mullah Krekar, now lives in Norway and is believed to have been involved in the bombings in both Morocco and Madrid. This change too will make it more difficult to combat international terrorism. For antiterrorism specialists, the world is becoming more complicated every day.

However, the third development is taking place in part because government security efforts have become a lot more vigorous in recent years. They have had reason to. In 1996, a truck bomb at the Khobar Towers, in Riyadh, Saudi Arabia, killed 19 American peacekeepers attached to the United Nations and wounded 372 others. In 1998, terrorists associated with Al Qaeda used truck bombs to destroy the American embassies in Dar Es Salaam, Tanzania, and Nairobi, Kenya. In 2000, another Al Qaeda team killed 17 American sailors and damaged the *USS Cole* in the harbor at Aden, Yemen. Though it took too long, the lessons of those events have been learned.

Military bases and other government installations today are much harder to attack than they were in the 1990s. As a result, would-be terrorists have been forced to seek out civilian targets. With the exception of some pipeline bombings in South America, nearly all of the facilities attacked in the last six years have belonged to the hospitality industry. Hotels, restaurants, and transportation systems are likely to remain in the crosshairs for as long as the battle against terrorism continues.

SAFETY FIRST

Despite the horrifying headlines that regularly arrive from around the world, many companies seem to have shrugged off the risk of a terrorist attack. According to a recent survey by the Business Roundtable, 85 percent of American firms have increased their spending on security since the terrorist attacks of September 11, 2001. Yet their budgets for this purpose have risen by only 10 percent, on average, in nearly three years. Even in this time of relatively stable prices, about half of that increase has gone just to keep up with inflation.

The situation is little better in the hospitality industry. Though some hotels have added security cameras to their lobbies and installed electronic locks on guestroom doors, many more have done nothing at all. A recent survey of hotels in the volatile Pacific Rim, locale of the bombings in Jakarta and Bali, found that only 25 percent had made any effort to bolster security.

That really is not good enough. Small facilities such as independent hotels and restaurants, which cannot afford to set up their own security operation, will find it increasingly necessary to hire a competent security firm to do the job for them.

While that mandate applies to everyone in the hospitality industry, there are places where it is particularly important. Las Vegas almost goes out of its way to offend the sensibilities of fundamentalist Islam, which bans gambling, alcohol, and any form of sexual activity by women that is not rigidly controlled by their husbands. If terrorists strike at the hospitality industry inside the United States, they are likely to hit Las Vegas first.

A hint at what even a small terrorist attack could accomplish there came in April 2004, when a power line failed at the Bellagio Hotel & Casino, causing a cascade of problems that eventually burned several thousand feet of cable. The resort was shut down for more than three days at a cost of about $3 million per day in lost revenue. A deliberate attack, calculated to cause as much damage as possible, could have been far worse.

IDENTITY CONCERNS

Security begins with people. This is especially true for the hospitality industry, where large numbers of workers are needed to serve even larger numbers of guests. Being absolutely certain who all those people are is the first step in defending against terrorism.

For any business, the most likely security threats come from disgruntled employees and former employees. Before people are hired, they should be screened thoroughly, not only to confirm their identity but to weed out those with significant criminal records, suspicious associations, or other potential risks. The screening procedure should be as rigorous at a hotel or restaurant as it is at an airport or airline. This will be particularly difficult for companies that hire large numbers of noncitizens, and particularly undocumented workers. Yet no company that skimps on this process can hope to be safe from attack.

In a world of terrorism, this requirement extends not only to the firm's own employees, but to those of suppliers, builders, and service contractors. Someone who comes to repair the air conditioning could also release anthrax into the system, and no one would find it easier to contaminate food than the people who deliver it. Suppliers and contractors who cannot guarantee that their employees have been screened as rigorously as the facility's own workers should be replaced by firms that can.

Having once screened their new hires, large-scale employers need to make certain each day that someone presenting an employee ID really is that worker and not an imposter. Even photographic identity cards can be tampered with, so something more secure is required.

That probably means biometrics, the use of automated systems to match people with their known physical attributes. Available technologies include fingerprint and retinal scanners, facial recognition software, and pen-sized accelerometers that can measure the precise hand movements used to sign one's name—data far more difficult to disguise than the signature itself. These techniques have undergone rapid development since 9/11, and many are now deemed reliable enough for practical application. Installing a biometric identity system and training security personnel to use it is expensive. Yet it is by far the best guarantee now available that someone who appears to be an employee really is who he claims to be.

Identifying guests with any certainty is still more difficult. For restaurants and other businesses where customer turnover is extremely rapid, it may be impractical or impossible. However, hotels, resorts, and conference centers all need to be certain who is staying with them. This will be simpler now that most foreign visitors need machine-read visas, fingerprints, and photo IDs to enter the country. A national identity card, if one is ever issued in the United States, could make the process easier still. These changes will be especially welcome for international meetings, where asking guests for fingerprints or other reliable identification has been an especially frequent and difficult challenge.

On an industry-wide level in the United States, there is one other change that could help to ease the process of "people security." This is to work with the Department of Homeland Security to identify potential problems. The Bureau of Citizenship and Immigration Services (formerly the Immigration and Nationalization Service), U.S. Immigration and Customs Enforcement, and U.S. Customs and Border Protection all can provide valuable information about security threats such as known terrorists who are believed to have entered the country. Developing close working relationships with these agencies should be a priority for the Travel Industry Association, the American Hotel & Lodging Association, and other leading industry groups.

SITE SAFETY

Ideally, no one could enter a hotel, restaurant, plane, or train before his identity had been confirmed and he had passed through a metal detector. Then security guards would monitor all public spaces to make certain that no one had slipped through inappropriately. That will never happen, of course, but most hospitality locations could do a lot better protecting their premises than they do today.

We can see evidence of this in the amount that hospitality venues spend on security. With all that they have to protect, average American hotels spend just 1 to 2 percent of their payroll on their security force. Contrast this with hotels in Israel, which spend, on average, about 8 percent of payroll on the security force.

In Israeli hotels, there is none of the chaos typical of hotels elsewhere. Guests are processed in an orderly, efficient, and highly security-conscious manner. They are likely to enter through a single lobby entrance that is protected by an airport-style metal detector. Guards patrol inside and out. At the most security-conscious hotels in Israel, identity checks are performed outside the hotel itself, and no one other than guests is allowed in at all.

Yet when it comes to hotel security, American casinos probably set the standard. At the state-of-the-art Borgata, in Atlantic City, more than 2,000 video cameras constantly watch the 125,000 square-foot casino floor, 70,000 square feet of event space, a 50,000 square-foot spa, a 7,100-car parking lot, employee areas, and access routes to more than 2,000 guest rooms. There even is an automatic face-recognition system to screen for known cheats—and to identify VIP guests so that they can be quickly targeted for special service. If the government ever provides a database of terrorist photographs, which has been suggested but not yet acted on, the system might be able to identify them as well.

At the Venetian, in Las Vegas, uniformed guards patrol the public areas, while others are stationed at the entrances and at a security booth in the lobby. Even before a major expansion, there were more than 200 guards in all, at least 40 on duty at any time; since then, both the number of rooms—now about 4,000—and the number of guards have doubled.

Place metal detectors at each entrance, and these casinos would be ready to face the worst that the age of terror is likely to throw at them.

It is easy to argue against that kind of security. Setting up the systems requires a big investment, and operating them involves substantial continuing costs. Guests at a luxury hotel might be more put off by the presence of armed guards and metal detectors than they are by lax security.

And there have been occasional excesses. For a time, the Bellagio Hotel and Casino, in Las Vegas, reportedly blocked driveway access with a vehicle parked across a blind corner. When guests stopped their cars, aggressive security guards dressed in black and without visible identification approached and demanded to look in their car trunks. Those who refused were rudely turned away. It was a bad mistake, and it lives on in harshly negative customer satisfaction reports that are widely available on the Internet.

Yet hospitality security need not be taken to extremes to accomplish its purpose. It just has to be good enough to send would-be terrorists in search of softer targets. That, at least, is possible. And there is every reason to believe that most guests would be willing to put up with a little inconvenience in return for the knowledge that they are as safe as they can be in an increasingly unsafe world.

This widespread prosperity should feed upon itself, with each trading nation helping to generate the continued well-being of its partners.

KEY TRENDS FOR SECURITY

1. The economy of the developed world will continue to grow for at least the next five years. Any interruptions will be relatively short-lived.

Summary: After a brief but painful recession, the U.S. economy has been growing steadily for nearly three years, through the first quarter of 2004. Job creation lagged far behind GDP growth, but it too appears to have begun a substantial recovery.

Similar improvements are being seen around the world. Many of the European economies are emerging from years of stagnation, while Japan is seeing its first significant expansion in a decade. India and China are achieving GDP growth that averages 6 percent or better each year.

Barring another terrorist incident on the scale of 9/11, or some equivalent shock, this widespread prosperity should feed upon itself, with each trading nation helping to generate the continued well-being of its partners. It can be sustained for some years to come.

Implications for Security: The gap between the world's have and have-not nations will continue to widen. In the Middle East and the developing countries, resentment against the prosperity of the West, especially the United States, will inspire terrorist incidents with growing frequency. Many of these attacks will strike at the hospitality industry.

This will be especially troublesome if Iraq continues in chaos and poverty under American domination. The prototype for this version of the future is the Palestinian *intifada*. The Iraqis are beginning to blame America for their problems, much as the Palestinians blame Israel for the problems in the Occupied Territories. Ultimately, they will respond in much the same way, and with no less determination. The turmoil in Fallujah and Najaf could be only the beginning.

The gap between haves and have-nots within the United States is growing as well. This could eventually inspire protest movements against business and government, but there is little possibility that they will resort to violence to gain their ends.

2. The world's population will grow to 9 billion by 2050.

Summary: The greatest fertility is found in those countries least able to support their existing populations. Populations in many developing countries will double between 2000 and 2050; in the Palestinian Territories, they will rise by 217 percent. In contrast, the developed nations will fall from 23 percent of the total world population in 1950 and about 14 percent in 2000 to only 10 percent in 2050. In 10 years or so, the workforce in Japan and much of Europe will be shrinking by 1 percent per year.

Implications for Security: Rapid population growth will reinforce American domination of the global economy, as the European Union falls to third place behind the United States and China. Among the poor nations, this will foster still more resentment of the world's most prosperous land.

Unfortunately, when populations grow faster than resources do, the general quality of life inevitably declines. Since the wealthy are largely immune to this loss, the poor and middle class not only suffer, but see that their rulers do not. And because political leaders the world over find it convenient to blame their problems on others, much of the resulting hostility will be aimed at the wealthy industrialized lands, who will be reviled as exploiters of the developing countries. Terrorist movements are one expression of the unrest that can be expected to grow as the world population does.

Barring enactment of strict immigration controls, rapid migration will continue from the Southern Hemisphere to the North, and especially from former colonies to Europe. Culture clashes between natives and immigrants are likely to destabilize societies throughout the developed world. Germany, Britain, and other lands traditionally welcoming to refugees and other migrants already are experiencing strong backlashes against asylum-seekers.

3. Militant Islam is spreading and gaining power.

Summary: It has been clear for years that the Muslim lands face major problems with religious extremists dedicated to advancing their political, social, and doctrinal views by any means necessary. Those problems often have spilled over into the rest of the world. They will do so again. By 2020, a strong majority of the world's twenty-five or so most important Muslim lands could be in the hands of extremist religious governments. The United States massively fortified the Muslim extremist infrastructure by supplying it with arms and training during its proxy war with the Soviet Union in Afghanistan. It is, in effect, repeating this mistake in Iraq.

Implications for Security: Virtually all of the Muslim lands face an uncertain, and very possibly bleak, future of political instability and growing violence. The exceptions are the oil states, where money can still buy relative peace, at least for now.

The West, and particularly the United States, is likely to face more, and more violent, acts of terrorism for at least the next 20 years.

Both Europe and the United States ultimately may face homegrown Muslim extremist movements. Thanks largely to waves of immigration during the 1980s and 1990s, Islam is the fastest-growing religion in both regions. There are credible reports that extremist clerics in Europe are successfully recruiting young Muslims to the cause of *jihad* against their adopted homes.

Western interests also will be vulnerable in many countries outside the Muslim core. The strong international ties formed among Islamic militants during the anti-Soviet war in Afghanistan have produced an extremist infrastructure that can support terrorist activities almost anywhere in the world.

This development must be taken even more seriously, because for the first time a Muslim country—Pakistan—has nuclear weapons, which Muslim extremists view as an "Islamic bomb," available to promote their cause. As the world has learned, some high-ranking Pakistanis already have been willing to donate nuclear technology to other Muslims. From here on out, the possibility of nuclear terrorism is a realistic threat.

4. Societal values are changing rapidly.

Summary: Industrialization raises educational levels, changes attitudes toward authority, reduces fertility, alters gender roles, and encourages broader political participation. This process is just beginning throughout the developing world. The future will be dominated by the materialistic values of Generations X and Dot-com.

Implications for Security: Reaction against changing values is one of the prime motives of cultural extremism, particularly in the Muslim world and in parts of India. As values continue to evolve in those lands, becoming more materialistic and Westernized as the younger generations achieve more influence, terrorism is likely to proliferate. It will be exported to the Western countries that radicals blame for the "contamination" of their traditional culture.

5. Oil prices are stable at $25 to $28 per barrel; they rise above that level only in times of trouble.

Summary: In autumn 2004, OPEC's aim is to hold the price of oil at relatively high levels, and the instability in the Middle East is making this relatively easy. However, keeping prices high requires a unity of purpose that member countries have never been able to sustain for very long. The cost of raising a barrel of oil from the ground in this region is around one-tenth the wholesale price. New oil supplies coming on line in the former Soviet Union, China, and other parts of the world will make it even more difficult to sustain prices at artificially high levels. Prices above $28 per barrel are simply unsustainable.

Implications for Security: Young men in Saudi Arabia and some other oil-rich states once grew up knowing that government subsidies guaranteed them a comfortable life. Today, they must earn a living on their own, often with inadequate preparation, in a troubled economy. Poverty rates are rising, even while the Saud family and its hangers-on remain extremely rich—this in the land of Mecca, dominated by the ultra-conservative Wahabi Muslim movement, and host to American troops, some of them female. This is a recipe for terrorism and revolution. Recent attacks linked to Al Qaeda are likely to be only the first in a long and bloody series.

6. Technology increasingly dominates both the economy and society.

Summary: In all fields, the previous state of the art is being replaced by new high-tech developments at an ever faster rate. Computers and telecommunications have become an ordinary part of our environment, rather than just tools we use for specific tasks. Biotechnology, and eventually nanotechnology, may do so as well. These developments provide dozens of new opportunities to create businesses and jobs, but they often require a higher level of education and training to use them effectively.

Implications for Security: As technology brings extra productivity, it retards job creation. We have seen the effects in the slow recovery of employment in the United States from 2002 through early 2004. Other developed countries are likely to feel the same effect in the future. This will increase the number of disaffected people who feel they have no place in society. In rigidly conservative countries, and in immigrant communities in more liberal industrialized nations, resentment toward the prosperous will grow.

New technologies often require a higher level of education and training to use them effectively. This too will limit opportunities for the unprepared.

Technology brings vulnerabilities of its own. Dependence on computer data systems and telecommunications networks means that a single virus or hacker attack can cost one company many hundreds of thousands of dollars. The Melissa virus in March 1999 reportedly shut down the computer systems of between ten and twenty-five *Fortune* 500 companies. There is no widely accepted way to measure the cost of virus attacks, but at least one estimate suggests that computer viruses cost up to $18 billion in 2000 alone.

However, new technology is one of the most valuable tools against terrorism. Improved detectors for metal and explosives will make it increasingly difficult to plant bombs on aircraft and ships and in government buildings.

7. Generations X and Dot-com will have major effects in the future.

Summary: Members of Generation X—roughly, the 30-plus cohort—and especially of Generation Dot-com, now in their 20s, have more in common with their peers throughout the world than with their parents' generation. They are entrepreneurial, well educated, and predominately English-speaking. Virtually all are materialistic, many are economically conservative, and they care for little but the bottom line—their own bottom line. Independent to a fault, they have no loyalty to employers at all.

Implications for Security: Radical conservatives in the Muslim and Hindu worlds view the materialism of younger generations as proof that the West is contaminating, and degrading, their society. The backlash against this perceived influence is one of the most powerful tools that unscrupulous leaders can use to motivate potential terrorists to "defend their faith" by attacking Westerners.

8. International exposure includes a greater risk of terrorist attack.

Summary: State-sponsored terrorism appears to be on the decline, as tougher sanctions make it more trouble than it is worth. However, nothing will prevent small, local political organizations and special-interest groups from using terror to promote their causes. And as the United States learned on September 11, the most dangerous terrorist groups are no longer motivated by specific political goals, but by generalized, virulent hatred based on religion and culture. On balance, the amount of terrorist activity in the world is likely to go up, not down, in the next ten years.

Implications for Security: The growth of international business brings new opportunities and targets for terrorism. The presence of Western-owned facilities in Muslim lands also provides some extra motivation for terrorism. This is particularly important for resorts and night clubs, where men and women mingle in ways not approved by radical Islam.

Western corporations may have to devote more of their resources to self-defense, while accepting smaller-than-expected profits from operations in the developing countries.

Like the attacks on the World Trade Center and Pentagon, and the American embassies in Kenya and Tanzania before them, any attacks on major corporate facilities are likely to be designed for maximum destruction and casualties. Bloodshed for bloodshed's sake has become a characteristic of modern terrorism.

Where terrorism is most common, countries will find it impossible to attract foreign investment, no matter how attractive their resources.

Though Islamic terrorists form only a tiny part of the Muslim community, they have a large potential for disruption throughout the region from Turkey to the Philippines.

The economies of the industrialized nations could be thrown into recession at any time by another terrorist event on the scale of September 11. This is particularly true of the United States. The impact would be greatest if the attack discouraged travel, as the hijacking of airliners to attack the World Trade Center and Pentagon did in 2001 and 2002.

The U.S. economy is being affected already by American antiterrorism measures. Since Washington began to photograph incoming travelers and required more extensive identification from them, tourism to America is off by some 30 percent. The number of foreign students coming to American universities has declined by a similar amount.

Part II

Sector Forecasts

Chapter 4

If This Is Tuesday, It Must Be Kuala Lumpur

The global market for tourism has just doubled, for many practical purposes. And that is only one of the changes that the tourist industry will be absorbing over the next ten to twenty years.

Around the world, the cost of travel is falling, while the middle class is becoming more prosperous and eager to go places. At the same time, demographic trends, changing values, and other developments are helping to bring some highly profitable turmoil to this segment of the hospitality industry.

Two long-standing trends will remain unchanged as far into the future as we can see: growth and globalization. Tourism is expanding rapidly, with more travelers every year and a wider variety of destinations and activities.

EXPANDING TRAVEL

The world's travel and tourism industry has gone through some grim times of late. First, air travel crashed after the September 11 terrorist attacks in the United States; in 2002, the number of passengers on international flights was down for the first time in more than ten years. Then SARS—severe acute respiratory distress syndrome—made Asia all but off limits to international visitors; Asian carriers lost half of their passengers. The invasion of Iraq cut transatlantic air travel by another 25 percent from the previous bad year; American domestic air travel was down by 15 percent. And no sooner was that worry past than the dollar collapsed on international currency markets, causing American tourists to stay home in droves. Orlando prospered, but Europe lost an estimated 20 to 30 percent of its tourist trade. In all, the industry has yet to regain the high-water mark it set in 2000.

Fortunately, bad times never last, and these seem to be just about over. In the United States, 2004 forecasts call for a rise in travel and tourism revenues to about $568 billion, nearing the $570.5 billion seen four years ago. Globally, the World Travel and Tourism Council (WTTC) predicts that all components of the travel market will turn out to have grown in 2004. Spending on travel and tourism, they estimate, will be up by 5.9 percent over 2003, to $5.5 trillion. The industry will create 3.3 million jobs worldwide.

That is important not just to the industry, but to the world economy. Travel and tourism is adding more than $1.5 trillion to the global GDP in 2004 and providing jobs for nearly 73.7 million people—and that is just the industry's direct impact. Add in suppliers and other industries that depend on travel and tourism, and the total impact is closer to $4.2 trillion—over 10 percent of the world's GDP—and 214.7 million jobs, or more than 8 percent of global employment.

Those numbers will be rising rapidly in the years ahead, just as they have for most of the last half-century. Over the next ten years, travel and tourism are expected to grow by an average of 4.5 percent annually. By 2014, that will amount to a market of more than $9.5 trillion, adding nearly $7 trillion to the world's GDP. Direct employment will not grow quite as quickly, but it will be up 1.7 percent annually, to nearly 87.5 million jobs, while indirect employment will account for some 260 million jobs around the world.

Looked at another way, in 1950 the travel industry recorded just 25 million international arrivals. (That includes both business and vacation travel, but personal travel regularly makes up about 80 percent of the total.) In 2001, arrivals were up to 693 million—and even that is just the beginning. By 2020, forecasters predict that there will be 1.5 billion, a solid majority of them vacationers. And the grimness of 2001 will be long forgotten.

PLACES TO GO, THINGS TO DO

The tourism market expands when potential travelers have more disposable income, and throughout the developed world, and much of the developing world, they do. In the United States, 13 percent of households now have annual incomes over $100,000. They spend an average of more than $3,600 per year on travel, nearly half again the national average. And 57 percent of these affluent consumers have purchased a luxury travel product over the last year. The number rises with income. Among households with incomes over $150,000, 64 percent have bought luxury travel products; over $200,000, the number is 68 percent. Similar trends are seen throughout Europe, Japan, and other relatively prosperous regions. When people have money, they spend it on travel.

Given so many economically comfortable travelers, countries from Brazil to Malaysia and Chile to Yemen have been working hard to attract their share of tourist dollars. Overall, they have been extremely successful, not just bringing in the wealthy, but attracting middle-class travelers as well. Heavy promotion, together with the spread of lower-cost tour packages and discounted air fares, have opened elite destinations to less wealthy tourists. Where Fiji, Tahiti, and—for more adventurous tourists—the Antarctic, once were playgrounds of the rich, merely-comfortable vacationers are now flocking to them. Cruise lines, too, are seeking middle-class customers, with great success. At the same time, relatively untraveled lands are fast building tourist industries. Nepal, Vietnam, Malaysia, Dubai, and South Africa all are drawing visitors, especially from within their own regions.

This same ability to spend has inspired a host of new tourism products aimed at the relatively well-off. "Theme" and "total immersion" travel experiences aim to provide guests with a complete escape from their daily routines. Old-fashioned dude ranches have been joined by French cooking classes in French chateaux, so-called "adrenaline vacations" like race-car driving schools and bungee jumping in New Zealand, sailing on a clipper ship, and research expeditions to tropical rainforests. One of the hottest markets is for "destination weddings," where the entire wedding party flies to Mexico or the Caribbean for an all-expenses-paid marriage celebration. With American weddings now averaging $22,000, a three-day marriage weekend for $2,500—guests pay their own way—can be awfully attractive.

TRAVEL MARKETS

Not all regions are benefiting from these trends equally. Europe and America remain the world's favorite travel destinations, while Africa is at best an also-ran. Here is a brief look at prospects for major regions of the world.

North America. Not long ago, industry imagined that travel in this region would follow its accustomed patterns. Nearly half of all international tourism would occur between the United States and either Canada or Mexico, while most of the rest would be made up by a steady flow of American tourists to Europe and Europeans to the United States. North America would remain secure in its place as the second-largest travel destination in the world.

It has not worked out that way. Travel to and from the United States has remained depressed by the fear of terrorism and by the high cost of going to Europe when the dollar does not buy nearly as much as it once did. Recent demands by American security officials have further suppressed travel to the United States. Entry rules now require that most visitors submit to being photographed and fingerprinted; eventually most also will have to carry a "biometric" passport that includes copies of their fingerprints and iris patterns. Since American authorities made it harder to enter the country, tourist arrivals have fallen to a level 30 percent from 2001.

This too shall pass. Growing prosperity in the United States, Canada, and Mexico will sustain the expansion of travel within North America at about 3 percent per year. Eventually, the United States will find its way out of the morass of Iraq, the dollar will regain its exchange value, and tourists will find their way between North America, Europe, and points East. Overall, international travel will grow by a bit less than 4 percent per year in this region, somewhat below the global average. Yet the United States will continue to lead the world in spending on and earnings from travel.

Europe. The continent too is in for slower growth than its tourist industry has been accustomed to. Overall, tourist arrivals are expected to expand by only 3 percent per year, bringing 717 million arrivals in 2020. Many of those visitors will bypass Western Europe, the traditional leader destination of choice. Both Northern and Southern Europe also are in for faster-than-average growth, as Asian tourists flock to Germany and Scandinavia, while others seek out the beaches of the Mediterranean. However, the fastest growth will be in travel to and from Central and Eastern Europe, where Soviet domination crippled economies and kept travel demand bottled-up for more than 40 years. By 2020, both Russia and the Czech Republic will join the world's top ten destinations for international tourism.

The Caribbean makes up only a small piece of the travel market, with just 3 percent of international tourist arrivals. Yet it is the overwhelming leader among cruise destinations, receiving nearly half of all cruises taken in the world. Credit this to balmy weather, spectacular beaches, a highly competitive travel industry, and proximity to the United States, which provides no fewer than 80 percent of all cruise passengers. None of these factors is likely to change, so tourist arrivals in the Caribbean should double between 1997 and 2010, and may nearly double again by 2020. However, there are natural limits to how many tourists can be packed into relatively small islands. Sustaining this growth rate will require the speedy development of resorts on relatively untapped islands. In the end, this could homogenize the Caribbean experience and send vacationers looking for less heavily traveled waters.

Central and South America, recognizing the economic benefits of greater tourism, have been positioning themselves as the natural destination for eco-tourists. This strategy will serve the region well in the next 20 years. From the lush rainforests of Costa Rica to the Amazon River Basin to the preserves of sea elephants, seals, and penguins of Tierra del Fuego, South America offers wonders to delight nature-minded vacationers. Cultural attractions also abound in pre-Colombian ruins and Andean villages far off the beaten path.

Developing these resources will not be easy, however. This region's attractions have survived to be worth visiting largely because they are so hard to reach, and many of them will be unable to accommodate large numbers of tourists without being changed in essential ways. Nonetheless, tourism to South America can be expected to grow by nearly 5 percent per year through 2020.

The Middle East does remarkably well on the international tourist market for an area with such a reputation for volatility and danger. Among all the world's regions, it was the second fastest growing tourist destination through-out the late 1990s. It will continue to grow in the years ahead, from 19 million tourist arrivals in 2000 to roughly 69 million in 2020.

Part of this growth can be attributed to the development of new attractions, like the spectacular *Bibliotheque* in Alexandria and the Al Arab Hotel in Dubai, where the seafood restaurant is reached by submarine. And even European tourists have begun to make their way to resorts on the Red Sea. However, the single biggest asset the region has to offer is Islam. Around the world, 1.3 bil-lion Muslims look to the Middle East for inspiration and spiritual leadership. Many of them are beginning to look there for luxury vacations as well. In 2001, some 42,000 Indonesian tourists visited Qatar, Yemen, and other destinations in the region, and the flow of Indonesian tourists to the Gulf states is expected to grow by about 7 percent per year.

Africa south of the Sahara has it all—all but tourists, that is. Sun-baked, surrounded by beaches, with a continent full of exotic wildlife, Africa still man-ages to attract only 4 percent of the world's international tourists, and nets just 2.5 percent of the profits—and more than a third of these go to the desert lands of Morocco, Tunisia, and Algeria in North Africa, not the lush southern region. Even with natural resources to recommend them, the combination of deep poverty and political instability is a hard sell.

This will be slow to change. Kenya recently received approval from Bei-jing as a destination for Chinese tour groups, and South Africa's Sun City is building a market among Asian tourists seeking a resort vacation closer to home than more traditional destinations. Yet overall growth in tourism to Africa will average about 5.5 percent over the next 15 years, according to the World Trade Organization, and nearly all of that will occur north of the Sahara, where growth rates are in double digits. So far as we can find, no one even bothers to estimate the growth of tourism in equatorial and southern Africa.

FORTY PERCENT OF THE WORLD

Asia merits close attention. There is just so much of it, and the outlook for tourism there is changing dramatically.

Just a few years ago, the international tourism industry in effect served less than 20 percent of the world's population, the roughly 1 billion people who lived in the United States and Europe and about 120 million Japanese. Other regions might provide interesting destinations for wealthy tourists from the in-dustrialized countries, but as sources of international tourism they might as well have not existed.

China and India in particular had more than 2 billion potential tourists in theory—populations of about 1.1 billion people in China and just under 1 billion in India—but essentially none in practice. Both national economies had been virtually stillborn, thanks to excessive regulation and centralized planning by governments philosophically opposed to free enterprise. As a result, neither country had a viable middle class to pay for vacation travel and related services. China also heavily restricted its citizens' movements outside the country; no international tourism was allowed until 1978.

In both countries, these conditions are changing rapidly. In 1978, China opened its economy to small private ventures such as crafts operations and family-owned restaurants. Over the years, a vibrant market economy has evolved, the Communist Party has begun to admit the capitalists it once despised, and China has joined the World Trade Organization. India, for its part, has been chopping away at the endemic red tape and corruption that had hobbled business development throughout the world's largest democracy ever since it gained independence in 1947.

The results have been remarkable. China's GDP quadrupled by 2000 and is now growing—according to Beijing's official figures—at between 8 and 10 percent every year. The Indian economy has grown by an average of about 6 percent per year since 1990. In both countries, the middle class is expanding rapidly. At the end of 2003, one study found that 19 percent of Chinese—247 million people—now qualify as middle class, and their numbers are growing by 1 percent per year. In India, there are more than 300 million in the middle class, and their numbers are growing even faster. "Middle class" does not mean quite the same thing in Asia as it does in the West—a net worth of $18,000 to $36,000 makes a Chinese family middle class, while in India this group spans yearly incomes with local purchasing power equivalent to anywhere from $20,000 to $600,000. In any case, many of them can afford to travel abroad—an estimated 85 million in China alone.

Many of them do, and many more are doing so each year. An estimated 4 million Chinese vacationed outside the mainland in 2001, 10 million in 2003 (one estimate puts the number at nearly 12 million in the first eight months of the year), with 16 million projected for 2005.

Tourism from India is growing as well. In 2000, an estimated 4 million Indians vacationed abroad, spending about $380 million. By 2005, an estimated 10 million will follow them to Europe, Australia, New Zealand, and places closer to home.

To date, these still are relatively small markets. By way of contrast, Americans made 144 million international flights in 2000, a large majority for tourism, before the September 11 terrorist attacks temporarily inhibited travel. Yet tourism from China and Japan are growing far more rapidly. The Pacific Asia Travel Association estimates that Chinese spending for international travel will reach $100 billion by 2008. By 2020, according to the World

Trade Organization, an army of 100 million Chinese will fan out across the globe, replacing Americans, Japanese, and Germans as the world's most numerous travelers. That same year, 50 million Indians are expected to tour overseas.

Nor is all this travel one-way. China soon will be not only the world's largest source of tourists, but the most popular destination as well, with 130 million arrivals in 2020. The 2008 Olympics in Beijing will hasten this trend, but they are only part of a massive effort to improve China's attractions and infrastructure. Both the government and many private tour operators are working to develop scenic, cultural, historical, and religious sites as tourist destinations, and Beijing has announced a plan to train 100,000 tourism specialists over the next ten years. The reward for all this effort will be an estimated 40 million new jobs in the tourist industry.

Yet it is Chinese and Indian vacationers who are beginning to reshape the map of world tourism. Although Europe remains the planet's favorite travel destination, and the top draw for Asian tourists with time on their hands, those out for a quick shopping trip or just a few days off are heading for places much closer to home.

In Europe, castles, the Autobahn, and snow are clearly big draws for many Chinese tourists. Scandinavia is hosting waves of tourists from the PRC, and Chinese vacationers racked up some 600,000 overnight stays in Germany in 2003, a number that is expected to double by 2008. Nearly all belonged to approved tour groups; individual tourists still were not allowed there without a personal invitation and a German visa.

Indian tourists are spreading out a bit further. Shopping holidays in Dubai, which is duty-free, and packaged tours to Paris, London, Switzerland, and Austria all are attracting visitors from the subcontinent in large numbers.

However, many more Asians are spending their vacations within the region. More than 7 million mainland Chinese sought R & R in Hong Kong last year, roughly as many people as the territory's native population, and that probably is just the beginning. This year, 1 million Chinese tourists are expected to visit Thailand, while 900,000 will travel to Malaysia and 700,000 will go to Vietnam. For Indian tourists, Hong Kong, Singapore (again duty-free), and Malaysia all offer shopping and quick getaways. Nepal has been a major draw for cultural tourism, though the expanding communist insurgency has begun to discourage travel there. Recently Sri Lanka has gained popularity for inexpensive beach vacations.

With so much tourist business at stake, many countries are working hard to attract the new Asian travelers. All of the Scandinavian countries have opened tourist offices in China, and Cuba has recently negotiated a memorandum of understanding that allows Chinese tour groups to visit. South

Africa is marketing Sun City and other resorts to Indian customers. Nepal is promoting no fewer than five new destinations in India. And the Australia and New Zealand tourist offices have mounted campaigns to draw visitors from both India and China.

This is a trend seen throughout the world. As travel and tourism expand, new destinations and new attractions are opening up rapidly all over the world. From small villages in Bolivia to five-star resorts on the beach in Morocco, the world's tourists will have a growing smorgasbord of destinations to visit. In the years ahead, not even the most experienced and jaded travelers will be able to feel they have seen it all.

KEY TRENDS FOR TOURISM

1. The economy of the developed world will continue to grow for at least the next five years. Any interruptions will be relatively short-lived.

Summary: After a brief but painful recession, the U.S. economy has been growing steadily for nearly three years, through the first quarter of 2004. Job creation lagged far behind GDP growth, but it too appears to have begun a substantial recovery.

Similar improvements are being seen around the world. Many of the European economies are emerging from years of stagnation, while Japan is seeing its first significant expansion in a decade. India and China are achieving GDP growth that averages 6 percent or better each year.

Barring another terrorist incident on the scale of 9/11, or some equivalent shock, this widespread prosperity should feed upon itself, with each trading nation helping to generate the continued well-being of its partners. It can be sustained for some years to come.

Implications for Tourism: Tourism will continue to grow by at least its accustomed 5 percent per year for at least the next ten years.

Growing prosperity in China and India will quickly increase the number of international tourists from those countries.

This will bring rapid expansion for destinations convenient to Asia. These include Nepal, Malaysia, and Thailand; Australia and New Zealand; and parts of Africa. Many new seaside resorts are likely to appear in the Seychelles, on the eastern shore of Africa, and in Southeast Asia, much as did in Mexico when Americans went looking for slightly exotic luxury.

The growth of tourist facilities in these far-off places will begin to draw more visits from adventurous and well-to-do Americans and Europeans.

Russia and the more stable parts of the former Soviet Union will contribute growing numbers of tourists, particularly to Western Europe and the United States.

2. The population of the developed world is living longer.

Summary: Each generation lives longer and remains healthier than the last. Life expectancy in Australia, Japan, and Switzerland is now over 75 years for men and over 80 for women, and it is growing throughout the developed world. As a result, the retirement-age population also is growing rapidly. It may expand even more quickly than official forecasts anticipate, because they assume that life expectancy will grow more slowly in the future. In fact, it is more likely that new medical technologies will lengthen our lives still more rapidly in the near future, and bring a better quality of life in the process.

Implications for Tourism: Older, but still vigorous travelers will be a growing market for international tourism. Well into their 70s, they will retain their youthful interest in pastimes such as scuba diving, hiking, and other low-impact activities with high "experience" value.

Nonetheless, facilities will require senior-oriented conveniences, such as larger signs with easy-to-read type, door handles that can be operated easily by arthritic hands, and fire and security systems that flash lights for those that are hard of hearing.

Club Med and its competitors will become "Club Medic," with nurses and emergency equipment on site and doctors on call, to care for guests who are less healthy and more fragile.

Special tours and other activities should be ranked for the amount of walking, energy, or agility they require, so that older customers can easily choose pastimes within their abilities.

It may also be necessary to increase staffing slightly, to provide older guests with extra help in checking in, coping with luggage, arranging for local transportation, and dealing with other chores that younger patrons could handle on their own.

They also want to feel that they are recognized (especially if they are repeat customers) and catered to. Older patrons appreciate being addressed by name, and as "Mr." and "Mrs." rather than as "you guys."

Because the oldest members of society also tend to be the wealthiest, luxury cruise lines and high-end tour operators should do well as the Baby Boomers enter their retirement years.

Retirees often are willing to travel off-season, spreading their vacations evenly throughout the year. This already is helping to mitigate the cyclical peaks and valleys typical of the tourist industry. Some 62 percent of American respondents to a *National Geographic Traveler*/Yahoo! Travel poll reported planning a winter vacation of at least five days in 2004.

Despite their relative wealth as a group, many seniors are extremely careful with their money. This will further raise the demand for vacation packages that are comfortable, staffed by attentive personnel, and cheap.

Mature travelers tend to be experienced travelers. Many are unforgiving of lapses in service, facilities that are less than the best, or excessively familiar tours or activities.

3. Societal values are changing rapidly.

Summary: Industrialization raises educational levels, changes attitudes toward authority, reduces fertility, alters gender roles, and encourages broader political participation. This process is just beginning throughout the developing world. The future will be dominated by the materialistic values of Generations X and Dot-com.

Implications for Tourism: The trend is toward extreme quality and convenience. Customers want constant pampering, luxurious accommodations, and fresh meals that seem like labors of love—all at a price that will not wound the consumer's conscience.

Travelers used to focus on destinations; now they want experiences. Vacations thus are becoming more active and participatory, as tourists become less interested in "go-and-see" and more eager to go-and-do. This is the trend behind the growth of adventure tourism.

"Authenticity" is another key value. Tourists who go to see other lands, rather than surf their beaches, want to find unique natural and cultural features that survive as close as possible to their original form. Travel experiences that remind guests of Navajo Indian blankets with "Made in China" tags will turn a destination into one more shopping mall, leaving visitors feeling that they might as well have stayed at home.

4. Consumerism is still growing rapidly.

Summary: A networked society facilitates a consumerist society. Shoppers increasingly have access to information about pricing, services, delivery time, and customer reviews on the Internet. In most industrialized countries, their needs are increasingly being written into laws and regulations, which are generally enforced.

Implications for Tourism: This is a mandate for quality. Brands with good reputations will have a strong market advantage over lesser competitors and unknowns.

It will take very few mistakes to undermine a reputation for quality, particularly when disgruntled consumers often voice their complaints over the Internet, where vacation-shoppers may see them for years.

A second-rate or poor reputation will be even harder to overcome than it is today.

5. Oil prices are stable at $25 to $28 per barrel; they rise above that level only in times of trouble.

Summary: In autumn 2004, OPEC's aim is to hold the price of oil at relatively high levels, and the instability in the Middle East is making this relatively easy. However, keeping prices high requires a unity of purpose that member countries have never been able to sustain for very long. The cost of raising a barrel of oil from the ground in this region is around one-tenth the wholesale price. New oil supplies coming on line in the former Soviet Union, China, and other parts of the world will make it even more difficult to sustain prices at artificially high levels. Prices above $28 per barrel are simply unsustainable.

Implication for Tourism: One of the major costs of tourism should remain generally under control, with oil prices falling to their normal range by 2006. This will make it possible for travel companies to earn acceptable profits while keeping prices relatively affordable.

6. People around the world are becoming increasingly sensitive to environmental issues such as air pollution as the consequences of neglect, indifference, and ignorance become ever more apparent.

Summary: The World Health Organization estimates that 3 million people die each year from the effects of air pollution, about 5 percent of the total deaths annually. The European Parliament estimates that 70 percent of the Continent's drinking water contains dangerous concentrations of nitrate pollution. Though government policies in some developing countries—and the United States, at the moment—rate industrial growth as more important than dealing with environmental problems, many others are working to clean up the air and water, save rainforests, and protect endangered species. Overall, the trend is clearly toward a cleaner, healthier environment.

Implications for Tourism: Demands for still more environmental controls are inevitable, especially in relatively pristine regions. Many of the more popular or fragile destinations may limit the number of tourists allowed to visit them each year.

Ecotourism will continue to be one of the fastest growing areas in the tourism industry.

China is being forced to build new resorts where Western tourists will not be exposed to power lines and cell-phone towers. Other developing countries will face the same imperative.

Destinations and tour operators with access to rainforests, wilderness areas, the ocean, and other unpolluted regions will find this trend highly profitable.

Environmental science tours and research projects with working scientists will continue to be a growing niche market.

7. Technology increasingly dominates both the economy and society.

Summary: In all fields, the previous state of the art is being replaced by new high-tech developments at an ever faster rate. Computers and telecommunications have become an ordinary part of our environment, rather than just tools we use for specific tasks. Biotechnology, and eventually nanotechnology, may do so as well. These developments provide dozens of new opportunities to create businesses and jobs, but they often require a higher level of education and training to use them effectively.

Implications for Tourism: New technologies should continue to improve the efficiency of airliners and cruise ships, helping to keep travel costs under control.

Tourism will benefit as Internet "virtual tours" replace printed brochures in promoting vacation destinations. Web sites cover not only popular attractions, but also provide current, detailed information on accommodations, climate, culture, currency, language, immunization, and passport requirements. These sites already have proved to be a major sales asset for some hotel chains. Resorts and other destinations are likely to find them an efficient way to approach new customers.

Consumers are increasingly shopping for travel services on the Internet, and posting their reactions there. One dissatisfied guest's negative report on the Internet can influence the buying decisions of potential customers for years.

For the travel industry, the move to online sales promises more efficient marketing and higher profits. Opt-in marketing campaigns online cost only $2 per sale (averaged over all industries), compared with $18 per sale for traditional direct marketing, and sellers have immediate feedback on the effectiveness of their campaigns.

Automatic translators similar to a PDA—and perhaps built into one—soon will make it possible for travelers to go off on their own in foreign lands without worrying about communicating with natives.

Technology also makes it possible to maintain information about repeat guests, who may find it increasingly tedious or difficult to provide necessary personal data. However, that technology must be entirely transparent to customers who may find it impersonal or intimidating.

This technology will allow hotels to perform the kind of extremely personalized marketing typical of the best Internet marketers, such as Amazon.com. Whenever a return guest arrives, he or she should be gently asked a host of questions: Do you want the same breakfast as last time? Black coffee with Equal? Shall we credit your stay to the same airline-miles program? Would you like dinner at the same restaurant? Reservations to the opera again? All this information can be automatically collected on the customer's first visit. It can be retained and used transparently to make future stays as comfortable as possible.

8. Generations X and Dot-com will have major effects in the future.

Summary: Members of Generation X—roughly, the 30-plus cohort—and especially of generation Dot-com, now in their 20s, have more in common with their peers throughout the world than with their parents' generation. They are entrepreneurial, well educated, and predominately English-speaking. Virtually all are materialistic, many are economically conservative, and they care for little but the bottom line—their own bottom line. Independent to a fault, they have no loyalty to employers at all.

Implications for Tourism: Younger consumers tend to be extremely well informed about their travel choices, thanks in large part to their comfort with the Internet. Net-savvy travel marketers have a strong advantage in reaching this market.

Generations X and Dot-com will be major customers for tourism in the future. Marketing to them will require a light hand, with strong emphasis on information and quality. Brands credibly positioned as "affordable luxury" will prosper.

Any perceived inadequacy of service will send them to a competitor for their next vacation. Under-40 customers make few allowances for other people's problems.

However, they are relatively tolerant of impersonal service. What they care most about is efficiency.

These generations also will be the industry's future employees. The good news is that they are well equipped to work in an increasingly high-tech world. The bad news is that they have little interest in their employer's needs and no job loyalty at all. They also have a powerful urge to do things their own way.

9. Time is becoming the world's most precious commodity.

Summary: Computers and other technologies are making national and international economies much more competitive. As a result, Americans have lost an average of 140 hours per year of leisure time. European executives and nonunionized workers face the same trend. In Britain, workers have lost an average of 100 hours per year of nonworking time.

Implications for Tourism: Work pressure is eroding vacation time throughout the industrialized world. One-third of Americans take 50 percent or less of the vacation time their jobs theoretically allow. In Britain, 25 percent of employees take only part of their vacation time. In Japan, where employees are legally guaranteed 17 days per year of vacation, the average worker takes only 9.5 days annually.

For those with little time but adequate funds, multiple, shorter vacations spread throughout the year will continue to replace the traditional two-week vacation.

For well-off travelers, time pressure is a strong incentive to use travel agents and shop for packaged tours, rather than doing their own vacation planning.

Less wealthy vacationers will speed the task of making travel arrangements and broaden their selection of affordable vacation packages by doing their shopping on the Internet.

Anything destinations and tour operators can do to save time for their customers will encourage repeat visits.

10. International exposure includes a greater risk of terrorist attack.

Summary: State-sponsored terrorism appears to be on the decline, as tougher sanctions make it more trouble than it is worth. However, nothing will prevent small, local political organizations and special-interest groups from using terror to promote their causes. And as the United States learned on September 11, the most dangerous terrorist groups are no longer motivated by specific political goals, but by generalized, virulent hatred based on religion and culture. On balance, the amount of terrorist activity in the world is likely to go up, not down, in the next ten years.

Implications for Tourism: Until the terrorist problem is brought under control—probably not soon—tourism to the more volatile parts of the Middle East will be a relatively hard sell for Western vacationers, despite the appeal of historic places.

This stigma is likely to spread almost instantaneously to any destination that suffers a major terrorist incident. That threat is likely to be one of the great unpredictable risks of the international tourist industry for at least the next ten years. It could last much longer.

Terrorist hazards are not limited to Muslim lands. The communist insurgency in Nepal already is inhibiting vacation travel from China and India.

American-owned facilities, and those where Americans congregate, will have to devote more of their budgets to security.

Some of the most important security measures will be invisible to customers, but highly intrusive for staff. These may include comprehensive background checks for new hires, much as airports need to screen such behind-the-scenes personnel as baggage handlers and fuel-truck drivers.

Disgruntled employees and former employees are the single greatest threat, because they are familiar with security procedures and weaknesses. Those recently fired are a frequent source of problems.

Chapter 5

Away on Business: The MICE Market

MICE—meetings, incentives, conventions, and exhibitions—used to be one of the easier, more profitable markets for the hotels and resorts that host them. Booking them took work, but each meeting signed meant a block of rooms filled, and payment for them was assured.

That has changed. Although the meetings and expositions industry has flourished, and still represents a worthwhile market, it has been struggling with difficult challenges. For the host destinations, this has meant more effort, smaller profits, and a lot less certainty. Where meeting organizers once worked six to eighteen months ahead, for many that lead time has shrunk to a few weeks. Customers promise a series of meetings, then book them one at a time. They demand meeting budgets in extreme detail, complete with greens fees. Worse, most are willing to pay only for rooms actually occupied, not for the number they reserved for expected participants.

This is a taste of things to come. In the years ahead, the global population will continue to grow and change, science and technology will tighten their hold on business and society, and the world will knit itself ever more tightly into a single market. As a result, both opportunities and trials will abound in this segment of the hospitality market.

More and more industries are relying on MICE to accomplish a variety of important goals. Industries set up expositions to introduce new products and services, to gauge their appeal, and to keep existing products before the public eye. Companies use meetings to promote the exchange of ideas with coworkers and competitors, and to train their people to deal with new products and procedures. They use incentives to inspire and reward better performance from their personnel. People attend meetings to "press the flesh" with colleagues whom they ordinarily meet only through the impersonal media of telephones, faxes, and e-mail. They also attend in order to escape daily routine in a way that still counts as doing business. All of these functions are becoming more important as technology raises the pressure to increase productivity and strips away opportunities for human interaction. Contrary to early fears, high tech makes "high touch" even more necessary, not less so.

Yet technology has its downside as well. Meetings, conventions, and expositions remain important for building new relationships, but the business world's growing reliance on e-mail has markedly reduced the need for personal contact in maintaining those associations. Thus, one primary impetus for meetings and expositions may have begun to wane.

Until recently, another major reason for industry expositions was the introduction of new products. By compressing the product cycle, technology is displacing that function as well. In high tech especially, manufacturers who finalize a new product in January can no longer afford to delay its introduction for a major trade show that may not take place until June; by then, it probably will be obsolete. For this function, smaller, task-specific meetings are displacing the giant industry blowouts that once hosted product announcements. This may help to explain the sense of emptiness reported by attendees at recent editions of COMDEX, a meeting once renowned for sardine-can congestion.

However, attendee shortages are a problem at many large gatherings these days, points out Skip Cox, president of Exhibit Surveys, in Red Bank, New Jersey. Although meeting organizers have traditionally earned 70 percent of their revenue from selling floor space to exhibitors, he comments, "Meetings live and die by attendees, and they were in significant decline even before the terrorist attacks of September 11 made people less willing to travel. In fact, traffic density has been falling for most of ten years, because people have been a lot more successful at selling display space than at getting people to attend. As a result, exhibitors are finding it a lot more difficult to compete for attention, and they get fewer contacts for their effort. The industry is going to have to refocus its attention on attracting people to meetings. We may see some 'right-sizing' as well."

This process is already under way, if the results of two polls are any indication. In one, Meeting Professionals International found that meeting planners in North America and Europe expected to see about 1 percent more meetings in 2003 than were held in 2002; yet meeting budgets were shrinking by more than 1 percent overall. At the same time, hospitality industry executives were expecting an increase of 6 percent in both the number of meetings and in revenue from the meetings they would host. This may have spelled disappointment for some hotels, resorts, and conference centers.

According to the second survey, carried out by Jacobs Jenner & Kent Market Research, 34 percent of the exhibition and convention executives responding expected fewer exhibitors at their meetings in 2003, 30 percent had sold less square footage, and 28 percent expected fewer attendees. This

shrinkage was far from universal, however. Some 46 percent expected more exhibitors, 41 percent had sold more square footage, and 39 percent expected
more attendees.

More recent reports have cited a gain in bookings at destinations near
major cities, particularly if they are flexible on price or can offer activities for
the families of meeting attendees.

The MICE market faces some challenges, which may help to explain the
differences uncovered by these polls.

Wall Street has been a continuing problem for meeting organizers. Its re-
lentless focus on earnings per share, and its refusal to look farther into the future than the next business quarter, have forced corporate executives to cut
corners wherever they can, even if it means eliminating functions that could
have been profitable in the longer term. Often, it is meetings that get the ax.

Mergers and acquisitions are another major factor driven in part by investor expectations. As a result of mergers, the hardware industry now is dominated by just five major companies. Forecasting International has long predicted
that there soon will be only three major airlines in the United States, a target date
that now seems likely to be met by 2006. And when two companies become one,
there are fewer potential exhibitors for the next meeting in that industry. Merg-
ing companies also tend to shed employees in the duplicated functions, and
thereby reduce the number of possible attendees for future meetings.

This is one aspect of a trend that FI calls "the bimodal distribution of institutions." As large companies merge and drive midsized competitors out of
business, thanks to their economies of scale, small "boutique" participants are
cropping up to serve niche markets in almost every industry. Working to attract
more exhibitors and attendees from among these micro-scale competitors may
be one way to make up for the losses at the top end of the corporate food chain.

Another trend that makes life harder for meeting managers is key account
selling. When companies focus their attention on the 20 percent of customers
who provide 80 percent of their sales, they are in daily contact with the clients
who matter to them most. Inevitably, they feel less need to see them in person
at large industry gatherings. This too has worked to slow the growth of demand
for meetings and expositions.

It also has helped to promote the growth of another important trend: Private events are quickly eroding the market for industry trade shows. Not only
for key accounts, but for potential customers, companies increasingly prefer
to meet their contacts in seclusion, where they need not battle competitors for
attention. Some of these closed meetings are enormous, and they will continue
to make up a growing part of the total market for meetings and expositions.

Though most meetings count on the local market for their success—an
estimated 40 percent of attendees come from within 400 miles of the meeting

site—international factors also are becoming significant for many exhibition managers. In recent years, exotic meeting places have grown increasingly popular, both for small, high-end gatherings of top executives and for the promotion of international trade. Some of the developing countries are particularly in favor as venues for meetings and expositions—despite occasional problems getting equipment in and out of the country—because they have low labor costs, likely participants want the "bragging rights" for having been to them, and the countries themselves are eager to showcase their assets.

Even more importantly, jobs themselves are moving overseas with increasing speed. Manufacturing jobs are heading to China and other low-wage countries. Telemarketing, sales, and customer service call centers are relocating to India and the Philippines. So are many thousands of computer programming jobs. Ernst & Young even has 200 accountants preparing U.S. tax statements at a processing center in Bangalore, India. Each of these offshore operations represents a few executives who will not be attending meetings, and occupying rooms, in the firms' native lands. Of course, they may offer an opportunity for destinations wishing to host conferences in Asia, and for organizers capable of arranging the meetings.

Yet, with all these specific factors to buffet the market for meetings and expositions, the most general consideration for the immediate future is still the most important. This is the global economy. If it improves, a rising tide lifts all boats, and the market for meeting and exposition space is likely to grow rapidly. However, a global recession would bring problems for all.

This is just one of a dozen trends that Forecasting International believes will be critical to the meetings and expositions market in the years ahead. What follows is a brief look at each of them.

PROSPERITY REBOUNDS

The slow, tentative recovery of the American economy is now looking remarkably solid, with more than a year of positive economic growth tallied six months into 2004, including the spectacular 8.2 percent rise in the third quarter of 2003. Forecasts now call for growth in the range of 4 percent or better for 2004. Similar gains are being seen in much of Europe, and even Japan's long-sickly economy appears finally to have entered a growth period.

This new prosperity is already being felt in the meetings-and-expositions market. Bookings reportedly are up from 25 percent to 50 percent for 2004, thanks in large part to the economic recovery. (Repeat business and relationship selling also come in for some of the credit.) Small meetings—100 guests and under—still book only a month or so ahead, but larger meetings are beginning to plan six months to a year ahead. Larger meetings are becoming just a bit more common than they were at the bottom of the slump.

All this is a long way from the boom days of the 1990s, and even then the market for meetings and expositions was tightening as companies tried to squeeze more return from every dollar of investment. Yet steady economic growth will ensure that major corporations and business organizations provide steady demand for meeting space.

The growing unification of the world into a single market will bring further demand for international meetings and expositions. Hotels and resorts with good connections to the largest international managers of meetings and expositions will be especially well positioned to benefit from this trend.

Destinations in some developing countries also will benefit from government efforts to build international trade and from the "trendiness" of exotic locales. However, they will have to reassure meeting managers about issues such as local manpower, equipment availability, and the financial risks of doing business under an unfamiliar legal system.

However, the threat of international terrorism will be a concern for international meetings for many years to come—and especially while American forces remain in Iraq, providing extra motivation for Muslim extremists. This will require hotels and resorts in many areas to take extra care in arranging security for meetings. It also will slow the growth in international meetings significantly below the pace it might otherwise attain.

One question yet to be answered is how much impact SARS—severe acute respiratory syndrome—and avian flu will have on meetings and expositions in Asia. In 2003, fear of SARS slashed attendance at industry gatherings in China, Taiwan, Japan, Singapore, and Hong Kong. If we see a new round of SARS outbreaks or the few cases of avian flu recently worrying doctors turn into another unexpected epidemic, it may not matter how the global economy performs. Asia could be off-limits to meetings and exhibitions for as long as it takes doctors to develop vaccines against these diseases. The first SARS death of the year was recorded in China in early May.

GROWING OLDER

Throughout the developed world, the retirement-age population is growing at an astonishing rate. For example, the over-65 cohort will rise from 12.4 percent of the American population in 2000 to more than 16 percent in 2020. The same trend is seen in Europe, Japan, and even in some developing countries. India's over-60 population is expanding from 56 million in 1991 to 137 million in 2021 and 340 million in 2051.

For destinations that host meetings and expositions, this offers one of the most vibrant markets that will be available in the next twenty years, as recent data shows. In 2002, attendance at trade shows overall shrank by 4.3 percent. By contrast, according to *Tradeshow Weekly,* professional attendance at medical and healthcare shows rose no less than 8.2 percent. And in a tight economic climate, the number of companies exhibiting increased by 1.8 percent.

This market can only grow in the years ahead. A wide range of new goods and services will cater to the needs of the elderly, and particularly for healthy, active seniors throughout the developed world. At the same time, the health care industry will continue to grow rapidly to meet the medical needs of less fortunate seniors. The need to introduce these products and services and keep them before the public will provide a fast-expanding market for meeting and exposition space. Exhibitions will also be used to test-market products redesigned for older consumers, another active niche market for the hospitality industry.

At the same time, workers in the traditional retirement years represent the fastest growing employment pool in many developed countries. It has yet to be fully or efficiently tapped. Retirement-age workers are especially well suited to the hospitality industry, because they are generally polite, well spoken, and available for part-time work.

INFOTECH UNITES THE WORLD

Telecommunications has all but eliminated geographic barriers. A message e-mailed from New York to Hong Kong arrives essentially instantaneously—and costs less than a phone call to New Jersey. Copies can be sent to hundreds of different destinations all over the world with little added cost. In the next few years, when telephone systems include hardware that can translate conversations among the most common languages in real time, the process of doing business internationally will be easier still.

This has both good and bad implications for hotels, resorts, and conference centers with an eye toward MICE. The Internet makes it possible for businesses throughout the world to compete on an even footing with industry leaders. This means that smaller destinations in developing countries will find it easier to target meeting planners who would like to find novel sites for high-end gatherings. It also is increasingly possible to market directly to clients such as companies planning small, private meetings, rather than going through intermediaries. And as the Net spreads through neglected parts of Asia and Africa, some of those locations too will become suitable sites for international meetings.

This also makes it easier for business executives to keep in touch with colleagues and customers, and that makes it easier to spend time at a meeting thousands of miles from the office. A few years ago, guests were impressed when hotels provided a modem jack on the telephone. Today, they are demanding wireless Net access from rooms to restaurants to poolside. This means investing in new hardware, and wireless Internet service is not even a strong competitive advantage. But the lack of it is an increasingly serious handicap when it comes to winning in the meeting market.

All this connectivity also has begun to change the way the hospitality industry does business. Potential customers now routinely shop for destinations, begin negotiations, register for meetings, and book their rooms on the Internet. This has forced hotel and conference-center executives to change their ways, but has made for more efficient marketing.

The downside of telecommunications—particularly e-mail, business TV, and computerized conferences—is that it has become easier for executives to maintain contact with their customers and colleagues without actually meeting them in person. These "virtual meetings" have begun to replace travel and face-to-face meetings. This is especially true of trips by one or two executives from site to site within big companies, which account for an estimated 80 percent of business travel. However, virtual meetings also are having an impact on conferences, where people used to reinforce their existing relationships. Now they can meet someone in person for the first time and "meet" them online whenever they have business to discuss. So-called "face time" remains important, but to some executives it seems no longer quite as important as it once was. This is particularly true for the younger generations, who grew up with computers and may have had close online friends whom they never actually met in the real world.

All this has helped to drain business from many large trade shows. For example, attendance at the giant COMDEX in Las Vegas peaked at 200,000 in 2000; two years later, it had slipped to less than 125,000 and parent company Key3Media Group soon filed for Chapter 11. (Of course, the general high-tech slump also contributed to COMDEX's troubles; exhibitors were off from 2,337 in 2000 to barely 1,000 in 2002.) Online conferences will not replace real-world events, but they will compete with hotels and resorts for the chance to deliver information to busy executives. In the long term, a lot of business that still happens in person today will migrate to the Internet.

Technology is having another effect as well. Thanks to developments such as computer-aided design and manufacturing, the product cycle is becoming increasingly compressed. As recently as World War II, it took thirty years to go from theoretical idea to the release of competing products in an established market; in computing, it now takes eighteen months or less. Competition among service providers is essentially instantaneous. Companies can no longer afford to wait for giant, industry-wide trade shows to introduce new products, so they are mounting their own smaller, highly focused events. These gatherings offer another hot market for destinations able to target corporate meeting planners.

SOCIETY GOES GLOBAL

Our beliefs and values are shaped by what we see and hear. Throughout the United States, people have long seen the same movies and TV programs. These media are achieving global reach. In the process, they are creating a truly integrated global society. Global migration, intermarriage, and the rapid growth of travel, for both business and pleasure, all are hastening this process. In the United Kingdom, some 21 percent of young adults answering a recent poll viewed themselves as primarily European, rather than British. Some 31 percent of French Gen Xers, 36 percent of Germans, and 42 percent of Italians also said they thought of themselves as Europeans.

Over the next half-century, growing cultural exchanges at the personal level will help to reduce some of the conflict that plagued the twentieth century. This is likely to produce a reactionary backlash in societies where xenophobia is common. Some of the most fervent "culturist" movements will spring from religious fundamentalism. Would-be dictators and strong-men will use these movements to promote their own interests, ensuring that ethnic, sectarian, and regional violence will remain common.

Thus, political risks are likely to grow in areas where there are strong religious or ethnic movements, especially when they may target Western or American interests. Antiforeign movements are increasingly common in Europe, but anti-American sentiments are widespread throughout the developing world. Terrorism especially will be a continuing problem for meeting destinations in the developing world, and particularly where there are large, conservative Muslim communities.

However, the trend toward a more homogeneous world culture is generally making life simpler for meeting planners and destination managers. In the most heavily traveled lands, it is quickly becoming easier to host international meetings and expositions, with less risk of unfortunate incidents owing to cultural conflicts. The continuing spread of the English language; the development of a task-focused, profit-oriented global business culture; and the slow, steady replacement of ethnic and sectarian interests by concerns for personal security and material well-being all will help to make international meetings more common and more manageable in the years ahead.

TOURISM EXPANDS

The hospitality industry will continue to grow by at least 5 percent per year for the foreseeable future, just as it has done for the last decade. Perhaps a bit ironically, this growth is likely to make the hospitality industry itself the largest single user of meeting and exposition services, both to promote its own offerings to consumers and to handle the industry's own increasingly large and frequent gatherings.

The downside of this trend is crowding, as many resort areas become increasingly packed with tourists. It will be harder for these destinations to attract major meetings, and the sardine effect will degrade the attendees' experience during leisure time at the meeting. This increasingly will send meeting planners to smaller hotels and resorts in out-of-the-way locations. It also will open new business for destinations that until recently might have found it more difficult to attract meetings and expositions.

However, taking advantage of these opportunities may require some difficult adjustments. Lawson Hockman, of the Foundation for International Meetings, points out that managers of small gatherings often have to work on a tight budget and thus are extremely reluctant to commit to paying for rooms that may not be filled. To gain their business, destinations may have to take on the liability of setting aside rooms for people who may never arrive. Hotels and resorts willing to accept that risk will have a big negotiating advantage over those that are not.

WE TRAVEL FASTER

By air and by sea, passengers are getting from one place to another at higher speeds, at lower prices, and with greater efficiency. As a result, by 2010, air travel for both business and pleasure will reach triple the 1985 rate. Larger capacity aircraft, such as the Airbus Industries A380 and Boeing 787, will contribute to this trend. The new Airbus plane is so large that companies will be able to hold onboard meetings while still on their way to meetings, just as they do on cruise ships today.

Going faster, cheaper means going farther in the same time and at the same price. Thus, more distant destinations become more attractive for meetings. This trend should bring more business for hotels and resorts in developing lands with spectacular scenery and other unique attractions.

Faster, more convenient travel options also will reduce the lead time needed to arrange smaller corporate meetings and other short-notice gatherings. It will be more difficult to tap into the market to host these hasty assemblies, and hotels and resorts that can build relationships directly with companies, rather than with meeting managers, will have a significant advantage over their less well-connected competitors.

SPECIALIZATION IS SPREADING

For doctors, lawyers, engineers, and other professionals, the size of the body of knowledge required to excel in a particular area precludes excellence across all areas. The same principle applies to artisans. Witness the rise of post-and-beam homebuilders, old-house restorers, automobile electronics technicians, and

mechanics trained to work on only one brand of car. Information-based organizations have already adapted to this trend. Most now depend on teams of
task-focused specialists to get their work done efficiently.

This trend creates endless new niche markets to be served by small businesses. It also brings more career choices, as old specialties quickly become obsolete, but new ones appear even more rapidly. And each subdivision of an industry
or market creates new companies and trade and professional organizations re-
quiring meeting and exposition management services. These proliferating niche
operators will provide a source of new demand for meeting space. Attracting them
will require hard, continuous work in new business development.

BETTER PAY FOR WOMEN

Women's salaries in the United States grew from 61 percent of men's in 1960 to
74 percent in 1991. This figure soon will top 83 percent. In the future, women's
average income could exceed men's. College graduates enjoy a significant advantage in earnings over peers whose education ended with high school. Today,
some 70 percent of young American women enroll in college, compared with
only 64 percent of young men.

To the extent that experience translates as prestige and corporate value,
older women should find it easier to reach upper-management positions. They
will strengthen the nascent "old-girl" networks, which will help to raise the pay
scale of women still climbing the corporate ladder.

More new hires will be women, and they will expect both pay and opportunities equal to those of men. Pay-and-benefits packages are likely to rise as
women find more high-quality opportunities in other industries. Competition
for top executive positions, once effectively limited to men, will intensify even
as the corporate ladder loses many of its rungs.

This is nothing new for the hospitality industry, which has long provided
some of the best job opportunities available to women, and has paid them fairly
for their skills. However, hotels, resorts, and meeting and exhibition managers
alike may find it a bit harder to hire top candidates, thanks to growing competition from industries once reluctant to give women authority and compensation equal to that of male executives.

WORK ETHIC WANES

Throughout industry, tardiness is increasing, and sick-leave abuse is common.
Job security and high pay are not the motivators they once were, because social mobility is high and people seek job fulfillment. Some 48 percent of those

responding in a Louis Harris poll said they work because it "gives a feeling of real accomplishment." Fifty-five percent of the top executives interviewed in that survey say that erosion of the work ethic will have a major negative effect on corporate performance in the future.

For the moment, this trend may be changing. In May 2003, the number of unemployed in the United States hit its highest point in twenty years. (Note that this is a raw number; as a percentage, the rate of unemployment remained under control.) And there is nothing like a bad job market to make people more interested in working harder to keep the paycheck they have. However, this is likely to prove a temporary reversal in a long-term trend.

The motivated self-starters on whom this industry depends will be increasingly hard to find. So will employees capable of working reliably on their own with meeting planners far from home. Finding them, grooming them for greater responsibility, and keeping them on staff will be among the hospitality industry's greatest management concerns of the next twenty years.

NEW GENERATIONS DOMINATE

The 19-year Baby Boom of 1946 through 1964 was followed by an 11-year "baby bust." Generation X thus produced the smallest pool of workers since the 1930s: There are just 44 million Gen Xers in the United States, compared with 77 million in their parents' generation. In Europe, the under-30 cohort represents just 22 percent of the population.

We should rename them "Generation E," for entrepreneurship, education, English, and e-mail, assets that members of this generation share throughout the world. Gen Xers, and especially Generation Dot-com, now in or entering their 20s, have more in common with their peers across the globe than with their parents' generation.

Throughout the world, Gen Xers are starting new businesses at an unprecedented rate. The Dot-coms are proving to be even more business-oriented, caring for little but the bottom line. Twice as many say they would prefer to own a business rather than be a top executive. Five times more would prefer to own a business than hold a key position in politics or government.

This attitude promises new demand from the meetings and expositions market. Each new company founded by a member of Generations X and Dot-com will translate into rooms occupied during industry gatherings, and many will add to the market for gatherings of corporate executives, product rollouts, and other single-firm meetings.

However, being completely "at home" on the Internet also could mean that Dot-coms and the generations that follow them are more comfortable dealing with colleagues they have never met in the real world. They may feel less need for in-person gatherings, and this could partially offset the expected growth in demand for meeting space.

One more new-generation attitude is likely to have a major effect on meetings: For all their hard-nosed attention to the bottom line, Generations X and Dot-com have a lot less interest in their careers than their Baby-Boom elders. To these younger workers, a job is just a means to an end. What really matters to them is friends, family, and fun. They are not likely to be much interested in attending meetings unless they can bring their families and put in some quality time in leisure activities.

SECONDS COUNT

As we have seen in previous chapters, time is rapidly becoming the world's rarest, most precious commodity. Like many other trends, this is reducing demand for large, general-purpose industry gatherings that may not repay the days, not to mention money, invested in attending them. However, it is increasing the need for small corporate retreats and other low-stress, high-productivity gatherings. These are likely to be one of the fastest-growing segments of the market for meeting space.

This offers opportunities for smaller destinations with unique attractions. In meetings of any size, many clients will appreciate cost-efficient, novel opportunities to relax in the leisure hours of their gatherings. Destinations that can supply them will have a significant marketing advantage over competitors whose primary appeal is the ability to accommodate a crowd.

BUSINESSES SHRINK

Thanks to computerized information systems, a typical large business in 2010 will have fewer than half the management levels of its counterpart in 1990, and about one-third the number of managers. That will bring at least some good for the hospitality industry, because it means lower management expenses, though at the cost of having fewer promotion opportunities for career-minded workers. However, like many of these trends, it is a mixed blessing for the meetings and expositions market.

One reason there are fewer managers is that the work they oversaw is now being contracted out. This offers new opportunities for the firms that now handle those chores. It should translate into new growth for a variety of service industries, which will need space for new meetings and their attendees.

One function that many companies are likely to farm out is the organization of MICE. This should make it easier for destinations to compete for business at those firms. Instead of trying to sell to one hard-to-identify manager who may handle meetings only for his division or department—and who could leave for another employer the following week—hospitality executives may be able to build a continuing relationship with a professional meeting manager who can speak for everyone at a major client firm, or for several smaller companies.

Yet overall, the trends suggest that the market for meeting space will grow even more challenging in the years ahead. As Francis J. Friedman, president of Time & Place Strategies, in New York City, points out, "Trade shows are the only medium where the customer pays to hear sales presentations." As the business world demands ever leaner and more efficient operations, that idea is losing its appeal. And as we have seen, smaller corporate meetings face challenges of their own. Thus questions arise: How will meeting organizers continue to flourish in this increasingly difficult environment? And how can destinations help them to succeed, and thus compete successfully for their future business?

An obvious starting point is to know what really matters to organizers charged with making their meetings a success. At FI, where we have occasionally run meetings of up to several hundred participants, we concentrate on four rewards that make it worth someone's while to attend a business gathering. Call them the "four Cs," if you want; we think of them as "C4," an explosive combination that makes meetings work. These are contacts, contracts, certification, and clarification.

Contacts, of course, are the people you meet. Can you impress enough of them so that they will call or e-mail you later? For most attendees, and especially for exhibitors, this is the real return on their investment in the meeting. Making first contact also is the one function of meetings that is most difficult to replace by e-mail and teleconferencing.

For the most successful attendees, who do impress potential new customers, or whose potential suppliers impress them, those contacts can result in contracts. Thus, large industry trade shows can have a measurable impact on the bottom line.

Certification comes from those workshops held at many association meetings. They provide a base of common knowledge that improves the efficiency of any industry. This is particularly important in highly technical fields, such as health care, where any deficiency in professional skills may cost lives.

Clarification can take many forms. It may be just a matter of asking the right question of an expert you would not have met outside the meeting. Clarification also can be more tangible: It's one thing to see a video of new equipment, but quite another to touch and see and hear it working in person.

Skip Cox, president of Exhibit Surveys, may not use exactly those terms, but he clearly has these issues in mind when he states that successful exhibitions or conventions adhere to just two basic principles: They deliver "highly valued information to all parties attending" and they provide "an environment that fosters and promotes personal interaction for the effective exchange of information."

In their recent survey, Jacobs, Jenner & Kent asked participants to cite the two most difficult challenges facing their events. More than forty problems made the list, and many echoed Mr. Cox's concerns. The single most common problem cited by respondents was "keeping the show relevant—aimed properly at the proper marketplace." Closely allied with this were issues such as convincing companies to market themselves at shows independent of the organizer's efforts, anticipating the next most effective elements in a constantly evolving effort to reposition their event, keeping attendees on the show floor, and providing enough value so that exhibitors and attendees would find it worthwhile participating in the gathering.

To maintain relevance, Skip Cox believes at least part of the answer may be downsizing. "The highly successful exhibitions and conventions of the future," he advises, "will be more focused, vertical trades shows that are rich in content, both of formal education and of exhibitors relevant to the attendees' interests. It will be easier to deliver high value information for a narrow field, discipline, industry segment, or area of technology." Attendees rate private corporate events as being particularly useful, Cox notes, specifically because they provide high value and specific information to meet the needs of "a very vertical audience."

Large industry gatherings also can be successful by imitating small ones, Cox adds: "Organizers will need to create well-defined vertical segments of their events and support each segment with rich content, a good representation of exhibitors relevant to each segment, and they must make it easy for attendees to 'consume' their segments of interest." An ideal mix includes large exhibitors who have a really good grasp of their field; smaller participants with diverse, highly specific viewpoints; and one or two top-notch speakers from outside the field, who can set industry developments into their broader perspective. This also is a good formula for panel discussions.

It may be an increasingly difficult ideal to meet, according to Francis Friedman. She divides meeting exhibitors into three categories: the largest companies with the biggest budgets, which make up about 10 percent of accounts; intermediate-sized companies, which represent about 40 percent of participants; and small companies with relatively small budgets, which are fully half of the meeting market. Ms. Friedman believes the importance of these groups to trade shows will be evolving rapidly during the remainder of this decade. This change may be important to destinations that host smaller meetings as well as the large trade shows.

Trade shows have traditionally focused on the large companies. As the most broadly knowledgeable members of their industries, large companies tend to hold the greatest interest for show attendees. As the organizers' most profitable customers, large companies merit key account selling and other targeted approaches. However, because they have many other opportunities to reach their own clients, large companies also are the least likely to be interested in attending a trade show. Their participation will continue to decline as they replace trade show exhibits with private meetings and other precisely targeted approaches to their customers. Over the remainder of this decade, Friedman predicts, this trend will shift the focus of trade shows to intermediate-sized and smaller companies. At the same time, it will open up more of the large-company meeting business to approaches from destinations wishing to host the smaller meetings that are becoming more important to these most profitable clients.

One issue cited in the JJ & K survey was of special importance to destinations. This was how to block enough rooms, but not too many, when growing numbers of attendees now book their own rooms over the Internet. Hotels, resorts, and conference centers all will need to work with meeting organizers to reduce the risk of bookings for rooms that may not be filled—one more problem cited in the survey. However, Jack Sammis, president of International Meeting Network, reports that "Both association and corporate buyers of meetings and exhibition space are turning to large 'outsourcing' companies that buy volume, negotiate the most favorable contract terms, and provide the most value to meeting attendees." His own firm, which specializes in helping associations arrange their meetings, has built its client base by 30 percent since September 11, he notes. It seems that destinations increasingly may find themselves working not directly with meeting sponsors but through some intermediaries.

In general, we are optimistic about the market for MICE in the next ten years. The global economy may be troubled, but it remains fundamentally sound. The economic union of Europe, America's stubborn refusal to slip back into recession, and many other indicators suggest that it will be stronger in the future. Thus, the number of meetings, conventions, and expositions to be hosted each year will continue to grow, even as companies find it increasingly profitable to use incentives to motivate and reward their workers.

Yet the meetings and expositions market is in for some interesting times. Growth may be more difficult to achieve than it was in the boom of the 1980s and 1990s. Yet even in a world of e-mail, videoconferencing, and the Net, human beings will always need to meet with each other; in fact, face-to-face interaction—what we think of as "high touch"—may be even more important in a world where most contact is mediated by high-tech appliances. Expositions may be smaller, meetings may shift to private venues, and even the largest gatherings are likely to focus narrowly on a few specific tracks aimed at segments of their markets; like any other industry, meetings and expositions will change with the times. However, they will still take place, and they will need hotels, resorts, and conference centers to accommodate them.

There are not only challenges ahead, but opportunities and rewards—and for savvy participants in this industry, the opportunities will be very rewarding indeed.

KEY TRENDS FOR MEETINGS AND EXPOSITIONS

1. The economy of the developed world will continue to grow for at least the next five years. Any interruptions will be relatively short-lived.

Summary: After a brief but painful recession, the U.S. economy has been growing steadily for nearly three years, through the first quarter of 2004. Job creation lagged far behind GDP growth, but it too appears to have begun a substantial recovery.

Similar improvements are being seen around the world. Many of the European economies are emerging from years of stagnation, while Japan is seeing its first significant expansion in a decade. India and China are achieving GDP growth that averages 6 percent or better each year.

Barring another terrorist incident on the scale of 9/11, or some equivalent shock, this widespread prosperity should feed upon itself, with each trading nation helping to generate the continued well-being of its partners. It can be sustained for some years to come.

Implications for MICE: A growing GDP brings prosperity and confidence to companies, encouraging them to spend on secondary activities such as meetings and expositions.

Growth in the world-leading U.S. economy should help expand the market for international meetings and expositions, as expanding trade begins to fuel further growth for all trading partners.

Fear of terrorism is likely to prevent any dramatic growth in international gatherings, for at least as long as American forces remain in Iraq.

2. The population of the developed world is living longer.

Summary: Each generation lives longer and remains healthier than the last. Life expectancy in Australia, Japan, and Switzerland is now over 75 years for men and over 80 for women, and it is growing throughout the developed world. As a result, the retirement-age population also is growing rapidly. It may expand even more quickly than official forecasts anticipate, because they assume that life expectancy will grow more slowly in the future. In fact, it is more likely that new medical technologies will lengthen our lives still more rapidly in the near future, and bring a better quality of life in the process.

Implications for MICE: Health services for the elderly are one of the fastest growing fields in business throughout the industrialized world. They also are the fastest growing market for meetings and expositions.

Growth in this field will continue through at least 2020, when the Baby Boom generation will finally be vanishing from the global stage.

However, this is subject to change. Any dramatic breakthrough in late-lift "wellness" could reduce demand for geriatric services and medical care and deprive MICE of its most promising market.

3. The growth of the information industries is creating a knowledge-dependent global society.

Summary: Information is the primary commodity of more and more industries. As a result, 80 percent of companies worldwide expect to have employees who work at home by 2005, up from 54 percent in 2003. By 2007, 83 percent of American management personnel will be knowledge workers, and Europe and Japan are not far behind. Computer competence is rapidly approaching 100 percent in these countries. The Internet makes it possible for small businesses throughout the world to compete for market share on an even footing with industry leaders.

Implications for MICE: Executives find it easier to attend meetings and other events, because e-mail and instant messaging make it easier to keep in touch with their office and customers.

"Virtual meetings" online are beginning to replace quick business trips by one or two executives. This trend is likely to accelerate as executives from Generations X and Dot-com take over from their less net-savvy Baby Boom predecessors.

CAD/CAM and other forms of high-tech streamlining have so hastened product development that no one can wait for the next trade show to roll out new products. This is eroding the market for major expositions, but may generate smaller, special-purpose meetings.

Smaller destinations find it increasingly easy to reach potential customers worldwide.

Faster travel and the chance to choose among more destinations also reduces the lead time required to schedule a meeting.

Destinations that can market directly to customers will have a further advantage over those who must work through third parties.

4. Growing acceptance of cultural diversity, aided by the unifying effect of mass media, is promoting the growth of a truly integrated global society. However, this is subject to local interruptions and reversals.

Summary: Information technologies promote long-distance communication as people hook up with the same commercial databases and computer networks, and above all with the Internet. Business travel, migration, intermarriage, and other forces also are mixing global cultures geographically, ethnically, socially, and economically. This trend is clearest in Europe, where 20 to 40 percent of young adults say they think of themselves primarily as European, rather than as citizens of their native country. However, in many countries there are powerful reactions against these changes. The German neo-Nazi movement is one example. This trend also feeds the extremist cultural and religious movements in the Middle East and Asia.

Implications for MICE: The spread of business-oriented culture should gradually build all aspects of this market.

As English becomes the universal language of business, it is becoming easier to arrange and conduct meetings.

The risk of cultural conflicts is declining, easing one major concern for planners of international gatherings.

5. Tourism, vacationing, and travel (especially international) will continue to grow in the next decade, as they did throughout the 1990s.

Summary: Once current worries over the threat of terrorism recede, American tourism will resume its traditional 5 percent annual growth. Other countries—particularly China and India—are contributing to this demand, as their economies grow and their citizens become more free to travel. Tourism will benefit as Internet "virtual" tours replace printed brochures in promoting vacation destinations and provide current, detailed information on travel conditions.

Implications for MICE: The tourism industry is a growing market for MICE.

Tourists are clogging many major resort areas, forcing MICE planners to seek out new destinations. For the largest gatherings, this can be a difficult challenge.

6. Advances in transportation technology will make travel and shipping faster, cheaper, and safer both on land and in the air.

Summary: New technologies are transforming the way we travel. A new generation of airliners will carry up to 250 people for 9,000 miles or 555 people up to 6,400 miles. Advances in automobile technology such as road-condition sensors, automated traffic management systems, and hybrid power systems all will be in common use by 2010.

Implications for MICE: Faster, cheaper travel makes more distant destinations more practical for incentives and relatively small corporate gatherings as well as international meetings and expositions.

7. Specialization is spreading throughout industry and the professions.

Summary: For doctors, lawyers, technical professionals, and even many artisans, the size of the body of knowledge required to excel in any one area precludes excellence across all areas. This is changing the way business gets work done, using teams of task-focused specialists and farming out work to consultants and contractors who specialize more and more narrowly.

Implications for MICE: This proliferation of niche markets offers many more opportunities for meetings and incentive packages.

Making these sales requires constant market development, often not just to the company but directly to the department.

8. Women's salaries are beginning to approach equality with men's.

Summary: Women's salaries in the United States grew from 61 percent of men's in 1960 to 76 percent in 2003. Women's salaries have been rising faster than men's since 1975. Women's salaries are rising in Japan as well. American women are likely to still do better in the future because some 64 percent enroll in college, compared with only 60 percent of young men, and because nascent "old-girl" networks will help to raise the pay scale of women still climbing the corporate ladder.

Implications for MICE: Fewer than for other industries; hospitality has always depended more heavily than most on female employees, and has paid them relatively well in return.

However, there will be more competition from other industries for the best new hires. This will require even better pay and benefits packages, with better opportunities for training and promotion.

This gives the largest players in the market an advantage over smaller firms with fewer chances to move up.

9. The work ethic is vanishing.

Summary: Tardiness is increasing, sick-leave abuse is common, and fewer workers respond to promises of high pay and job security. For Generation X, the post–Baby Boom generation, work is only a means to their ends: money, fun, and leisure. Top executives say this will reduce corporate performance in the future, but many show no greater ethical standards, as seen at Enron, WorldCom, and other major companies.

Implications for MICE: Finding motivated, reliable workers is likely to be much harder in the years ahead, with more competition for them from competing employers.

Keeping them motivated will require constant attention and creativity from managers and upper executives.

10. Generations X and Dot-com will have major effects in the future.

Summary: Members of Generation X—roughly, the 30-plus cohort—and especially of Generation Dot-com, now in their 20s, have more in common with their peers throughout the world than with their parents' generation. They are entrepreneurial, well educated, and predominately English-speaking. Virtually all are materialistic, many are economically conservative, and they care for little but the bottom line—their own bottom line. Independent to a fault, they have no loyalty to employers at all.

Implications for MICE: The younger generations are extraordinarily entrepreneurial. Their new companies will provide a fast-growing market for MICE.

However, their comfort with e-mail and virtual meetings may reduce their need to meet colleagues and customers in person.

The companies started by these new entrepreneurs will include many in the hospitality industry. This promises more intense competition in all aspects of the field, including MICE.

11. Time is becoming the world's most precious commodity.

Summary: Computers and other technologies are making national and international economies much more competitive. As a result, Americans have lost an average of 140 hours per year of leisure time. European executives and nonunionized workers face the same trend. In Britain, workers have lost an average of 100 hours per year of nonworking time.

Implications for MICE: The need for small, high-productivity events is growing at the expense of larger, less intense gatherings.

Though faster travel means that destinations can hope for sales to more distant customers, nearer meeting locations still have an advantage.

Destinations with a broad range of leisure activities on-site, giving guests more opportunities to relax and enjoy themselves during brief leisure moments, will have a strong competitive advantage over those that are merely "near" attractions. This could shift more MICE activity to cruise ships, where all of the leisure activities can be found within a few hundred feet.

12. A typical large business in 2010 will have fewer than half the management levels of its counterpart in 1990, and about one-third the number of managers.

Summary: Thanks to computers managers can effectively control up to twenty-one subordinates, rather than the traditional six. Thus, fewer mid-level managers are needed, flattening the corporate pyramid and leaving few opportunities for promotion. Downsizing, restructuring, reorganization, outsourcing, and cutbacks of white-collar workers will continue through 2006.

Implications for MICE: Arranging MICE is one secondary function that many companies are sure to farm out. This should help to support the market for meeting management.

Where companies retain this function in-house, destinations and meeting managers should find it easier to identify the right executives to approach for future contracts.

13. Institutions are undergoing a bimodal distribution: The big get bigger, the small survive, and the midsized are squeezed out.

Summary: For at least twenty years, economies of scale have allowed the largest companies to buy their smaller competitors or drive them out of business. At the same time, thousands of tiny, agile companies are prospering in niche markets. We see this pattern among automakers, computer companies, airlines, banks, and many other industries.

Implications for MICE: When companies combine, they reduce the number of possible buyers for MICE and related services. They also eliminate duplicate functions, reducing the number of employees available to attend industry gatherings.

At some point, the trend toward consolidation will reach meeting management companies and other segments of this industry, as it has so many others.

Chapter 6

Water, Water Everywhere: The Cruise Industry

Cruising is hot, hot, hot, and not just when the weather turns sultry. Passenger loads have grown from a mere 500,000 in 1970 to 7.4 million in 2002, and 9.5 million in 2003. More than 80 ocean-going cruise lines with over 250 ships now visit some 2,000 destinations, and guests can choose from over 30,000 different cruises each year. Bookings are expanding by 8 percent annually, the fastest growth rate in the hospitality industry.

Yet it has not all been clear sailing for the cruise sector. In 2001, some 10 million people booked passage on the world's cruise lines. The terrorist attacks of September 11 slashed that demand. In the following weeks, no fewer than seven ocean-going lines and one river cruise line either went out of business or filed for bankruptcy protection. Drastic price cuts brought business back—in the first half of 2002, ticket sales actually were up 4.3 percent over the previous year—but the discounts decimated profit.

In early 2004, this was a continuing problem. Ticket prices remained depressed. According to one estimate, up to 50 percent of berths and cabins were being sold at unannounced discounts, up from just 20 percent before the September 11 attacks. Passengers complained that service had suffered as a result.

The industry has other troubles as well. Capacity is rising even faster than demand; at least 42 new cruise liners are in the yards, many of them scheduled for delivery in the next year, and nearly 20 of them are "super-ships" of over 100,000 tons each. The epidemic of the Norwalk virus among passengers in 2002, a small but highly publicized outbreak on the *Norwegian Sky* in May 2003, and the threat of SARS and avian flu all have passengers worrying about their health as well as their safety. The engine room explosion aboard *Norway* also raised concerns. And a Florida lawsuit that accuses Royal

Caribbean International of bilking passengers of $150 million in phony government fees and port charges will stand as a black eye for the industry even if the company is exonerated.

All this brings up obvious questions: Can even these livable times last, or do worse problems lie just over the horizon? How long will cruise prices remain depressed? How can cruise operators turn growing demand into solid profits? How can they adapt to the challenges of a fast-changing world?

In fact, the cruise market continued to improve in 2004, with an estimated 10.4 million passengers for the year—an increase of 10 percent, compared with 8 percent in an average year. And by mid-year, the number of discounted berths and cabins had fallen back to its pre-9/11 level of 20 percent. As for the rest . . .

We have some ideas. What follows is how the most important forces affecting the cruise lines will play out.

U.S. ECONOMY

Nothing is as important to the cruise industry as the American economy. No less than 80 percent of cruise tickets are sold to Americans. According to one recent study, only 13 percent of Americans have taken a cruise, but half dream of doing so. Many of these potential customers may at least consider taking a cruise when they feel economically secure. But in bad economic times, the American cruise market shrinks, and it takes radical price cuts and other inducements to fill berths.

So this comes as good news: The American economy has regained a lot of its strength. In the first two quarters of 2004, GDP expanded at a bit more than 4 percent annually. This marks 12 quarters of continuous growth since the bottom of the downturn in 2001. While the Conference Board's Index of Leading Indicators dipped in June and July 2004, these were only slight decreases after eleven months of nearly continuous growth. After long delay, in March 2004 the economy even began to add more than enough jobs to employ all the new manpower that enters the workforce each month. Between March and June, more than 1 million new jobs appeared in the United States with a few more opening up in July and August.

We now believe that the economy has begun a new period of stable expansion that should see GDP growth in the area of 3 to 4 percent for at least the next year. This is important news for cruise lines whose potential customers have been finding it hard to commit themselves to a costly vacation. This is one case where a rising tide floats all cruise ships.

AGING POPULATION

Throughout the developed world, people are living longer and, on average, growing older. (Demographically, one does not necessarily imply the other.) Life expectancy in Australia, Japan, and Switzerland is now over 75 years for men and over 80 for women. In the United States, every generation has lived three years longer than the previous one. An 80-year-old in 1950 could expect 6.5 more years of life; today's 80-year-olds are likely to survive 8.5 more years.

As a result, and because birthrates are declining throughout most of the industrialized world, older people now make up more of the population than they used to. Their numbers will continue to grow. People over 65 were only 8 percent of the population in the developed world in 1950, but 15 percent in 2000, and will grow to 27 percent in the next half-century, according to the Center for Strategic and International Studies. In Germany, people of retirement age will climb from under 16 percent of the population in 2000 to nearly 19 percent in 2010 and 31 percent in 2050. Japan's over-65 population, 17 percent of the total in 2000, will rise to 22 percent in 2010 and nearly 37 percent in 2050.

This is important because older people are now the wealthiest segment of society, and the most likely to have the time for an extended cruise. According to the 2000 Market Profile Study conducted by the Cruise Line International Association, Baby Boomers now make up the largest market for cruises; 42 percent of those polled had taken a cruise, compared with only 32 percent in the over-60 group. However, well-to-do seniors generally take the longest and most luxurious cruises. Unlike younger, family- and budget-minded passengers, they tend to prefer smaller ships, giving up tennis courts and ping pong tables in return for all-out pampering. As the giant Baby Boom generation ages, the upper end of the cruise market can only grow rapidly.

Seabourn Cruise Line has hitched its ocean-going wagons to a younger market. Yet in the process, it has poised itself to benefit from the aging trend.

"Over the last two years, the year-round average age of our guests has fallen from around 59 to about 55 years," says Richard Meadows, vice president of sales and marketing. The line is attracting younger customers in part by offering one-week Mediterranean cruises for mid-career Baby Boomers. "At the same time, we balance the product for our other customers by making the one-week cruises combinable for two, three, or even up to five weeks with a different port content," Mr. Meadows adds. When Seabourn's 50-something passengers reach their leisure years, they will have built considerable brand loyalty to their accustomed hosts.

The growth of the over-65 market will moderate the habitual seasonality of tourism, because retirees can travel off-season, and prefer to do so when it can save them some money. This should help to even out the cash flow of cruise operators.

To serve these demanding customers, some cruise lines have adapted their ships to the needs of older passengers. Others should follow their lead. Obvious features for the elderly include safety handholds in bathrooms and showers, larger signs with easy-to-read type, and large, levered door handles for arthritic hands. Older cruisers also need special services such as help in moving their belongings and information about the physical demands of side trips. Such amenities will be increasingly important in the years ahead.

TOURISM GROWS

The number of Americans traveling to foreign countries (excluding Canada and Mexico) grew by 5 percent per year from 1981 through 1996. It will continue for the foreseeable future. For many vacationers, cruises are one of the most desirable forms of international travel.

Those American tourists soon will be joined by the growing middle classes of India and China. By 2010, China is expected to be the single largest source of international tourists in the world, displacing Americans, Japanese, and Germans as the planet's busiest travelers. Already, more than 85 million Chinese are believed to be able to afford international vacations. By 2020, 100 million Chinese tourists will fan out across the globe. If just 1 percent of them take a cruise each year, they will more than double the cruise market. Long before that, cruise lines will begin to offer cruises and on-board amenities suited to Chinese and Indian tastes, while native Chinese and Indian cruise lines will appear to serve their local market.

Recently, short-distance activities have added to the bottom line of flexible, market-savvy cruise operators. These include shipboard meetings, brief "cruises to nowhere," scenic cruises during fall foliage season, and trips to nearby destinations—for example, from the Gulf coasts of Florida and Texas to Mexico. We expect similar cruise operations to appear in the Indian, Asian, and Japanese markets.

One more source of change is the growing number of destinations for cruises. In addition to new resorts and adventure experiences, many passengers will be attracted by unique facilities such as the extraordinarily beautiful *Bibliotheque,* a recreation of the fabled Library of Alexandria, whose exterior walls are covered in passages from the Rosetta Stone. Another spectacular new destination is the Al Arab Hotel, a literally ship-shape 60-story edifice in Dubai where diners travel to the underwater, glass-ceilinged seafood restaurant by submarine. Word has it that in 2004 there are 100 new hotels under construction in Dubai, one of them nearly 100 feet under water and accessible only by elevator. Serving these profitable niche markets will require small, luxurious ships suited to shallow ports and discerning cruisers.

HIGH TECH, HIGH TOUCH

The more dependent we become on technology, the more we require the attention of a friendly, courteous human being to soothe our jangled nerves. Fortunately, that very high-tech environment increasingly brings us the human contact we crave. The finest cruise ships now provide the best of both worlds, using technology to provide comfort, connectivity, and entertainment at sea and a large, well-trained staff to tend the passengers' every need.

For example, Hapag-Lloyd's opulent, German-speaking *Europa* offers a state-of-the-art "Cruise Infotainment System" that combines a capable PC and Internet connectivity with 24-hour video and audio on-demand in all suites. Outboard power pods pull the ship through the water with absolutely no vibration or noise. The two suites for the disabled provide electronically operated beds with hydraulic lifts. High tech all the way.

Yet the vessel's most spectacular features are the appointments provided for guests, including the attention of 1.7 highly trained crew members per passenger. Cabin stewardesses serve nearly every stateroom; the 12 premium accommodations have a butler. Deck stewards spritz sunbathers with cooling Evian water. Fresh flowers abound. Penthouse guests enjoy a fully stocked bar, handmade chocolates, and caviar on request. No wonder *Berlitz Ocean Cruising & Cruise Ships 2003* gives *Europa* five-stars-plus, the only ship in the world to attain that rating.

However, what may be the epitome of high touch is found on the Seabourn line, where every member of the staff begins each cruise by studying photographs of the passengers. By the end of the second day, they can address every guest by name. It is a courtesy that astonishes many first-time passengers and is appreciated by all.

In the future, computer data mining will enable cruise lines to do the kind of personalized marketing to cruise passengers that is now being pioneered in hotels and resorts. Crew members will not only be able to recognize guests, but will "remember" what meals and entertainment cruisers enjoyed on previous voyages and be able to suggest appropriate activities for their current trip.

Not every vessel, nor even every line, can hope to provide guests with that level of luxury and attention. Yet this is the balance all must work toward, a combination of high-tech conveniences with personal attention that leaves passengers feeling pampered—and eager for their next voyage.

ECONOMICAL ENERGY

Cruise ships will never be cheap to run, but at least they will not be burdened by high oil prices—though this is a difficult claim to make in September 2004, when crude oil prices are nearing $50 per barrel for the first time in history. Despite its best efforts, OPEC has been hard pressed to keep petroleum from falling below its target of $25 per barrel ever since the United States announced its decision to invade Iraq. New oil supplies coming on line in the former Soviet Union, China, and other parts of the world will make it even more difficult to sustain prices at artificially high levels. So will the return of Iraqi oil to the global marketplace, under American control. In all, oil will generally remain between $25 and $28 per barrel for the foreseeable future. This is one factor that will not bleed profits from cruise operators.

CLEANING UP

Several years ago, a research vessel crossed the middle of the Atlantic, taking samples of what it found. When they reached land, the scientists told of packaging materials, clumps of tar, and even human waste, floating hundreds of miles from land. The report made headlines in newspapers and magazines across the United States.

Gone are the days when vessels could casually dump their wastes near land. Yet it does happen. Ten years ago, Regency cruises was fined for dumping plastic bags 30 miles off Florida, something banned by U.S. law anywhere at sea. More recently, Royal Caribbean, Norwegian Cruise Line, and Carnival all have been fined—in one case up to $27 million—for dumping oily bilge water, plastic trash, raw sewage, and even toxic chemicals. Crystal Cruises' *Crystal Harmony* was banned from Monterey Bay after dumping sewage and bilge water in October 2002.

Many cruise lines have gone a long way to clean up their act. Royal Caribbean now processes all its bilge water on trips to Alaska and carries an environmental compliance officer on each trip there. Crystal Cruises switched to more expensive, less polluting fuel several years ago and voluntarily reported the Monterey Bay incident. Modern cruise ships are equipped with extensive treatment plants for bilge water and sewage and with storage facilities for other wastes. Yet there is clearly room for improvement.

Those enhancements will be mandatory. U.S. regulations now ban discarding raw sewage and food wastes within three miles of shore and limit the amount of oil in dumped bilge water to just 15 parts per million, but allow gray water to be discharged anywhere. FI believes these rules will be tightened drastically. Those rules will be enforced by satellite surveillance and other technologies. In the future, alarms will sound if wastes are dumped near land, and discharge of raw sewage and other noxious substances will be banned anywhere at sea. New ships may require double hulls in critical sections to prevent loss of toxic materials in a collision.

TECHNOLOGY IMPROVES TRANSPORT

Outboard power pods on ships such as the new *Queen Mary 2* are one such innovation; they propel ships efficiently, quietly, without vibration, and make even the largest vessels far more maneuverable. Better stabilizers, satellite navigation, computerized controls, and even the computer-aided design systems that make it possible to build a new ship in two years instead of five all are improving the business of cruising. And the discovery that cleaning propellers does even more than cleaning hull bottoms to save energy is making the ships cheaper to run.

At the same time, design innovations are helping to better the cruise experience. The sterns of Seabourn's *Pride, Legend,* and *Spirit* carry a water sports platform that extends to provide enclosed swimming and a marina for kayaks, peddle boats, windsurfers, and even a ski boat. (Thanks to this kind of amenity, these sister ships earned five stars from Berlitz.) On *Queen Mary 2,* one of the five pools has a retractable glass roof to combine the best features of indoor and outdoor swimming.

Many other new technologies will be less noticeable, but equally appreciated by guests. Jerry Leeman, WW Food Service Segment Manager at IBM's Retail Store Solutions division points out that technology is making it possible to personalize customer experiences in the grocery, retail, and food service markets. Cruise passengers will expect that same level of technology-driven personal care on shipboard.

In the years ahead, these and many other novelties will continue to make cruising more economical for operators and more pleasurable for their passengers. Expect to see floating islands that act as artificial ports, ocean-going condominiums for hard-core cruise enthusiasts, even more efficient engines and waste management systems, more small and modern coastal vessels optimized for the run to Alaska and the New England foliage season, and all manner of new amenities for guests.

CYBER-CRUISING

These days, you can take it with you, and pretty much have to. The Internet, that is. It's a rare user of e-mail who can stand to be away from his in-box for more than a day or two at a time, and many cruise passengers love being able to share vacations with friends and relatives almost as they happen. Hotels unable to offer 24/7 Internet access for guests already are losing revenues to those that can. There will be over 1 trillion Net users in the world by 2005, including a substantial majority of cruisers.

In response to this trend, many lines are providing more convenient Net access for their guests. *Europa* offers 24-hour Internet access free in every stateroom. Silversea is phasing stateroom Internet access into all its ships. Several ships have added Internet cafes, where passengers can surf while they graze. Five years from now, expanded Internet access will be standard fare on nearly all cruise lines.

IBM's Jerry Leeman points out that guests will also expect to be able to communicate through their PDA or cell phone to the onboard ship customer information system. They will want to be able to check dinner reservations and plan activities anywhere aboard ship at any time. Cruise ships soon will require a "virtual concierge" to supplement their human staff.

The exponential growth of the Internet has one more implication for cruise operators, one that some cruise executives we have talked with are reluctant to accept.

The Internet is revolutionizing the travel industry. An estimated 93 percent of travelers with Internet access now seek travel information online—and according to *The Unofficial Guided to Cruises 2003* the amount of travel information available through the Internet has grown by 1,000 percent in just two years. The Travel Industry Association of America says that 39 million travelers actually booked their trips over the Internet in 2002, up 25 percent from the previous year. Of those customers, 77 percent bought plane tickets, while 57 percent made hotel reservations and 37 percent booked rental cars.

This has had a big impact on some companies, especially in the airline market. Southwest Airlines reports that about 37 percent of its bookings are now made over the Internet. British Airways expected 50 percent of its bookings to arrive over the Internet this year. In Europe, about 90 percent of budget airline bookings now come through the Internet.

According to Forrester Research, the number of households arranging leisure travel online will grow by at least 32 percent through 2007. At that point, Internet bookings will be worth nearly $50 billion.

Thus far, the cruise industry has lagged well behind this trend. Some 95 percent of cruise bookings are made through travel agents, and many industry executives expect that to continue. In announcing the recent promotion of Carnival president Bob Dickinson to CEO, the company used the opportunity to stress his close relationship with and commitment to travel agents. (He does advise them to put in more time on weekends, when customer calls are five times more common than during the business week.) Princess executive Dean Brown declares in the newsletter *Cruise Week* that "Cruise lines booking direct is one of the most distracting things that a retailer can look at." Only 5 percent of the company's business is booked direct, he adds, and travel agents provide at least one-fifth of new growth. Virtually every cruise line has a Web site, but many are little more than billboards designed to hone the corporate image.

It cannot last. Internet users are accustomed to the convenience of shopping online. They expect the companies they do business with to provide the information they need on the Net, where it can be browsed at will, 24/7. And as cyber-wary seniors begin to leave the market, they will be replaced by Net-savvy Gen-Xers and Dot-coms who have little patience with the stately pace of offline sales. The transition to Net-based marketing will largely bypass the luxury market, where customers prefer to have others do the tedious work of putting the travel package together. Two-earner families, those on a budget, and habitually informed consumers already have begun to take much more of the cruise shopping process into their own hands.

Ultimately, it may be that there are too few travel agents to meet the cruise lines' needs. The number of agents dropped from 35,000 to 26,000 in just the eighteen months ending in June 2002—and that was before airlines eliminated commissions for sales on most domestic flights. Cruise lines cannot support all the world's travel agents on their own, and it seems that no one else has much interest in doing so.

This transition will be gradual, but it is inevitable. Five years from now, travel agents will be much less important to the cruise lines, while the Internet will account for a significant and growing portion of bookings. Only the extreme luxury market will be immune to this trend, as wealthy seniors continue to prefer the pleasure of being waited on by travel agents to the efficiency of online cruise shopping. Outside that niche, the only question is which lines will be early adopters of Internet sales and which will find themselves playing catch-up.

TIME IS PRECIOUS

Two-earner households just don't have much of it. Neither do affluent singles. In the United States, workers spend about 10 percent more time on the job than they did a decade ago, and the number is still rising. European executives and nonunionized workers face the same trend.

In this high-pressure environment, consumers are increasingly desperate for any product or service that offers a taste of luxury—and many of them can afford to pay for it. There is no luxury tastier than a cruise.

Catering to this market will require some obvious adaptations: more short cruises, more three-day "cruises to nowhere," more departures from ports within driving range of their homes, still more attention to children's activities and facilities for the families of young, harried parents. (The average age of first-time cruise passengers is now under 40.) Given that Carnival Cruise Lines carried more than 300,000 children in 2001, while cruise ships are now being docked at lesser ports from Norfolk to Boston, it seems these changes are well in hand.

Time has another aspect, which also presents opportunities for cruise operators. Older passengers often are concerned with "life milestones"— anniversaries, birthdays, and other opportunities for family gatherings. This is a clear market for brief, relatively inexpensive cruises. It is likely to grow as the economy improves and the retirement-age population grows.

BANG, YOU'RE DEAD!

They mean it literally, as suicide bombings and other attacks have proved from Saudi Arabia to Bali. Terrorism is a long way from dead, despite optimistic pro-nouncements from Washington since the invasion of Iraq. In fact, there is every reason to believe that Al Qaeda is reconstituting itself and a new round of large-scale attacks may not be far off.

To date, only one cruise vessel has ever been attacked by terrorists, the *Achille Lauro* in 1985. Yet a ship full of happy, prosperous vacationers is an ideal target for extremists. Some 94 percent of American travelers rate hotel safety as a prime factor in deciding where to stay. It would take just one inci-dent to make terrorism a top concern for cruise passengers as well.

This is a growing concern also because cruise ships are increasingly being used as floating hotels. In February 2004, the *Queen Mary 2* docked in Rio de Janeiro so that cruisers could enjoy *carnivale,* giving would-be terrorists access to a stationary target. And during the summer Olympics in Greece, many cruise vessels were moored in the harbor throughout the event to supplement scarce landside hotel space. Despite a $1.2 billion security program that includes a new sonar system to protect the harbor against attack by submarine, this was one of the most obvious opportunities for a terrorist spectacular we have ever seen. That Greek authorities managed to defend these ships successfully was a very impressive accomplishment.

For cruise lines elsewhere, many other security measures already are in place. On-board bon voyage parties, once a normal part of cruising, have been eliminated, as only passengers are allowed on ship. Entering port in the United States, ships now pick up six "sea marshals" along with the pilot. Two remain on the bridge, two watch over the engine room, and two patrol the remainder of the vessel. In Miami, divers from the local fire department carefully exam-ine the ship for clinging mines. And a Coast Guard cutter leads the ship into port, watching for high-speed attackers such as the small boat that assaulted the *U.S.S. Cole* in Yemen.

In the years ahead, cruise operators will be forced to tighten security even beyond current standards. They will have to screen not only passengers, but everyone who has contact with the vessel—food loaders, baggage handlers, port pilots, and their own disgruntled employees and former employees. One thing they will not have to do is screen baggage, a job too expensive to handle at individual ships. That will be taken care of as people enter the dock, either by government employees or by private security firms under contract to the Department of Home Security or to industry associations. Already, some cruise lines have stopped the age-old practice of putting name tags on at the airport for fear that would-be terrorists will slip a bomb or hazardous material into a bag before it ever reached the ship.

Security is as important for small inland cruises as it is for ocean-going liners. On the Potomac, tour boats glide past within striking distance of the Kennedy Center, where a bomb could endanger 40,000 people. Many ships that cruise down the Mississippi and other waterways also pass within easy reach of populous, vulnerable targets. Tourists on these vessels undergo no security checks at all, but that is about to change. Coast Guard regulations now require the screening of tour boat passengers. Ships entering major ports are searched by the Coast Guard, while Navy SEALs examine the hull for explosives, and further security procedures now stretch leaving the ship into an ordeal that can last for hours.

All this represents a difficult adjustment for both cruise passengers and the companies that carry them. There is something about being treated as a potential hijacker that conflicts fundamentally with the sense of luxury and pampering that cruisers signed up for and cruise operators aim to provide.

We will just have to get used to it. From now on, boarding a ship is going to look more and more like running the gauntlet at a busy airport. The alternative is even worse.

SAVVY CONSUMERS

A networked society is a consumerist society. Shoppers today can search the Internet for information about pricing, services, delivery time, and peer reviews of all manner of goods and services. Already, the monthly Internet newsletter *CruiseReports* delivers reviews of cruise ships, complete with passenger comments, directly to the reader's e-mail box. Over the next few years, this trend will sweep through the cruise industry as well. Disappoint one passenger, and thousands of potential customers will hear about it.

Norwegian Cruise Line showed how not to handle problems in April 2003, when ice in the Gulf of Finland forced *Norwegian Dream* to cancel stops at Helsinki, Tallinn, and—unforgivably—St. Petersburg, the high point of the trip. Passengers learned of the changes only when they checked in at Dover, and they were offered compensation of only $100 to $200 each, amounts that sent irate cruisers on stage to harangue fellow passengers in a near-revolt. As one dismayed agent commented, "They've come a long way to see St. Petersburg, and $150 ain't going to cut it." The Internet carried that tale around the world, no doubt in the words of the angriest customers.

A world of savvy, demanding, networked consumers requires still greater effort to give passengers the best possible cruise. It may be even more important to soothe their frustrations when something goes wrong.

SHOCK AND AAHS

Throughout the business world, institutions are undergoing what FI calls bimodal distribution: The big get bigger. The small survive, and some of them do quite well. But midsized competitors are squeezed out, because they are not flexible enough to prosper in niche markets and cannot achieve the economies of scale enjoyed by the Wal-Marts of their industries.

Similarly, purveyors of high-end luxury products flourish; look at any spectacularly good restaurant. The fast-food chains also make it; cheap, Spartan products fill a need for those who cannot afford better. But midpriced family restaurants eventually go broke.

We see this trend among auto manufacturers, computer makers, farms, banks, and very clearly in the airline industry. We are beginning to see it among cruise lines.

Those companies that failed or took refuge in Chapter 11 after the 2001 terrorist attack represent the vulnerable middle of the industry, underfunded and without the kind of core market it takes to survive. For the mass market, there is Carnival Cruise Lines; in the luxury end, there are Silversea and Carnival's subsidiary, Seabourn.

Carnival's ships are big, from roughly 85,000 to 110,000 tons, with stateroom capacities that range from about 2,100 to nearly 3,000 passengers. The atmosphere is relentlessly upbeat, with constant music and passenger games, but there is none of the emphasis on luxury typical of some other lines. The food is adequate, the cabins large enough, the glasses plastic, at least on deck and in the Lido Buffet. This is the McDonald's of the cruise industry, and it is spectacularly successful. Carnival's mass appeal has made it the largest cruise line in the world.

At the other end of the spectrum, we need to look at just one ship, the spectacular new *Queen Mary 2*, which sailed on its maiden voyage for Carnival's Cunard subsidiary in January 2004. This is the largest, fastest cruise ship ever built—150,000 tons, nearly a quarter-mile long, 100 feet taller than the Eiffel tower, able to carry 3,090 passengers across the Atlantic at speeds up to 30 knots.

Carnival set out to make the world's most luxurious cruising ship. The result, built at a cost of $780 million, is likely to provoke shock and "aah"s. Even its smallest staterooms offer 194 square feet of sumptuous appointments, its largest—two Grand Duplex apartments at the stern—can be combined with the penthouses above to create a single apartment with an unprecedented 8,288 square feet of floor space. Even the most modest accommodations, to whatever extent the concept of modesty applies to any part of this vessel, is equipped with a 20-inch television and attached computer keyboard providing digital video, music, and audio books on demand, with 24-hour e-mail access. There are fourteen bars, ten restaurants, five swimming pools, a gymnasium, and a spa with twenty-four treatment rooms, and even a putting green.

In the words of one observer, "This is the ship God would have made if he had the cash flow." Carnival does, thanks to its firm hold on both the mass market and luxury ends of the cruise industry.

However, *QM2* will not be the world's largest cruise ship for long. In fact, Royal Caribbean's new *Mariner of the Seas* already carries more passengers, 3,114, and the line has a 1,114-foot long, 3,600 passenger ship named *Ultra Voyager* scheduled for launch some time in 2006.

As this business grows more competitive, large and successful cruise lines increasingly will follow one of these models. Some will cater to relatively unsophisticated first-time passengers. Others will aim for discriminating cruise enthusiasts who can pay to be pampered. Smaller players will specialize in niche markets such as coastal cruises or expedition, nature, or adventure excursions. Midsized, midrange operators will slowly disappear. That is just the way things are in the global economy.

COMPETITIVE ADVANTAGE

At both ends of the spectrum, the battle for market share will grow ever more challenging. That too is in the nature of worldwide competition. There are several tools and offerings that cruise lines will use to make it in this difficult environment.

One is specialized attractions for niche markets. Theme cruises already are popular. There have been highly successful trips specializing in adventure themes, astronomy, bridge, chess, computer science, education, film festivals, gays and lesbians, murder mysteries, and nudism. We will see many more such enticements in the future. In fact, the future itself could be a marketable theme, with lectures covering technology, medicine, economics, social issues, and other important, fast-changing fields.

Well-known celebrities, entertainers, and guest lecturers fall into this same category. Whenever someone writes a bestselling book, acts on a hit television show, or sings a pop song, they create a niche market for cruise lines. We would not be surprised to learn that the winners from *American Idol* already are booked on Carnival or one of its mass-market competitors.

YIELD MANAGEMENT

A key marketing technique just being adopted by the cruise industry is yield management. The basic idea is simple. Companies keep careful track of how their products are selling. If time is growing short and something needs to be moved out the door, it is discounted and advertised heavily until it sells.

This is basic marketing, computerized, turbocharged, and driven up-to-the-minute sales and inventory statistics. It can work remarkably well. In one typical case, after the SARS epidemic broke out in Asia, *Crystal Harmony* was abruptly repositioned to Los Angeles. Bookings were heavily discounted and sold out in just five days.

Yield marketing cries out for the Internet, where prices can be changed around the world at the touch of a few keys. Predictably, some of its most effective practitioners in the travel industry are online discounters such as Expedia, Travelocity, and Orbitz. However, profit-minded cruise lines will want to bring this in-house, to route cash flow to their own balance sheets. This means that a dramatic expansion of Web sites and the adoption of Internet-oriented sales techniques are all but inevitable. In five to seven years, cruise operators will be every bit as dependent on Internet sales as the airline industry.

TEN TRENDS

In his feature, *Budget Travel*, Arthur Frommer recently surveyed developments in the cruise industry. He found ten trends, many of which paralleled Forecasting International's observations. Here is his list:

- Continued discounting of ticket prices, often unannounced.
- A growing variety of ships, from multi-thousand-passenger megaships to 100-passenger vessels capable of visiting the smallest ports.
- More cruises from ports such as New York and San Francisco, which are within convenient driving distance for many passengers.
- A renaissance in freighter cruising, which ten years ago had almost vanished; today more than 40 freighters carry patient vacationers to a wide variety of ports not served by traditional cruise lines.
- New itineraries, particularly in formerly neglected areas such as Asia and Africa.

- More theme cruises for fans of music, history, murder mysteries, haute cuisine, and other specialized interests. This July, *Norwegian Dawn* will even carry what is being billed as "the first gay cruise with family values," led by former talk-show hostess Rosie O'Donnell.

- Many more cruises by luxurious sailing ship, a relaxed and relatively inexpensive alternative to traditional motor vessels.

- A wider variety of cruise lengths, with voyages stretching from three to seven nights up to fourteen or fifteen, appealing to older travelers with plentiful free time.

- If cruising is hot, the Antarctic may be the hottest destination of all. Demand is so strong that vessels carrying up to 800 passengers are now plying this trade.

- Batteries, and a lot of other things, not included. Amenities from meals to miniature golf are being paid for separately, a trend that is sure to continue.

THROUGH 2010

It should be a good time for efficient, market-savvy cruise lines. Carnival CEO Bob Dickson reports that early in 2004 he had already seen a significant uptick in bookings from the lows of the recent recession. "Obscenely low pricing will not last," he predicts. "As demand rebuilds, pricing will go up." Forecasting International agrees.

Some of our other forecasts here may be more controversial. Yet if some of FI's views about the future of cruise lines appear to be radically different from current industry practices, most are simple extensions of current trends. They all grow directly from the market forces we see operating today.

Tomorrow's cruise lines will be even more flexible, even more in tune with the needs of their changing, and growing, markets. As a result, we believe they will be some of the most dynamic and profitable companies in the world.

KEY TRENDS FOR THE CRUISE LINES

1. The economy of the developed world will continue to grow for at least the next five years. Any interruptions will be relatively short-lived.

Summary: After a brief but painful recession, the U.S. economy has been growing steadily for nearly three years, through the first quarter of 2004. Job creation lagged far behind GDP growth, but it too appears to have begun a substantial recovery.

Similar improvements are being seen around the world. Many of the European economies are emerging from years of stagnation, while Japan is seeing its first significant expansion in a decade. India and China are achieving GDP growth that averages 6 percent or better each year.

Barring another terrorist incident on the scale of 9/11, or some equivalent shock, this widespread prosperity should feed upon itself, with each trading nation helping to generate the continued well-being of its partners. It can be sustained for some years to come.

Implications for Cruise Lines: People take cruises when they feel economically secure and take less expensive vacations when they do not. In the next few years, many more people will feel they can afford to take a cruise.

This is relieving the price pressure on cruise lines, so that fewer tickets will be discounted. This should improve profitability for the next several years.

2. The population of the developed world is living longer.

Summary: Each generation lives longer and remains healthier than the last. Life expectancy in Australia, Japan, and Switzerland is now over 75 years for men and over 80 for women, and it is growing throughout the developed world. As a result, the retirement-age population also is growing rapidly. It may expand even more quickly than official forecasts anticipate, because they assume that life expectancy will grow more slowly in the future. In fact, it is more likely that new medical technologies will lengthen our lives still more rapidly in the near future, and bring a better quality of life in the process.

Implications for Cruise Lines: Older people make up a growing segment of the cruise market.

Because they form the wealthiest segment of industrialized societies, retirement-age consumers also are the most likely to take cruise vacations, particularly for the longest and most luxurious cruises.

Younger travelers form a profitable market for family-oriented cruises. However, one of the biggest advantages of catering to them is the opportunity to build brand loyalty for their later lives, when they will be the most profitable cruisers.

Retired people are free to take trips when they wish, rather than when it suits an employer. They are beginning to even out the traditional seasonality of travel.

Older passengers need amenities suited to their physical limitations. Examples include signs with larger type, lever door handles rather than knobs, safety grips in bathrooms and showers, and extra help with their luggage.

3. The growth of the information industries is creating a knowledge-dependent global society.

Summary: Information is the primary commodity of more and more industries. As a result, 80 percent of companies worldwide expect to have employees who work at home by 2005, up from 54 percent in 2003. By 2007, 83 percent of American management personnel will be knowledge workers, and Europe and Japan are not far behind. Computer competence is rapidly approaching 100 percent in these countries. The Internet makes it possible for small businesses throughout the world to compete for market share on an even footing with industry leaders.

Implications for Cruise Lines: Internet cruise booking will become much more important to the industry, eventually displacing travel agents in all but the luxury market.

Cruise ships increasingly will require Internet connections in every room for 24/7 access to the guest's e-mail, either free or at a very modest price.

Data mining can provide cruise lines with an opportunity for extremely personalized marketing, much as it already does for cutting-edge hotels and resorts.

4. Tourism, vacationing, and travel (especially international) will continue to grow in the next decade, as they did throughout the 1990s.

Summary: Once current worries over the threat of terrorism recede, American tourism will resume its traditional 5 percent annual growth. Other countries—particularly China and India—are contributing to this demand, as their economies grow and their citizens become more free to travel. Tourism will benefit as Internet "virtual" tours replace printed brochures in promoting vacation destinations and provide current, detailed information on travel conditions.

Implications for Cruise Lines: The market for cruises will grow at least as fast as the travel market in general. If the American economy again begins to expand rapidly, rather than at the measured pace seen in early 2004, cruising should grow even more rapidly. Many consumers view cruising as one of the most desirable forms of vacation, even if they have never taken a cruise themselves. In affluent times, they will be even more inclined to indulge their wish for luxury by signing up for a voyage.

Within ten years, the number of Chinese and Indian cruisers will justify providing amenities, and even designing cruises, specifically for their tastes. By 2020, we expect to see several new cruise lines based in China and India and catering to the needs of local vacationers.

The growth of tourism will inspire the development of many new destinations, giving cruise ships new ports of call to interest their passengers. Some of those destinations will be developed with the growing Asian tourist markets in mind.

5. Consumerism is still growing rapidly.

Summary: A networked society facilitates a consumerist society. Shoppers increasingly have access to information about pricing, services, delivery time, and customer reviews on the Internet. In most industrialized countries, their needs are increasingly being written into laws and regulations, which are generally enforced.

Implications for Cruise Lines: This is one more force behind the disintermediation of travel. The cruise industry cannot resist this process permanently.

Net-savvy consumers will expect to find much more information online about ship facilities, prices, options, and port attractions, so they can compare possible cruising choices when planning a vacation.

Disappointed cruisers will voice their complaints online, where a single negative report can influence the choices of future consumers for years.

6. Oil prices are stable at $25 to $28 per barrel; they rise above that level only in times of trouble.

Summary: In autumn 2004, OPEC's aim is to hold the price of oil at relatively high levels, and the instability in the Middle East is making this relatively easy. However, keeping prices high requires a unity of purpose that member countries have never been able to sustain for very long. The cost of raising a barrel of oil from the ground in this region is around one-tenth the wholesale price. New oil supplies coming on line in the former Soviet Union, China, and other parts of the world will make it even more difficult to sustain prices at artificially high levels. Prices above $28 per barrel are simply unsustainable.

Implications for Cruise Lines: The single greatest "disposable" expense of running a cruise ship should remain under control, with oil prices falling back to their normal range by 2006. This will help to keep tickets affordable and profits acceptable.

7. People around the world are becoming increasingly sensitive to environmental issues such as air pollution as the consequences of neglect, indifference, and ignorance become ever more apparent.

Summary: The World Health Organization estimates that 3 million people die each year from the effects of air pollution, about 5 percent of the total deaths annually. The European Parliament estimates that 70 percent of the continent's drinking water contains dangerous concentrations of nitrate pollution. Though government policies in some developing countries—and the United States, at the moment—rate industrial growth more important than dealing with environmental problems, many others are working to clean up the air and water, save rainforests, and protect endangered species. Over all, the trend is clearly toward a cleaner, healthier environment.

Implications for Cruise Lines: Restrictions on dumping of refuse and waste will become much tighter in the years ahead, and will be much more strictly enforced.

Ships will be forced to use more, and more capable, antipollution technologies. These will be a significant new expense for cruise lines.

8. Advances in transportation technology will make travel and shipping faster, and cheaper by land, sea, and air.

Summary: New technologies are transforming the way we travel. A new generation of airliners will carry up to 250 people for 9,000 miles or 555 people up to 6,400 miles. Advances in automobile technology such as road-condition sensors, automated traffic management systems, and hybrid power systems all will be in common use by 2010. Similar developments are seen in every sector of transportation.

Implications for Cruise Lines: Outboard power pods, better stabilizers, improved satellite navigation and weather, and other technologies are making cruise ships faster, more comfortable, and more efficient.

Design innovations made possible by technology are creating new experiences for cruisers. These include extensible marinas and swimming areas and retractable glass roofs, as on the *Queen Mary 2.*

In the future, much more ambitious innovations will be seen; artificial island ports and cruise ships the size of modest cities can be expected within 20 years.

9. The Internet is growing logarithmically and globally.

Summary: In spring 2004, Net users numbered around 945 million worldwide. This population is expected to reach 1.1 billion by 2005, 1.28 billion by 2006, and 1.46 billion by 2007. One reason for this is the rapid expansion of Net connectivity in some developing lands. India had only 170,000 Net subscribers in 1998; by 2004, it had 39 million. In early 2004, China's population of Net users amounted to 96 million. Americans had declined from 42 percent of Net users in 2000 to under 20 percent in 2004.

Implications for Cruise Lines: Vacationers accustomed to instant Net access will be increasingly unwilling to leave their e-mail at home. High-speed, 24/7 Net access in all staterooms will be standard, as it is now for business-class and luxury hotels.

This is a major force behind the growth of consumerism among potential cruise passengers.

The Internet will be an increasingly important tool for the millions of potential cruisers in the Indian and Chinese travel markets.

10. Time is becoming the world's most precious commodity.

Summary: Computers and other technologies are making national and international economies much more competitive. As a result, Americans have lost an average of 140 hours per year of leisure time. European executives and nonunionized workers face the same trend. In Britain, workers have lost an average of 100 hours per year of nonworking time.

Implications for Cruise Lines: Harried two-earner households are eager for any luxury they can find—and many of them can afford to pay for it. Many see a cruise vacation as the ultimate luxury.

What many of them cannot afford is time. Growing numbers will take brief "cruises to nowhere," long-weekend coastal cruises, and short segments of longer cruises, preferably leaving from regional ports near their homes.

11. International exposure includes a greater risk of terrorist attack.

Summary: State-sponsored terrorism appears to be on the decline, as tougher sanctions make it more trouble than it is worth. However, nothing will prevent small, local political organizations and special-interest groups from using terror to promote their causes. And as the United States learned on September 11, the most dangerous terrorist groups are no longer motivated by specific political goals, but by generalized, virulent hatred based on religion and culture. On balance, the amount of terrorist activity in the world is likely to go up, not down, in the next 10 years.

Implications for Cruise Lines: Cruise ships are an ideal target for terrorists willing to sacrifice themselves so long as they can take large numbers of people with them. This represents a significant risk to the industry, particularly as government facilities and land-locked attractions become harder to attack.

Government mandates are likely to require even tighter security precautions on cruise ships.

A successful attack on a cruise ship could stifle the industry's growth for several years.

Chapter 7

Clipped Wings: Troubled Times for the Airlines

The Biblical four horsemen of the Apocalypse were War, Famine, Pestilence, and Death. Since 2001, the airline industry has faced three of them—all four, if you count the recent absence of meals on many long-distance flights. It has not been a good way to begin a century.

We have a reputation as optimists who can see the bright side in most situations. This is undeserved; we simply go where the data lead, without the emotional and philosophical biases that make habitual pessimists of some other forecasters. But in the case of the airline industry, there is no getting around it: The recent past has been grim, and the future offers only modest improvements.

Before looking ahead, we need to measure just how far the airlines must go simply to recover from recent catastrophes. The events themselves are familiar; the magnitude of their impact may not be.

ONE MORE PERFECT STORM

These days, it seems that anyone who has suffered business reverses blames them on a "perfect storm," a disastrous combination of forces and events that could not have been foreseen or defended against. If any industry has the right to use this excuse for its troubles, it is the airlines. The first two horsemen of the air-pocalypse struck without warning, and none of the three has allowed any effective defense against them.

Death arrived first, on September 11, 2001, when Al Qaeda terrorists hijacked four aircraft from United and American Airlines. As the World Trade Towers collapsed, so did air travel. In the month after the attack, U.S. domestic passenger miles dropped 20 percent from the previous October; international passenger miles were off 37 percent. Schedule cuts at the top ten U.S. air carriers reduced flights by 17.5 percent from a year earlier. Before 2001 was over, the American airline industry shed some 79,000 jobs, one in ten of the people it had employed before September 11. Other countries saw similar declines. Airlines belonging to the International Air Transport Association (IATA) carried 1.35 billion scheduled passengers in 2001, more than 3 percent fewer than in 2000, the first year-on-year decline since 1991.

The effects of 9/11 continued on far into 2002. American air carriers alone lost an estimated $10 billion that year, up from $7.7 billion in 2001. Globally, industry losses in 2001 and 2002 amounted to $25 billion, according to IATA Director General Giovanni Bisignani.

By early 2003, it had begun to seem that the worst might be over. Then Pestilence appeared, as doctors recognized that a new and virulent disease was spreading rapidly in much of the Far East. For a time, severe acute respiratory syndrome, or SARS, inhibited travel even more than the threat of terrorism had done. IATA estimates that in May 2003 SARS cut international passenger traffic 21 percent below the level seen 12 months earlier, when post-9/11 anxiety was still near its peak. The effect was worse by far among Asian carriers, which lost nearly 51 percent of their passengers during the worst of the period. Travel to Singapore and Hong Kong plummeted to just 10 percent of the previous year's level. Air traffic also declined more than 20 percent in North America during the outbreak and 5.5 percent in Europe.

No sooner was SARS under control than War arrived in the form of America's invasion of Iraq. Worries that terrorists might attack more planes in response to the invasion again kept many potential travelers on the ground. Transatlantic traffic in April 2003 was down just over 25 percent, while American domestic flights were off by 15 percent. At the same time, crude oil prices soared, carrying jet fuel to $1.05 per gallon that May; it had been only $0.62 per gallon in January 2002.

The result was predictable: Soon after 9/11, Sabena went out of business, while Swissair survived only with a government bailout. In the United States, Midway Airlines filed for Chapter 11 bankruptcy protection; U.S. Airways entered bankruptcy, restructured, and has emerged; and United Airlines filed for bankruptcy in December 2002. Other airlines filing for bankruptcy protection or the equivalent since the 2001 terrorist attack include Avianca, Air Canada, National, and TWA. When asked what other airlines might go under, one travel analyst replied, "Almost any of them."

CURRENT STATUS

All these unexpected developments have been catastrophic for the world's airlines. In the two years following September 11, carriers in the United States lost every penny they made between 1995 and 2000. They have had to take on so much debt just to survive that they will need $20 billion by 2007 to restore their balance sheets to the levels seen in 1999. The situation has been little better elsewhere.

"Our industry has lost at least three years of growth and development," comments IATA's Bisignani. "This year [2003], we can expect to lose almost five billion U.S. dollars on international services. If we include domestic traffic, losses could approach ten billion. Effectively, every round-trip international passenger was given twenty-five dollars by the airlines in 2003."

The situation has been hardest in the United States, which accounts for 40 percent of the world's air traffic. In 2003, only 600 million people flew on American carriers, compared with 634 million forecast before 9/11; that number is not expected to reach the level seen in 2000 until at least 2006. Ten of 16 airlines surveyed by the federal Bureau of Transportation Statistics (BTS) ran in the red in the first quarter of the year. Before 2003 was over, the airlines were expected to lose yet another $8 billion. In midsummer, 2,000 jets—about 13 percent of the fleet—were parked in the Mojave Desert as carriers abandoned flights in order to boost their load factor, the percentage of seats with passengers in them.

In June 2004, the situation looks better in some ways, worse in others. Passengers are coming back to the airlines in substantial numbers. In January, Ulrich Schulte-Strathus, head of the Association of European Airlines, predicted that passenger numbers would rise by 7.5 percent in 2004, compared with a negligible 1 percent the previous year. In February, revenue passenger miles for U.S. airlines were up for the seventh month in a row, while passenger traffic grew by 10 percent. Airlines have actually been retrieving some of those mothballed aircraft—mostly smaller planes—from the desert to handle the demand. In the Asia-Pacific sector, passenger traffic is expected to grow no less than 14 percent in 2004, bouncing back neatly from the SARS-induced slump in 2003.

At the same time, carriers throughout the world have cut costs and improved their efficiency. Some 400,000 jobs have been squeezed from the industry, including a total of 100,000 in the United States, and those lucky enough to remain at work have had to endure widespread pay cuts. Capacity is down as well, because the airlines have cut flights, especially from overserved routes.

To make up for this, many airlines have formed alliances in which carriers can renumber planes, market flights, book seats, and share profits on aircraft actually operated by someone else. This also allows smaller airlines to offer service to destinations they could not otherwise reach. For example, the Sky Team alliance, dominated by Air France and Delta, gives partners like Aero Mexico, Alitalia, Czech Airlines, and Korean Air access to 512 airports in 114 countries.

For U.S. air carriers, these changes have brought load factors to nearly 80 percent in April and May 2004, the best they have been in years. European airlines are running with load factors of 70 to 75 percent, while most Asian carriers are just below 70 percent.

However, all these improvements have been more than offset by a catastrophic rise in the cost of fuel, due to a combination of Iraq war worries, limited refining capacity in the United States, and OPEC policies that have driven the cost of crude oil above $40 per gallon for the first time in history. Every penny per gallon increase in the price of jet fuel costs American air carriers $180 million, according to John Heimlich, chief economist of the Air Transport Association. There have been a lot of extra pennies. In the United States, jet fuel averaged 90 cents per gallon in 2003, $1.10 in January 2004, and $1.30 in March. Prior to the rise, U.S. airlines had been expected to score their first break-even year in recent memory. By May, they were facing a loss of at least $2 billion and perhaps as much as $3 billion—roughly the increase in their fuel bills. Carriers in Europe and Asia were not doing any better.

Post-9/11 security improvements also have added to the cost of doing business. Airlines in the United States had paid out over $500 billion for security upgrades by early 2004, and Federal authorities believed the carriers' share of the cost should have been more than $700 billion—and were seeking to bill the airlines for the extra cost.

And there is a growing fear that Pestilence may return to inhibit the travel market, as it did in 2003. By June 2004, there had been only a few cases of SARS since the last outbreak, all in China, which was acting vigorously to control the disease. However, a new strain of bird flu had killed at least 12 people in ten Asian countries. All confirmed cases appeared to have been contracted directly from infected birds, but virologists worry that the disease could soon gain the ability to pass from one human patient to another. Bird flu has a much higher mortality rate than SARS, so human-to-human transmission could produce an epidemic that would kill millions. In the process, it could kill air travel in the affected region for years.

It is against this background that some long-standing trends and a few new developments will play themselves out. What follows are some of the most critical issues the airline industry must deal with in the years ahead. They add up to very mixed prospects for the future.

MONEY MATTERS

Like other sectors of the travel and hospitality industry, airlines are exquisitely sensitive to their economic environment. Would-be tourists with empty pockets tend to stay at home, and businesses facing lean times view travel budgets as fat ripe for the trimming.

So it comes as good news that the American economy is looking healthier than it has in several years. In the first two quarters of 2004, the U.S. gross domestic product rose at an annual rate of about 4 percent. In March, new jobs finally started to appear in significant numbers for the first time in more than two years—353,000 in March and just over 1 million in all by the end of June. It takes just 150,000 new jobs each month to absorb the new workers coming into the labor market, so it looks like some of the people laid off during the downturn were finally going back to work.

According to the Conference Board's Index of Leading Economic Indicators, this new strength is likely to be with us for some time. It rose by 0.3 percent in May for its ninth increase in ten months and incurred only a tiny decline in June. Burgeoning federal debt—not something we generally welcome—has kept the U.S. dollar down on international currency markets, making American exports more attractive to foreign buyers; this is one more reason to hope for a brighter economic future.

Elsewhere, economic news is mixed. Growth has been sluggish to nonexistent in Europe since 2002. In 2003, the European Union's growth rate came in at just 0.4 percent. Germany, Italy, and the Netherlands were in recession during the first six months of the year, and widespread strikes put the French growth rate in negative numbers as well.

This may be changing. France and Germany cut taxes in 2003, and there are signs that the powerful German labor unions have lost some of their clout. Both these developments have led economists to hope that the sluggish French and German economies are due for better times.

Their wishes appear to be coming true. In France, the GDP had been shrinking by 0.6 percent or more since 2002, and consumer spending has remained sluggish, thanks to unemployment in the range of 9 percent. Yet the economy turned in unexpectedly positive growth of 2.5 percent annually in the fourth quarter of 2003 and 3.1 percent in the first quarter of 2004. By April, the Conference Board's leading index for France had been positive or break-even for nine consecutive months, sagging only slightly in May. In 2004, the French GDP is expected to grow by 2 to 3 percent.

The German economy—the largest in Europe—also has been in decline for several quarters, but appeared to bottom out in September 2003. In the second half of the year, GDP growth averaged 0.9 percent. It is not clear how long or strong the recovery will be. The Conference Board's leading index for Germany actually declined in January and February 2004, thanks in part to a substantial drop in residential construction. However, the most recent forecasts still call for a growth rate of 1.6 percent in 2004 and 1.75 percent in 2005.

Elsewhere in Europe, economies are stable to improving. In Britain, growth is steady at around 1.9 percent per year, with 3 percent expansion forecast for 2004 and 2005. In Italy, a stagnant GDP is expected to rise by 1.8 percent in 2004. In all, the European economy as a whole grew by 0.4 percent in 2003, and slightly better performance can be expected in 2004.

In the years ahead, one more economic factor will work to the airlines' benefit. This is the expansion of the European Union, which gained ten new members in April 2004. Opening these economies to free trade will give the wealthy countries of western Europe new markets and a source of relatively cheap skilled labor, while companies in eastern Europe will get access to prosperous western consumers. This should bring new growth in travel between the two halves of the continent and open some profitable new routes to European airlines. The average distance between the EU capital in Brussels and the capitals of the ten new member countries is 1,400 km.

In all, the next few years hold considerable promise for European air carriers. If they cannot look forward to boom times, they can at least hope that the economic turbulence of 2001 and 2002 is finally behind them.

The three giant economies of Asia deserve special note. Japan was in recession, or near it, for more than a decade, but that seems to have changed. GDP growth, which had struggled to reach 1 percent through most of 2003, shot all the way up to 7.3 percent in the fourth quarter and 6.1 percent in the first quarter of 2004. Exports surged as well, but most of the growth appeared to be in the domestic market, a solid indication that the future should be brighter than the past. The Conference Board's leading index for Japan had been up for ten straight months by February 2004, but it leveled off in March and declined slightly in May. GDP growth seems to be slowing as well. In June, it still is not clear how Japan's economy will perform in the remainder of the year, much less in 2005. However, it now seems there is little danger that Japan will slip back into recession.

The Chinese economy had no need to recover from a slump. The Chinese economy grew by 9.1 percent in 2003, 9.9 percent in the fourth quarter of the year, and an astounding 10.7 percent in the first quarter of 2004. By spring 2004, the economy was showing signs of being seriously overheated, and Chinese officials had raised interest rates twice in an effort to keep things under control. The country was running a trade deficit with most of the world—the United States being a prominent exception—because it was forced to import raw materials in order to keep its factories running fast enough to keep up with demand. Chinese economic planners hope to bring that back to 7 percent, without triggering a sharper slowdown. Thus, a dip to 9.6 percent growth in the second quarter of 2004 actually came as good news: It seems that the Chinese economy may be slowing gently to a growth rate it can sustain, rather than collapsing into a recession as some economists had feared. Together with the country's enormous population, broad expanse, and growing ties with the rest of the world, this astonishing economic success will make China one of the biggest growth areas for both internal and external air travel for years to come.

The third Asian powerhouse is India, home to one-sixth of the world's people. In 2001, FI spent nearly a year studying India for a major corporate client.

At that time, we concluded that the Indian economy would grow at an average rate of 6.5 percent per year at least through 2005, and probably through 2010. This was 2 percent higher than consensus estimates, and thus far it is proving to be too conservative. The Indian economy expanded by 8 percent in 2003, and economists predict a growth rate as high as 7.3 percent in 2004. India's middle class is growing by an estimated 30 percent per year. Over the decade ending in 2007, the middle class is expected to triple in size, while the wealthiest class will expand by a factor of six. Demand for air travel in this region can only grow in proportion.

TOMORROW'S PASSENGERS

India and China are poster children for our second trend. The world's population is well on the way to doubling in forty years. Among the industrialized countries, America is growing by far the fastest, thanks to high birthrates among Hispanic immigrants and religious conservatives. However, the fastest population growth is in the developing and undeveloped countries. In Niger and the Palestinian Territories, populations will more than double between 2000 and 2050. In Yemen, Angola, and Congo, they will expand by over 160 percent.

Yet for the airline industry, the most important growth regions will be China, India, and the Muslim lands. According to the U.N., China is on track to grow by some 260 million people between 1995 and 2025, bringing its population to nearly 1.5 billion; the total could be much greater if the birthrate turns out to be even slightly higher than the extremely conservative assumptions used to form the estimate. India still has a high birthrate; its population is expected to pass 1.3 billion in 2021, up nearly one-third in twenty years. By 2050, there could be more than 2 billion people living in India. Growth rates in the Muslim lands vary widely. In Pakistan, it is about 2.6 percent per year, enough to bring its population from 130 million in 2000 to 220 million in 2020. Indonesia is growing at only half that rate. At the current rate of growth, by 2050 Pakistan could be the third most populous country in the world.

This matters to the airlines, because population growth represents new passengers. It matters even more because the Indian subcontinent is the prime source of guest workers for the Middle East, and most of them travel by air. In addition, more than 1 million people annually fly to Saudi Arabia for the Haj, the once-in-a-lifetime visit to Mecca required of all Muslim faithful. These markets will grow rapidly in the years ahead.

It matters still more because population growth is fastest in the cities of the developing world. Between 2000 and 2030, the global population will grow by an estimated 2.2 billion. Of this, 2.1 billion people will be added to the world's cities, primarily in places like India, China, and Indonesia. In 1950, there were just eight megacities, with populations over 5 million, in the world. (Newer definitions put the minimum population for a megacity at 10 million.) By 2015, there will be 59 megacities, 48 of them in less developed countries. Of these, 23 will have populations over 10 million, all but four in the developing lands. These vast concentrations of people—places like Delhi, Mumbai, São Paolo, and Dhaka—are likely to be among the fastest growing aviation markets in the world.

HIGH ALTITUDE, HIGH TECH

Not that long ago, when someone spoke of new airline technology, many people automatically thought of traveling on the *Concorde* and the faster, cheaper, miraculously sleeker new supersonic transports that would follow. By 2010, diplomats and the busiest executives would even bounce around the world on suborbital rocket planes, hopping from New York to New Delhi in just two hours.

Those dreams have evaporated in the heat of market reality. Now that the *Concorde* has been retired from service, it looks like commercial supersonic flight is an idea whose time has gone. Today's version of advanced aircraft technology is a lot less exciting, but a lot more practical.

Some of the most promising developments deal with the environment, which remains a much more important issue in most of the world than it has been in the United States of late. Researchers are working hard to improve fuel economy, reduce air pollution, and cut the noise associated with jet operations.

Air travel now produces about 12 percent of global CO_2 emissions. That should drop significantly in the coming decade. Yet by 2010, researchers hope to cut aircraft CO_2 emissions by another 20 percent and NO_X emissions by 60 percent.

More efficient burning means that fuel economy should rise as well. Today's jets burn an average of about 3.5 liters of fuel per 100 passenger-kilometers. This makes them 70 percent more fuel efficient than the airliners of forty years ago, but that is only the beginning. Airbus says that per-seat fuel consumption of its A380, scheduled to enter service in 2006, will be around 13 percent lower than a Boeing 747, with total expenses per-seat mile 15 percent lower. Boeing's 787, planned for 2008, is intended to cut fuel use by 15 to 20 percent, thanks to the use of highly efficient engines and much lightweight composite in its airframe.

Noise is another important environmental issue for the aviation industry, particularly in Europe, where 7 percent of the population lives within the sound "footprint" of a commercial airport and standards are much tighter than in the United States. Today's jet aircraft are typically 20 dB—75 percent quieter than the jets of 1960. That is just the beginning. Researchers hope to bring aircraft noise down another 6 dB by 2010 and perhaps 10 dB by 2020.

However, these are incremental advances. Some of the most sweeping changes are likely to appear not in the aircraft themselves, but in the systems that guide them from one place to another. These days, the global positioning system (GPS) keeps hikers from getting lost in the wilderness and guides drivers of luxury cars to the nearest gas station. It also enables pilots to fix their positions within a few feet of latitude, longitude, and altitude. Far more is possible.

In North America, most commercial aircraft make their way over long distances via designated air lanes, like drivers following a freeway. Straight-line flights from one point to another are relatively uncommon. This is in contrast to the situation in Europe, where most flights take the direct route and few of them are longer than 90 minutes.

In large part, the American system grew out of technological limitations that no longer apply. Before GPS, air traffic controllers just found it easier to keep track of planes that moved along easily predicted paths. It has worked fairly well for the hub-and-spokes traffic system, which routes tens or hundreds of flights per day through a few major airports.

However, there are serious disadvantages to this practice. The standard airways have limited traffic capacity, and many of them are getting crowded. And it takes more time and fuel to slip into the system and follow the airways to your destination than it would to fly in a straight line.

GPS makes the airways pretty much obsolete. The combination of satellite navigation and air traffic computers can fix any number of airplanes within a few feet of their actual positions, making sure that two aircraft never try to occupy the same space. This makes it practical to fly point-to-point, even over the longest routes to the busiest airports.

It also becomes possible to pack more airplanes together safely into less altitude, and the FAA now plans to cut the vertical separation required between airplanes from 2,000 feet to only 1,000. Thus twice as many airliners will be able to take advantage of the most efficient flight levels, saving both fuel and travel time.

Nav Canada, which provides air traffic control north of the border as the FAA does within the United States, believes that satellite navigation will allow unlimited free flight in its region by 2010. At that point, planes will fly directly to their destinations by the quickest, most convenient route, taking advantage of favorable winds. This will save still more fuel and open space for many more aircraft in the system. It could also further a reshaping of the airline industry that began more than twenty years ago.

BIG AND SMALL

We have written of bimodal distribution before. Giant players flourish due to economies of scale, and boutique operators prosper by delivering the kind of tailored service that mass marketers cannot. Midsized companies, lacking either advantage, disappear. This process has been especially hard on air carriers, which are vanishing at record rates. Globally, the number of airlines is expected to drop from around 500 in 2002 to only 60 in 2010.

However, in this industry the mechanism of attrition is a bit different. This is important, because it will continue to shape air travel in the next two decades as it has done for the last twenty years.

There are no small, high-service airlines analogous to the boutiques seen in other industries. Instead, carriers compete almost exclusively on price. And it is seldom the largest participants that compete most effectively. Discount carriers generally run tighter operations, pay their employees less, often buy used planes in good condition rather than investing in new equipment, turn them around faster between flights, and pack their passengers tighter. These efficiencies give the discounters lower costs per passenger mile and better profits despite offering cheaper prices than their larger competitors.

As a result, discount operators are flourishing even as full-fare carriers fight to survive. Low-fare lines held just 4 percent of the American market in 1991. By early 2004, they accounted for 25 percent. In 2003, even business travelers were buying air tickets that averaged 51 percent cheaper than standard business rates. Thus, Southwest Airlines, the pioneer of cut-rate aviation, managed to make $45.5 million in the first quarter of 2003, a time when United had an operating loss of $608 million and American hemorrhaged no less than $735 million. Air Tran built up its capacity by 28 percent over the year ending in June 2003 and will take delivery of 35 new aircraft over the next three years. Jet Blue has expanded from 21 aircraft in December 2001 to 41 in April 2003, and expects to operate 83 aircraft by the end of 2005.

All this is reshaping consumers' travel habits. In Europe, vacationers used to book package tours, organized and sold by major tour operators. Not anymore. In 2003, more than 20 percent of visitors arriving in Mallorca, for example, arrived by discount airline and booked their hotel rooms on the Internet. And because they paid less for air fare, many upgraded to more expensive hotel accommodations.

Early in 2004, several discount airlines in the United States even were moving into the international market, long a private preserve of the full-service, full-price carriers. Several already are serving the Caribbean and Latin America, while others plan to offer discount service to Europe and Asia by the end of the year.

Discount airlines also have achieved steady growth in Europe, where some 500 routes are now served by 20 discount airlines. According to one estimate, low-fare carriers now handle 40 percent of passenger traffic within Britain and between Britain and the continent. By 2010, low-fare and no-frills airlines such as Ryanair and easyJet are expected to capture at least 25 percent of the market throughout the European Union.

Despite the jammed seating and food choices that top out at a small bag of pretzels, low-cost carriers are winning passengers for more reasons than cheap travel. The Airline Quality Ratings, compiled by professors at Wichita State University and the Wichita State Aviation Institute, rate fourteen airlines that carry at least 1 percent of American domestic passengers. Criteria measured in the survey include on-time performance, staff courtesy, baggage handling, and the number of customer complaints. The 2003 survey ranked fourteen airlines. JetBlue came in first, with low-fare carriers taking three of the top four places.

In the United States, the discounters have one more advantage as well. United, US Airways, and the other giants exist to serve as many cities as possible. They do this by collecting passengers from smaller cities and consolidating them at about thirty major hub airports for long-distance travel. Running a hub-and-spokes system is not cheap, and it drives costs up for the major carriers by an estimated 15 percent. Discount airlines specialize in flying between cities that offer enough traffic to fill their planes and avoid the expense of hub operations.

Executives at the giant airlines argue that the hub-and-spokes model is the only way air travel can work in the United States. Of the 30,000 city-pair markets where air service is available, only 5 percent have enough traffic to support nonstop, point-to-point flights. For example, Syracuse, New York, offers 43 departures each day. Flights run nonstop to 11 hub cities and provide one-stop access to more than 175 destinations. Flying point-to-point, if it takes 75 passengers to justify running an airplane for them, Syracuse could support only one flight per day to each of seven destinations.

Discount airlines can offer cheap fares in part because they serve only markets that can fill planes for point-to-point travel. And the top 5 percent of city-pairs that give the discount airlines their living account for 73 percent of all passengers flying in the United States.

However, this picture is changing. The major airlines have not just been cutting prices—by up to 77 percent on some routes!—to compete with the leaner, meaner discounters. They have been eliminating service and starting their own low-fare operations. Non-hub airports have lost 19 percent of their air service since 1998; short-haul flights by the "Big Six" airlines have declined 43 percent since late 2001, and about two-dozen cities have lost all service by the major airlines. Fully half of the aircraft flown by the traditional airlines early in 2004 are smaller regional jets with no first-class seats. Most of the "Big Six" carriers have reduced flights to some of their hubs and pulled out of some smaller communities. None of them flies to Africa any more, nor to the Middle East (other than Israel), Eastern Europe, Indochina, Scandinavia, nor any of the states of the former Soviet Union, save for a single flight to Moscow. It is getting harder and harder to tell the difference between the major airlines and the discounters, save that their seats cost up to 30 percent more, even on the same routes.

At the same time, local populations are growing. Demand for air travel grows with them, so many more markets should be able to fill planes each day. And with satellite navigation, it becomes a lot easier for the air traffic control system to handle that kind of flight schedule. Point-to-point air travel may be destined to make the hub system obsolete, except for the longest routes. That would open a lot more U.S. markets to discount service. This is not good news for the major airlines.

Some aviation experts are convinced, others not. Boeing is betting the store on direct-route air travel. Airbus clearly is just as convinced that the hub-and-spokes system is here to stay. We can see this in the new models the two companies are bringing to market.

The Boeing 787 is a midsized, long-range carrier. Though details are yet to be fixed, it is expected to come in somewhere around 225 passengers, and the company says it will definitely be capable of 8,000 miles in a single hop. This plane clearly aims to provide nonstop service between midsized cities that today would be linked by a hub. Boeing is so sure that point-to-point travel will take over the market that it has committed to the project with only a couple of modest orders from Nippon Airways and Japan Air Lines. It will be the first time the company has built a new plane without major support from a domestic airline.

In contrast, the Airbus A380 will be a double-decker giant with seating for 555 passengers, plus a lounge and walking-around room of a kind not seen since airlines dumped the 747 piano bar to make room for more seats. It makes sense only in a hub-and-spokes system, where it can serve as the long-haul carrier for passengers with a variety of origins and destinations.

The two firms have put hard numbers to their visions of the future. Boeing believes that about 24,000 new airliners will be sold in the world over the next twenty years, not counting the smallest planes suited only to regional service. Of those, it says that 68 percent will be midsized single-aisle aircraft like its 787; only 3 percent will be mass movers larger than the current 747. Airbus puts the market closer to 15,000 new jets, plus 3,000 planes being refurbished to like-new standards. It believes that 52 percent of sales will be in the 787 category and 11 percent will be vast hub-to-hub airplanes like its A380, which thus far is the only model destined for its intended class.

At FI, it seems to us that both companies may be half-right, in principal if not in their exact numbers. It will be a long time before the hub-and-spokes system disappears completely. Too many small cities cannot support direct service, and even some medium-sized communities must combine their passenger loads to support international flights. Yet both technology and population growth clearly point toward more point-to-point service, at the expense of the hub-and-spokes carriers.

Nearly all of the American full-fare airlines have tacitly accepted the point-to-point model by setting up their own discount operations. The European airlines will make this transition soon, though it will not be easy for them. In late 2003, Cranfield (U.K) University's Air Transport Group warned that excess seating capacity already could drive some of Europe's low-cost air carriers out of business. At this point, we expect both Boeing and Airbus to find markets for their new models—but there are likely to be a lot more 787s than A380s in the air twenty years from now.

THE BOTTOM LINE

The post-9/11 downturn in air travel will have a lasting impact on the airline industry. Boeing estimates that 5 percent fewer passenger-miles will be flown in 2020 than would have been the case in the absence of 9/11. That puts the market roughly four years behind the growth curve that analysts once expected. This fits well with FAA projections. Three years ago, the agency forecast that passenger volumes in the United States would reach 1 billion in 2010 and 1.1 billion three years later. It now says that growth will recover soon to the 5.1 percent annually seen prior to 9/11. Yet American carriers will not fly 1 billion in a year until 2014.

This all adds up to an environment much like the one that existed before September 11. Undercapitalized, inefficient carriers will struggle to survive—and that second category will include some of the biggest names in air travel. Full-fare carriers will continue to offer wider seating, in-flight Internet service, and even a few bunks for weary passengers on long flights, all in an effort to justify premium prices. They will find it a hard sell, as even business travelers put up with the discomforts of flying coach in order to save money on all but the longest routes. The number of major hub-and-spokes airlines in the United States will decline from seven to five, then four, and eventually perhaps to only three. The same trends will be seen in Europe, and to a lesser extent, Asia. Yet in each region the most efficient, best capitalized competitors will reap ample rewards.

But behind these forecasts there are a few assumptions, and they should be made clear because they could prove wrong. In predicting a recovery, we assume that the cost of jet fuel will come down before it drives many of the major airlines out of business. This is likely, if only because OPEC has always found it impossible to inflate the price of crude oil for very long. We will be surprised if there is not a significant break in time for the American presidential elections in November 2004.

We assume also that there will be no major outbreak of bird flu, nor an epidemic of SARS that lasts for more than a few months. Bird flu in particular has the potential to halt most international air travel for a year or more. We assume that it will not only because there is, as yet, no evidence that the virus has learned to leap from one human patient to another.

The third assumption may be the weakest link in our forecast; it could go not merely wrong, but horribly wrong. We assume that there will be no repetition of the September 11 terrorist hijackings. Another spectacle in which airliners full of terrified passengers slam into buildings with thousands of occupants, or die in some equally spectacular way, could put the global airline industry into a depression from which it would not emerge for years. And, in May 2004, there have been disquieting rumors for months that Al Qaeda has an encore performance already in the works.

KEY TRENDS FOR THE AIRLINES

1. The economy of the developed world will continue to grow for at least the next five years. Any interruptions will be relatively short-lived.

Summary: After a brief but painful recession, the U.S. economy has been growing steadily for nearly three years, through the first quarter of 2004. Job creation lagged far behind GDP growth, but it too appears to have begun a substantial recovery.

Similar improvements are being seen around the world. Many of the European economies are emerging from years of stagnation, while Japan is seeing its first significant expansion in a decade. India and China are achieving GDP growth that averages 6 percent or better each year.

Barring another terrorist incident on the scale of 9/11, or some equivalent shock, this widespread prosperity should feed upon itself, with each trading nation helping to generate the continued well-being of its partners. It can be sustained for some years to come.

Implications for the Airlines: Business travel will slowly recover from its low in the recent recession, bringing new demand for seats, particularly on long-distance flights. (However, this does not necessarily suggest that executives who have grown accustomed to discount fares will soon be willing to pay for business-class seats, even if those seats are available.)

Leisure travel will recover as well, and probably more quickly than business travel. These passengers increasingly will prefer low-fare carriers.

The Asia-Pacific markets, particularly India and China, will grow much more quickly than demand in North America and Europe.

2. The world's population will grow to 9 billion by 2050.

Summary: The greatest fertility is found in those countries least able to support their existing populations. Populations in many developing countries will double between 2000 and 2050; in the Palestinian Territories, they will rise by 217 percent. In contrast, the developed nations will fall from 23 percent of the total world population in 1950 and about 14 percent in 2000 to only 10 percent in 2050. In 10 years or so, the workforce in Japan and much of Europe will be shrinking by 1 percent per year.

Implications for the Airlines: Demand for air travel will grow at least as quickly as the world's population.

3. Oil prices are stable at $25 to $28 per barrel; they rise above that level only in times of trouble.

Summary: In autumn 2004, OPEC's aim is to hold the price of oil at relatively high levels, and the instability in the Middle East is making this relatively easy. However, keeping prices high requires a unity of purpose that member countries have never been able to sustain for very long. The cost of raising a barrel of oil from the ground in this region is around one-tenth the wholesale price. New oil supplies coming on line in the former Soviet Union, China, and other parts of the world will make it even more difficult to sustain prices at artificially high levels. Prices above $28 per barrel are simply unsustainable.

Implications for the Airlines: For so long as jet fuel remains overpriced, the full-service airlines have no hope of becoming profitable. This problem should ease when oil prices return to their normal range, most likely by 2006.

Full-service airlines eventually will be forced to enact a ticked surcharge to cover the cost of fuel. However, doing so will drive still more of their passengers to the discount carriers.

4. People around the world are becoming increasingly sensitive to environmental issues such as air pollution as the consequences of neglect, indifference, and ignorance become ever more apparent.

Summary: The World Health Organization estimates that 3 million people die each year from the effects of air pollution, about 5 percent of the total deaths annually. The European Parliament estimates that 70 percent of the continent's drinking water contains dangerous concentrations of nitrate pollution. Though government policies in some developing countries—and the United States, at the moment—rate industrial growth more important than dealing with environmental problems, many others are working to clean up the air and water, save rainforests, and protect endangered species. Overall, the trend is clearly toward a cleaner, healthier environment.

Implications for the Airlines: Pollution controls will continue to be a growing burden for the airlines. However, the need to eliminate pollution eventually will help to make the air carriers more efficient and profitable.

5. Advances in transportation technology will make travel and shipping faster and cheaper by land, sea, and air.

Summary: New technologies are transforming the way we travel. A new generation of airliners will carry up to 250 people for 9,000 miles or 555 people up to 6,400 miles. Advances in automobile technology such as road-condition sensors, automated traffic management systems, and hybrid power systems all will be in common use by 2010. Similar developments are seen in every sector of transportation.

Implications for the Airlines: New technology should cut fuel use by as much as 10 percent per passenger mile over the next ten years.

New safety technologies, such as fuel tanks filled with inert gas, should eliminate some potential accidents in the future, saving more than 1,000 lives in the next ten years.

By eliminating the need for America's hub-and-spokes air travel network, satellite navigation will dramatically reduce the cost of air travel in the United States over the next ten years. It also will improve the profitability of the major airlines—or at least of those that survive until the transition has been made.

6. International exposure includes a greater risk of terrorist attack.

Summary: State-sponsored terrorism appears to be on the decline, as tougher sanctions make it more trouble than it is worth. However, nothing will prevent small, local political organizations and special-interest groups from using terror to promote their causes. And as the United States learned on September 11, the most dangerous terrorist groups are no longer motivated by specific political goals, but by generalized, virulent hatred based on religion and culture. On balance, the amount of terrorist activity in the world is likely to go up, not down, in the next ten years.

Implications for the Airlines: No matter what else goes right, there will be a sword over the industry's neck for at least the next ten years.

New security precautions will continue to drain profits from the airlines, particularly in the United States.

It is essential that the airlines set up to screen all checked baggage before it goes onto an airplane, just as they do carry-on luggage.

7. Institutions are undergoing a bimodal distribution: The big get bigger, the small survive, and the midsized are squeezed out.

Summary: For at least 20 years, economies of scale have allowed the largest companies to buy their smaller competitors or drive them out of business. At the same time, thousands of tiny, agile companies are prospering in niche markets. We see this pattern among automakers, computer companies, airlines, banks, and many other industries.

Implications for the Airlines: High-priced, full-service airlines have only just begun to cope with competition from the discount carriers. No-frills airlines will continue to gain market share at the expense of the full-fare lines.

Boeing's 787 is likely to find more of a market than the Airbus A380.

Competition among the discount airlines will be even more intense than between the discounters and the full-fare carriers.

Chapter 8

Tasty Trends for the Restaurant Industry

In Japan, hungry customers pack into Tokyo's Friendly Cajun Café. In Europe, gourmet restaurants are doing much less business than usual, but American hamburger chains are blamed for soaring rates of obesity on the continent. And in the United States, those same fast-food restaurants are adding low-carb, high-nutrition menu items for health-conscious consumers who will no longer eat french fries. Around the world, the restaurant business is changing.

Inevitably, many changes are driven by economics. The details vary from country to country, but throughout the developed world we are seeing a common theme of nascent recovery after some difficult years. Restaurants are expected to benefit from this welcome development.

In the United States, the threat of a "double-dip" recession seems to have passed. After two difficult years, the economy finally expanded by 3.1 percent in 2003 and in May 2004 seems on track for about 4 percent growth this year. Retail sales, factory orders, and the Index of Leading Indicators all have been rising consistently, often more strongly than economists anticipated. Even job growth, which consistently underperformed forecasts by a wide margin throughout the early stages of the recovery, began to rebound strongly in March and April 2004; by June, more than 1 million new jobs had been added to the economy. All this augurs well for the nation's restaurants.

Europe also is beginning to recover from the economic sluggishness of recent years. Growth on the continent ran at just 0.9 percent in 2002 and 0.4 percent in 2003. In substantial part, this was due to the weakness of the dollar on international currency markets, which discouraged American tourism and cut demand for relatively expensive European exports. Now retail sales, sentiment indicators, and even manufacturing have begun to pick up. France turned in 2.5 percent growth in the fourth quarter of 2003, its first positive showing in two years, and 3.1 percent in the first quarter of 2005. The Conference Board's index of leading indicators for the country is pointing solidly up. In Germany, both consumer and industrial demand are rising, and the economy is expected to grow by 1.6 percent in 2004 and 1.75 percent in 2005. Britain managed to avoid a recession during the recent downturn, despite a severe drought in London's critical financial sector, and the GDP is expected to grow by about 3 percent annually in 2004 and 2005. Unemployment remains high in parts of Europe—around 9 percent in France and 10 percent in Germany—but things are clearly looking up.

China had a remarkable economic boom in 2003, with GDP growth averaging 9.1 percent for the year and 9.9 percent in the fourth quarter. In the first thee months of 2004, the economy grew by an unsustainable 10.7 percent, a rate so hot that Chinese economic officials were trying to slow its growth so as to avoid an outbreak of inflation. In the second quarter, growth declined to "only" 9.6 percent, and economists were breathing a sigh of relief, as it appeared that China might be settling back to a growth rate that it can sustain.

Even Japan is growing solidly for the first time in a dozen years. The economy expanded by a satisfying 7 percent in late 2003, this after more than four years in which the growth rate averaged just 0.3 percent. By April 2004, the Conference Board's index of leading indicators for Japan had been up no less than twelve months in a row.

All this spells good times for the world's restaurants, which prosper when people feel they can afford to splurge. Restaurant sales in the United States are expected to grow by 4.4 percent this year, to a record $440.1 billion. Adjusted for inflation, the growth rate will be about 2 percent, up from 1.3 percent in 2003.

In Japan, restaurant sales are growing rapidly as the economy improves. Some 65 percent of consumers eat out at least once a week, and an estimated 75 million restaurant meals are served daily.

In China, both full-service and quick-service restaurants have been enjoying a boom, as affluent, but busy customers flock to eat out. McDonalds, KFC, Pizza Hut, and local quick-service operators such as the Hulian Supermarket Chain, Xiao Fai Yang, and Beijing Quanqude all have been growing rapidly. Chinese quick-service sales are expected to grow by 5.5 percent per year for the foreseeable future. Much of this expansion is being driven by government policy, which encourages the Chinese people to spend their money rather than saving it in order to generate further growth.

As the dollar regains some of its strength in currency markets, American tourists should return to Europe and Japan, and head back to more upscale accommodations. Restaurants in tourist destinations, where sales have been off by up to 50 percent from previous years, should find it much less of a struggle just to survive. This will be even better news in London, where a wave of bankruptcies decimated the restaurant business during the financial sector's lean times.

Returning prosperity in the United States should promote the current growth among restaurants a cut above the traditional casual-dining segment. This trend may be felt in Europe as well, once the current appeal of American-style fast food begins to wane.

However, low-end earners and those under heavy time pressure will opt for quick-service restaurants. Their numbers are likely to grow as automation continues to reduce the need for human labor and outsourcing exports well-paid American jobs to poorly paid foreign lands.

Of course, economic conditions are just one of many factors that influence the world's restaurants. At FI, we see many trends that will help to shape this industry in the years ahead. Some are limited to the United States; others are felt worldwide, or soon will be. Most are very broad waves that are sweeping societies at large; a few are specific to restaurants. In no particular order, here are twelve of the most important trends for the restaurant industry:

DINERS CHANGE, RESTAURANTS ADAPT

Throughout the developed world, people on average are growing older. In the United States, those over 65 made up 15 percent of the population in 2000; by 2050, 27 percent of Americans will be in their traditional retirement years. Japan's over-65 population will skyrocket from 17 percent in 2000 to 22 percent in 2010 and more than 36 percent in 2050. Germany, France, Britain, Italy, and many other countries also are aging, on average.

They are growing more diverse as well, thanks to a wave of migration that is bringing millions of people from the eastern hemisphere to the western hemisphere, and from south of the equator to the northern lands. In the United States, the Hispanic, Asian, and Middle Eastern populations all are expanding rapidly. In 2000, Latinos accounted for about one-eighth of the U.S. population. By 2050, they will be nearly one-fourth. And the number of Asians is almost doubling from 11.2 million in 2000 to 19.6 million in 2020. Similar changes are being seen in Europe, where hundreds of thousands of immigrants arrive each year from Eastern Europe, North Africa, the Middle East, and the Indian subcontinent.

Baby boomers still dominate restaurant clientele. They visit full-service restaurants with per-person checks in the $10-to-$20 range more than any other age group. They will continue to power the casual-dining market for many years to come. In addition, several fast-food vendors in the United States are trying to create a new middle ground known as "fast casual" in an attempt to expand beyond the saturated fast-food market. This innovation aims to take advantage of boomers and their children who grew up on fast food but cannot yet make the leap to the higher-ticket casual dining.

A more diverse population spells growing demand for ethnic cuisines formerly outside the mainstream. In Europe, a generation of immigrants from North Africa, the Middle East, Pakistan, India, and Bangladesh have been opening restaurants that offer their native cuisines for nearly 20 years. This new fare has proved popular with indigenous Europeans.

New immigrants and their first-generation children prefer the foods they grew up with. This is helping to drive the American boom in Asian, Latin, and Caribbean restaurants. In early 2004, the fastest growing segment is Mexican restaurants, thanks to a growing Hispanic population, with a growing income. (So-called "Nuevo Latino," the latest craze, combines Latin and Caribbean influences.) This trend is particularly strong in California, Florida, and other areas with large Hispanic communities. American Hispanics have an estimated $452 billion.

All this fits well with buying habits in the United States, where baby boomers and their descendants have long sought out novelty and variety. They are looking not just for food, but for new and exciting experiences. This extends to new cuisine, exotic surroundings, and almost anything that is just plain "different." What these restaurant customers seek is not so much nutrition and convenience, but the experience of dining out. The trend is to dining as entertainment. Witness the rise in America of Thai food, with its emphasis on chili oil, coconut paste, fish sauce, lemon grass, and other relatively exotic flavors. The popularity of Cajun food in Japan and pizza and ice cream in China are similar trends.

The drive toward flavor and experience is behind the American fad for tapas—the Spanish equivalent of dim sum—and "grazing," which offer more different flavors in a single meal. These changes increasingly are finding their way into quick-service restaurants. Arby's Roast Turkey Ranch and Bacon sandwich features Asian-style tamarind sauce, while McDonald's has been experimenting with Latin-flavored items. If these innovations are successful, they will soon be exported to outlet Europe and Asia. Though these specific fads may pass, the notion of packing more intensity and experience onto one table is with us to stay.

In the years ahead, we can expect to see more American restaurants featuring foods from out-of-the-way parts of Asia, the Caribbean, Latin America, and North Africa, with a modest boom in Indian fare; more European restaurants offering cuisine from many of these same regions; and still more restaurants in Japan specializing in American regional fare.

Even more intense flavors lie ahead as well. Aging baby boomers will need them to maintain their feeling of novelty and excitement as their taste buds lose their sensitivity.

As the boomers grow older, other changes are in store. Already, retirees struggling with fixed incomes are competing with young people for restaurant jobs. This should help to minimize tightness in the labor market owing to the relatively small size of the current generations and may provide a more stable, reliable pool of workers in a traditionally volatile industry. Farther ahead, any restaurants are likely to find that a major part of their business consists of delivering take-out meals to local retirement communities.

TOURISTS EAT, TOO

The world's boom in tourism has only been slowed, not stopped, by concerns such as the threat of terrorism and the unfavorable exchange rates for the dollar in 2003 and early 2004. Once those worries have passed, the number of Americans traveling abroad will begin to grow again at its accustomed 5 percent per year. It will expand for the foreseeable future.

The opening of European borders has caused a boom in continental tourism, especially among the younger generations, who routinely speak several languages. Young people from Italy, France, England, and Germany today are nearly as likely to spend vacations, and even long weekends, in each other's countries as in their own.

For restaurants in tourist destinations, this is good news, and not only because visitors from prosperous foreign lands will again be dining out. Because growing numbers of travelers are taking their vacations off-season, they should help to even out the cyclicality of cash flow for restaurants, just as they have been doing for other hospitality businesses.

This is particularly significant for higher-end full-service restaurants, which report that up to 30 percent of their sales—and more than half in some major European tourist destinations—are to vacationers and business travelers.

DINING FOR HEALTH AS WELL AS PLEASURE

Early in 2004, the federal Centers for Disease Control and Prevention warned that fully two-thirds of Americans are overweight. Obesity, the agency added, is fast closing in on heart disease (itself weight-related) as the nation's leading cause of death.

This is a global problem; in fact, the epidemic has been nicknamed "globesity." According to the International Obesity Task Force, 1.7 billion people around the world need to lose weight, and 312 million are obese—at least 30 pounds over their maximum recommended weight. About 36 percent of children in Italy, 30 percent in Spain, and 22 percent in Britain are now overweight or obese. Only the poorest nations of Africa are immune to this trend. As a result, the incidence of diseases such as type 2 diabetes, hypertension, coronary heart disease, osteoarthritis, and several types of cancer is skyrocketing throughout the world. So are death rates.

Figures like these—no pun intended—are bringing new power to the health movement that began in the United States more than 20 years ago. In the industrialized West, growing numbers of consumers are changing the way they eat and care for themselves, not only at home but when dining out. This trend is being felt in restaurants throughout the United States and is beginning to appear overseas.

Smoking also is in decline. Only 21 percent of Americans smoked cigarettes as of January 2000, down from 30 percent in 1983. Early in 2004, Ireland even banned smoking in its pubs; this was the first sign that smoking may be going out of favor in Europe as well as the United States. The number of smokers is rising rapidly in much of Asia, but we expect this trend to be reversed as the true cost of this habit makes itself clear in rising rates of cancer, heart disease, emphysema, and other ills.

Restaurants in the United States are working hard to adapt to the health concerns of their guests. Even before the low-carb fad took off, 71 percent of Americans reported that they were trying to include more fruit and vegetables in their diets, rather than meats and baked goods. Now the low-carb Atkins and South Beach diets are the hottest things in the fat-fighting market. TGI Friday's reports that 19 percent of its frequent casual-dining customers are following the Atkins plan. Beef producers report that not even the discovery of mad cow disease in December 2003 could slow meat sales within the United States; carb-conscious dieters kept beef prices near record highs.

Menus are being adapted to fit this trend, with high-protein meals displacing some choices that are stronger in carbohydrates and fats. TGI Friday's and Ruby Tuesday both have introduced series of low-carb items to their menus. Pit Stop Pasta, in Escondido, California, has even come out with a low-carb "pizza in a bucket," delivering all the toppings but none of the crust. (FI does not expect this to be a big hit with customers.) In the United States, at least, we will see similar menu changes with every diet fad that manages to remain popular for more than a few months. Europe probably is ten years behind in this trend.

Restaurants not actually changing their menus are counting carbs and promoting Atkins-friendly choices. Many say this has helped them to keep customers who might otherwise have been lost. We expect it to become standard practice in many casual-dining establishments.

Salad entrees are rapidly becoming more popular, particularly in the casual dining restaurants, while both casual-dining and fine-dining restaurants report a market increase in sales of seafood. These trends are likely to continue for several more years.

Mediterranean cuisine also is gaining popularity in the United States, even as its appeal wanes in Europe, thanks largely to medical studies that have praised it as heart-healthy food.

Health-minded consumers are demanding more nutrition information, even in restaurants. Calorie and content details are likely to begin appearing on American menus to supplement heart-healthy symbols.

This trend has proved hard on quick-service chains, which are struggling to overcome a long-standing reputation for heart-*un*healthy fare. A 2001 Harris Poll showed that about one-third of Americans ate at fast-food restaurants less often than a year before, citing health reasons. As a result, many chains are adding salads, low-carb dishes, and other diet choices to their menus. However, hamburgers remain the dominant item on fast-food menus and are likely to remain so for many years to come.

Supersizing is out, smaller portions in—for the moment. This has all the earmarks of a short-lived fad.

Consumers also are shunning desserts, with sales down some 2 percent in 2003 alone. This is in part a money-saving measure in a tight economy, but weight-watching is clearly important. Restaurants increasingly are responding by offering smaller, lighter, cheaper desserts, reducing selection, and focusing on other parts of the meal.

CONSUMERISM COMPOUNDS

The Internet has brought shoppers vast new sources of information about product quality, pricing, delivery time, and store services. At the same time, advocacy groups and regulations have been promoting better content labels, nutrition data, and other consumer-oriented requirements. This continuing growth of consumerism is inevitably making itself felt in the world's restaurants.

Savvy consumers demand high quality at the best possible price, and in good economic times quality is more important. In this, consumers in the United States and Europe are following the lead of their peers in Japan, where only the freshest and highest quality foods are salable. Their concern for quality is pushing the entire restaurant industry to improve its performance in this critical area.

This gives restaurant chains one more advantage over their single-site competitors. The ability to market a brand will remain a powerful tool in attracting quality-conscious consumers. However, the sterile uniformity of the most homogenized restaurant chains is out. Consumers increasingly are shopping for quality food delivered in an ambience of warmth and comfort.

Chef-owned restaurants will find it increasingly difficult to establish a foothold, save in the largest cities, where one person's reputation can attract customers in sufficient numbers to sustain a business.

Consistent quality is important for another reason as well: Consumers increasingly get their information from the Internet. A single dissatisfied customer in Dubuque can damage a chain's reputation all over the country.

This trend will become more important in Europe as the Brussels bureaucrats of the European Union spin off ever more consumerist regulations and more upscale American restaurant chains expand their continental operations.

HIGH TECH, HIGH TOUCH

As technology permeates our daily lives, and further reduces us to small, highly pressured cogs in the global economy, our need for comfort and personal attention is growing rapidly. Restaurants increasingly are providing a haven where we can sit back, relax, and feel a little bit pampered. This is one powerful force behind the growth of the new upscale restaurant chains that are quickly building a niche between casual dining operations and the luxury restaurants.

Technology is bringing even more obvious changes outside the diner's view. Automated equipment, more sophisticated order and inventory systems, and other improvements in information technology will continue to cut operating costs for both quick-service and full-service restaurants. For example, automated food service prep machines are being integrated into the process of fulfilling customer orders. French fryers can be connected to point-of-sale hardware and automatically lower fries into the oil as orders are placed. Automatic drink dispensers fill orders with no human intervention. Anything that is repetitive and requires consistency will be replaced over time with robots.

Corporate-level accounting, personnel records, and similar functions all can be shipped to reliable offshore data services with a significant impact on the bottom line.

However, technology is raising some other costs. After a brief respite in the 1990s, the price of health care is again rising at double-digit rates, thanks in substantial part to the high cost of new medical technologies. As new diagnostic and treatment methods reach clinical use, they will continue to drive up the cost of employee medical benefits. This trend is likely to continue so long as smoking and obesity remain common. In Europe, these costs will be felt as higher taxes rather than as direct expenses.

At the same time, restaurants are finding that technology makes it pay to retain employees, even if salary costs are slightly higher. Overall, it costs less to keep a skilled employee than to provide training and benefits for a new hire. In the long run, retaining practiced workers lowers costs and increases guest satisfaction. This trend is growing faster in the full-service restaurants than in quick-service extablishments.

XS AND DOTS

Though the Baby Boomers still dominate Western culture, their children and grandchildren are a growing force in society. They are influencing the restaurant business in a number of ways.

Members of the post-boomer generations have more in common with their peers throughout the world than with their parents. They share values, fashion sense, and a host of other factors that mark them as something new and different. They are materialistic; individualistic, yet cooperative in groups; tech-savvy; and given to extremely short attention spans.

They also are relatively rare. Generation X, roughly the 30-plus cohort; the Dot-coms, now in their 20s; and their younger siblings, yet to be authoritatively nicknamed, are far smaller than the 40-plus age group. Though there are more entry-level workers today than there were just five years ago, there still are fewer than employers need. In the United States, more than half of restaurant operators say they are finding it increasingly hard to hire enough workers, and particularly hourly workers. The shortage is tightest among cooks, but this problem is felt in all positions.

The worker shortage affects quick-service restaurants more severely than full-service locations. One-third of American quick-service operators report that recruiting and retaining employees is a major challenge, compared with only 14 percent of full-service operators with average check sizes over $8. This problem can only grow more difficult in the near future.

Generation X should be renamed "Generation E," for entrepreneurial. Throughout the world, they are starting new businesses at an unprecedented rate.

The Dot-coms are proving to be even more business-oriented, caring for little but the bottom line. Twice as many say they would prefer to own a business rather than be a top executive. Five times more would prefer to own a business rather than hold a key position in politics or government.

If this sounds like good news for business, it's not. The bottom line these generations care about is their own, not their employer's. They have grown up to expect affluence, and even wealth; just how they will achieve it is not clear, given that many in the United States are undereducated even for most working-class jobs. But the Xs and Dot-coms also watched their parents remain loyal to their employers, only to be downsized out of work. The lesson was not lost on them. They will quit and move across the country at even the hint of a job that offers better pay or opportunities for training. The data are not readily available, but we strongly suspect that this is as true in the other developed countries as it is in the United States.

The generations now entering the job market are likely to be even less reliable than their older peers. Turnover rates have declined slightly among both hourly and salaried workers in the current tight job market. They are likely to rise sharply now that the economy is finally beginning to create enough new jobs to go around.

If this sounds like the work ethic is in trouble, you are catching on. For younger employees, work is only a means to their ends: money, fun, and leisure. In this, Americans are just catching up with a trend that swept Europe when government pensions and labor laws guaranteed workers there free time and much greater security. Tardiness is increasing, sick-leave abuse is common, and job security and high pay just aren't the motivators they once were. Fifty-five percent of the top executives interviewed recently say that erosion of the work ethic will have a major negative effect on corporate performance in the future.

To meet their need for reliable workers, restaurants will have to adopt all the standard recruiting techniques: raise starting salaries, provide better benefits, and expand training programs.

For today's entry-level workers, training for future jobs is a key issue; they simply do not believe in traditional careers and long-term employment, even if the restaurant industry were in a position to offer enough satisfying, well-paid positions to go around. So an essential factor in retaining young workers is to position restaurant jobs and training very clearly as stepping-stones to more desirable positions in other industries later in the recruit's working life.

Better training programs also will be needed to ensure a high quality of service from generations not basically inclined to pay attention to detail.

In this context, displaced baby-boom workers and post-retirement job seekers become even more important as a source of reliable employees.

One more effect of this change will be to drive restaurants to implement robots and artificial intelligence to run and maintain a smooth flow of production in the restaurant. Many of the skills required to maintain smooth operation will be conducted remotely at a central or regional location. Intelligent machines, in-store real-time video, and network connectivity will allow one manager to control several locations.

CLOCK-WATCHING

Computers, electronic communications, the Internet, and other technologies all are making national and international economies much more competitive. Labor productivity has been skyrocketing in recent years, partly because of these new technologies, but also because companies are driving their employees to do more faster. American workers accomplished nearly 30 percent more work per hour at the end of 2003 than they did in 1992. They also spent about 10 percent more time on the job than they did a decade ago. European executives and nonunionized workers face the same trend.

In this high-pressure environment, dining out is becoming ever more important, both as a convenience to harried workers and as an opportunity to relax and enjoy life after the stresses of work. In a study by the National Restaurant Association, 79 percent of American diners said that eating out was a better use of their leisure time than cooking and cleaning up. Those workers will continue to expand the market for casual and higher-end dining.

"The multi-unit operators will continue research to ensure that their menu price points will drive the time-conscious harried workers to their restaurants," comments Paul Wise, dean emeritus and former head of the hospitality program at the University of Delaware. "The frequency of returning customers is a growing important element of success in an increasingly competitive environment."

The need to save time is one driver for the spread of American-style family restaurants in Japan. By 2006, their numbers will have nearly doubled in ten years.

However, the greatest beneficiaries will be quick-service restaurants that can provide tasty, nutritious fast food in a pleasant environment.

One growing market is the "grab-and-go" breakfast. Though 77 percent of breakfasts are still eaten in the home, that number is likely to decline as working lives become ever more demanding. Many potential customers will opt for a donut or energy bar and coffee in the car. Others will stop at their preferred quick-service restaurant for something more substantial.

GOVERNMENT WATCHDOGS

Since the U. S. Congress passed regulatory reform laws in 1996, more than 14,000 new regulations have been enacted. Not one proposed regulation was rejected during this period. The Federal Register, where proposed and enacted regulations are published, was nearly 50 percent larger in 1998 than it had been just ten years earlier—50,000 pages in all.

In Brussels, officials of the European Union are churning out new regulations at an even faster pace, creating more uniform consumer and workplace regulations throughout the continent.

Predictably, this growing burden of legal requirements is falling at least as heavily on the restaurant industry as it does on other businesses. In addition to all the general work-related rules, laws proposed in the United States and Europe would provide nutritional data to consumers in real time, even in restaurants where menus are based upon local fresh produce and meats.

To keep up with the competition, corporate computer networks will be required to access data that may be required to run a restaurant in the future. They will automatically check on changes in corporate and industry standards, government regulations for food safety, and other information critical to business planning.

Beyond that, there really is not much to be said about the spread of government regulations. Restaurant operators will have to spend a growing fraction of their time coping with them, just as their peers in other industries do. It's just one more cost of doing business.

SECURITY THAT ISN'T SOCIAL

The September 11 attacks on New York and Washington have inspired a wave of laws and regulations intended to keep would-be terrorists out of the country, or at least unable to harm others. This transformation has added a whole new level of legal and regulatory demands on all businesses.

A bioterrorist attack on the food industry could be the most important terrorist risk in the developed world. Directly and indirectly, the food industry generates 13 percent of the U.S. GDP and employs one in eight Americans; in some European countries, the numbers are slightly higher. This makes food a target to gladden the heart of any terrorist.

Restaurants are the most accessible bull's-eyes in the industry, with the highest concentrations of relaxed, vulnerable civilians. Restaurant attacks would have enormous shock value. To date, most have been straightforward bombings of establishments where Americans and other westerners congregate. Such attacks have occurred in Germany, Bali, Morocco, and many other lands. They will happen again. They are possible almost anywhere in the world, because most borders present relatively few obstacles for the would-be terrorist. This is especially a concern for the European Union, because anyone who has entered one EU country can travel freely throughout the continent.

However, food contamination may be an even greater threat. It has happened before. As early as 1984, followers of Baghwan Shree Rajneesh contaminated eleven salad bars with salmonella in a plot to take political control of Wasco County, Oregon, by preventing nonmembers from voting in a local election. The group reportedly possessed cultures of typhoid fever as well; the salmonella was just a proof-of-concept experiment. Nonetheless, it sickened more than 700 people.

It could have been far worse. To take just one possible scenario, imagine what would have happened if the person who mailed anthrax bacteria to

American politicians and journalists in 2001 had instead taken a lunch-time job at a restaurant near Wall Street or in London's financial district, or even had signed on at his local McDonald's. The results might not be as immediate and dramatic as a bomb tossed through the front door, but they could prove just as devastating.

Restaurant operators should consider hiring security experts to look for vulnerabilities in their locations and operations. Consistent with the comfort and pleasure of their customers, they may want to take precautions to make themselves harder targets for would-be terrorists.

Because food contamination is an obvious tactic for terrorists, restaurants will be under growing pressure to know exactly whom they are hiring and to maintain detailed records about their employees.

One new and important overhead item is insurance coverage against terrorist incidents. In the United States, case law now holds that professional hosts such as restaurants and meeting planners are liable for injuries to their guests caused by a terrorist attack on their site.

THE RICH GET RICHER

We have written in other chapters about bimodal distribution, the tendency of large, successful companies to keep growing and small ones to flourish in niche markets, while midsized competitors are bought up or driven out of business. We have seen this pattern among automakers and computer companies, banks and hotels. We see it among restaurants as well. The consolidation seen among chains in this sector can only continue. Expect a continuing stream of mergers, acquisitions, and deal-making in the restaurant industry in the years ahead.

The growing popularity of restaurant chains positioned nearer the middle of the price and service range appears to be something of an exception to this trend in the United States. We expect it to spread to Europe before this decade is over. Restaurants in the fast-casual market—such as Baja Fresh and Panera—offer a wider range of menu options and more inviting décor than quick-service chains, but much less service than casual-dining establishments. Similarly, places like the Bonefish Grill, Cheesecake Factory, and its even higher-end spinoff, the Grand Lux Café offer a more upscale experience than the casual-dining chains but less service and ambience than luxury restaurants. Market segmentation clearly allows more diversity among restaurant chains than is found in most other industries. When combined with a unique identity and a reputation for quality, economies of scale can make for a winning combination in almost any part of the market.

However, the growing proliferation of restaurant names—whether chains or single-location, neighborhood restaurants—is likely to cut into profits in the years ahead. According to the National Restaurant Association, nearly two-thirds of fine-dining restaurants and half of casual-dining and family-dining chains say that it is becoming more difficult to maintain customer loyalty than it used to be.

This is one more place where technology will come to the rescue. By collecting information about individual customers, restaurants will be able to customize their future dining experiences. As guests become accustomed to entering a grocery store, downloading their grocery list, and receiving specials coupons designed for their individual preferences, they will start to expect this same experience when they enter their favorite restaurant chain. They will want to know which items have appeared on the menu since their last visit, and which contain peanuts or other ingredients that they dislike or that might trigger their allergies. The menu will be personalized to their individual tastes. In the immediate future, this will apply largely to full-service restaurants. However, the trend toward individually customized menus will extend to quick-service locations as well.

IN ALL . . .

These trends spell interesting times for the world's restaurant operators—and according to popular tradition, the wish that someone live in interesting times is an old Chinese curse, not a blessing. Yet at FI we are optimistic about the future of the restaurant industry.

There are some difficult challenges ahead, particularly with regard to staffing and overhead. Yet the restaurant industry has both a decades-long record of success and all the assets it requires to build a bright future. In prosperous, growing, and increasingly stressful nations, it supplies two of the basic necessities of life: food and comfort. And if 90 percent of independent restaurants go out of business in their first year, well-run chains and the best independent operators have always looked forward to a long and productive future. So it is today.

The restaurant industry's unique market—every man, woman, and child in every country—is huge and receptive, and its challenges are manageable. For the world's restaurant operators, a bright and prosperous future appears to be all but assured.

KEY TRENDS FOR RESTAURANTS

1. The economy of the developed world will continue to grow for at least the next five years. Any interruptions will be relatively short-lived.

Summary: After a brief but painful recession, the U. S. economy has been growing steadily for nearly three years, through the first quarter of 2004. Job creation lagged far behind GDP growth, but it too appears to have begun a substantial recovery.

Similar improvements are being seen around the world. Many of the European economies are emerging from years of stagnation, while Japan is seeing its first significant expansion in a decade. India and China are achieving GDP growth that averages 6 percent or better each year.

Barring another terrorist incident on the scale of 9/11, or some equivalent shock, this widespread prosperity should feed upon itself, with each trading nation helping to generate the continued well-being of its partners. It can be sustained for some years to come.

Implications for Restaurants: Restaurant sales will grow at least as quickly as economies in general, and probably a bit faster. This should bring good times for restaurant operators throughout the industrialized world.

Upscale restaurants will benefit from the growing prosperity of their customers, as patrons who might have dined slightly down-market feel able to spend a bit more for a meal.

However, quick-service chains also will benefit as hard-pressed workers with only a few minutes to spare choose to "grab and go," rather than spend time preparing their own meals.

2. The population of the developed world is living longer.

Summary: Each generation lives longer and remains healthier than the last. Life expectancy in Australia, Japan, and Switzerland is now over 75 years for men and over 80 for women, and it is growing throughout the developed world. As a result, the retirement-age population also is growing rapidly. It may expand even more quickly than official forecasts anticipate, because they assume that life expectancy will grow more slowly in the future. In fact, it is more likely that new medical technologies will lengthen our lives still more rapidly in the near future, and bring a better quality of life in the process.

Implications for Restaurants: Older diners will make up a growing portion of restaurant clientele.

Older workers also will be available to make up the slack left by the small size of younger generations.

Older diners will seek out stronger flavors to make up for the declining sensitivity of their taste buds.

3. Tourism, vacationing, and travel (especially international) will continue to grow in the next decade, as they did throughout the 1990s.

Summary: Once current worries over the threat of terrorism recede, American tourism will resume its traditional 5 percent annual growth. Other countries—particularly China and India—are contributing to this demand, as their economies grow and their citizens become more free to travel. Tourism will benefit as Internet "virtual" tours replace printed brochures in promoting vacation destinations and provide current, detailed information on travel conditions.

Implications for Restaurants: Tourists increasingly are taking vacations out-of-season, softening the seasonality of income that has long been typical of restaurants in tourist destinations.

Surviving restaurants in European tourist destinations should soon recover the business they lost during 2002 and 2003, when terrorist worries, the war in Iraq, and the low value of the dollar all discouraged international travel by Americans.

4. Consumerism is still growing rapidly.

Summary: A networked society facilitates a consumerist society. Shoppers increasingly have access to information about pricing, services, delivery time, and customer reviews on the Internet. In most industrialized countries, their needs are increasingly being written into laws and regulations, which are generally enforced.

Implications for Restaurants: Restaurants will have to cope with a growing burden of consumer-oriented regulations.

Restaurant chains with a reputation for quality will have an enormous advantage in advertising to knowledgeable consumers.

Single-location restaurants will be at a growing competitive disadvantage, save in major cities where the reputation of a top chef can carry them.

Any problems with quality are likely to be immortalized on consumer-oriented Internet sites, where they will discourage potential customers long after they have been corrected.

5. Technology increasingly dominates both the economy and society.

Summary: In all fields, the previous state of the art is being replaced by new high-tech developments at an ever faster rate. Computers and telecommunications have become an ordinary part of our environment, rather than just tools we use for specific tasks. Biotechnology, and eventually nanotechnology, may do so as well. These developments provide dozens of new opportunities to create businesses and jobs, but they often require a higher level of education and training to use them effectively.

Implications for Restaurants: Our growing dependence on sterile, hard-edged technology is one of the most powerful forces behind our need for modest luxuries, like restaurant meals.

Restaurants will depend more and more on automation to make up for shortages of workers and to ensure more uniform quality of meals and service.

6. The work ethic is vanishing.

Summary: Tardiness is increasing, sick-leave abuse is common, and fewer workers respond to promises of high pay and job security. For Generation X, the post–Baby Boom generation, work is only a means to their ends: money, fun, and leisure. Top executives say this will reduce corporate performance in the future, but many show no greater ethical standards, as seen at Enron, WorldCom, and other major companies.

Implications for Restaurants: Productivity is likely to suffer as Baby-Boom executives are replaced by their Generation X and Dot-com successors.

7. Generations X and dot-com will have major effects in the future.

Summary: Members of Generation X—roughly, the 30-plus cohort—and especially of Generation Dot-com, now in their 20s, have more in common with their peers throughout the world than with their parents' generation. They are entrepreneurial, well educated, and predominately English-speaking. Virtually all are materialistic, many are economically conservative, and they care for little but the bottom line—their own bottom line. Independent to a fault, they have no loyalty to employers at all.

Implications for Restaurants: Higher salaries, better benefits, and opportunities for training all will be increasingly important in motivating and retaining younger workers.

Younger workers will require a more "hands-off" management style than previous generations have been willing to accept.

Post-retirement workers will be needed, both to make up for the shortfall in the younger generations and to ensure that some employees, at least, will be motivated and reliable.

8. Time is becoming the world's most precious commodity.

Summary: Computers and other technologies are making national and international economies much more competitive. As a result, Americans have lost an average of 140 hours per year of leisure time. European executives and nonunionized workers face the same trend. In Britain, workers have lost an average of 100 hours per year of nonworking time.

Implications for Restaurants: Dining out is becoming ever more desirable, both as an escape from our increasingly pressured working lives and as a better use of time than cooking and cleaning up after meals.

Harried workers with only a few minutes to spare will continue to patronize quick-service restaurants. However, they will favor outlets with the tastiest food and most pleasant, relaxing environments.

Fast-casual restaurant chains will continue to prosper as cheap, convenient, more comfortable alternatives to quick-service meals.

9. International exposure includes a greater risk of terrorist attack.

Summary: State-sponsored terrorism appears to be on the decline, as tougher sanctions make it more trouble than it is worth. However, nothing will prevent small, local political organizations and special-interest groups from using terror to promote their causes. And as the United States learned on September 11, the most dangerous terrorist groups are no longer motivated by specific political goals, but by generalized, virulent hatred based on religion and culture. On balance, the amount of terrorist activity in the world is likely to go up, not down, in the next ten years.

Implications for Restaurants: Today, virtually every establishment has "international" exposure, because borders are relatively porous, even in the post-9/11 environment. This is particularly true in the European Union, where anyone who enters one member country has unimpeded access to all the rest.

Restaurants are a prime target for terrorist attack, because they host large numbers of relaxed, unsuspecting victims, and because people watching news reports—the real targets of the attack—can easily picture themselves happily enjoying a meal when the attack occurred.

Contamination of food with toxins or pathogens is a serious risk, and one that is difficult to protect against.

Restaurants and chains unable to maintain their own security departments will need consultants to identify risks, design security programs, and screen possible new hires.

10. Institutions are undergoing a bimodal distribution: The big get bigger, the small survive, and the midsized are squeezed out.

Summary: For at least twenty years, economies of scale have allowed the largest companies to buy their smaller competitors or drive them out of business. At the same time, thousands of tiny, agile companies are prospering in niche markets. We see this pattern among automakers, computer companies, airlines, banks, and many other industries.

Implications for Restaurants: Mid-priced, family-oriented restaurants will continue to face difficult times as large, value-oriented chains outcompete them at one end of the scale and high-quality, high-luxury establishments capture their customers on the other.

The fast-casual segment will continue to grow at a comfortable rate for at least several years.

As chains proliferate and target a relatively fixed population of diners, it will be increasingly difficult to maintain customer loyalty.

Chapter 9

The Past Is Prologue

Picture your next vacation as it might be in 2075. In early July, you and your family ride the space elevator to a port terminal 62,000 miles over the equator. There you join nearly 2,000 other budget-conscious tourists on an interstellar cruiser the size of an ocean liner. After a stately embarkation, you sail out through interplanetary space, past the giant storms of Jupiter, close enough to Saturn to walk on its rings, and on into the inky blackness beyond. Just four luxurious days later, you arrive at alpha Centauri, the star closest to our own sun, tour a small but spectacular system of planets, and get out at. . .

Er, well, probably at a theme park in Orlando, where the whole journey took place in a few hours of virtual reality. Alas, the smart money in physics is still betting that Einstein was right about never going faster than the speed of light. We will never travel to the stars unless we learn to hibernate and spend centuries en route. $E = mc^2$: It's not just a good idea, it's the law.

Nonetheless, many other changes will come to the hospitality industry over the next few decades. None will be as dramatic as star travel, but some may be nearly as important to the participants.

What follows is a timeline of probabilities. Unlike the brief science fiction scenario above, the developments below are rooted in today's realities. A majority deal with new technologies, for obvious reasons: Technology changes a lot faster than social factors, and it often is the driver that eventually forces societal change. Our dates are "guesstimates"; they could be a few years off in either direction. However, we at Forecasting International will be surprised if many of these predictions fail to materialize.

And when we are wrong, it is likely to be because even bigger changes made them obsolete. When forecasters peer out into the further distances—say, beyond the next ten years—our mistakes are usually failures of the imagination. The far future is always stranger than we can anticipate.

2010

Invisible Idiot.   That is how one early language-translation program, converting from English to Russian and back again, interpreted the phrase, "Out of sight, out of mind." The software available online today does not do much better, as anyone who has tried to read foreign-language e-mail can attest. But within a few years, well-equipped tourists will be carrying pocket computers capable of translating idiomatic speech from any of half a dozen major languages into any of the others, in real time. Just talk into the box, and that Parisian waiter will know exactly what you want. Whether he likes your accent well enough to bring it is another matter.

Who Are You?   In the age of terrorism, governments want to know for sure. During this period, probably by 2012, passports and visas will be replaced by biometric identity cards that carry records of your fingerprints, retinal blood vessels, and other permanent, unique proof that you are really you.

Watch the Birdie.   Or not. If you can see it, the tiny digital camera built into your sunglasses will capture it for your friends back home. Expect basic VGA resolution by 2008, higher-quality snaps a couple of years later.

Condo Cruising.   The first cruise ship with apartments owned by the passengers (price tags from about $900,000) is already sailing from one luxury destination to another, with stops at the Olympics and other major tourist events planned. How quickly other ships follow its lead depends on the global economy, but FI expects that half a dozen of these ultimate RVs will take to the water by 2012.

Superclothes.   For adventurous vacationers headed to deserts, mountains, and other hostile areas—one of the hottest areas in tourism, sometimes literally—industrial-strength couturiers are developing "active" attire that cools or warms the wearer, as needed, and collects and stores solar energy to keep your GPS going without heavy batteries. Look for them at trendy outfitters around 2010.

Going, Going, Almost Gone.   Travel agents, that is. They already are an endangered species, their numbers down from 35,000 in the United States at the end of 2000 to only 26,000 by mid-2002. That is the latest number we have seen, but if there are more than 20,000 agents left today, we would be amazed. Only the cruise industry still relies on travel agents for their bookings, a throwback to the days when cruises were reserved for the wealthy elite. Though some prominent executives are reluctant to accept the obvious, their patronage is not enough to support even those agents who have survived this long. Neither can their distaste for online booking and other agentless forms of customer service long offset the economies and efficiencies of direct sales. By 2015, tourists could visit travel agencies as they would tour the back country of New Guinea, to see a vanishing way of life.

Altered Airports.   Those self-service ticket kiosks appearing in major airports will proliferate rapidly and spread to train stations, sports arenas, concert venues, and other transportation hubs and destinations. As a result, airport personnel rosters will shrink by 20 percent no later than 2010. At the same time, radio ID tags will guarantee that luggage arrives where its owners do. And to compensate for the loss of ticket agents, who now act as a first screen for possible terrorists, airport security departments will grow by 10 percent.

See the World—From Above.   The X-Prize competition is offering $10 million to the first private team that sends three people on a suborbital junket into space and manages to repeat the feat within two weeks. At least three entrants have made atmospheric test flights, and one is almost certain to make near-space flight practical within the next five years. After that, it will take less than a decade to build the first large-scale space tourism industry. Seats will sell for a lot less than the $20 million paid by Dennis Tito and Mark Shuttleworth to visit the International Space Station. The hardest part is likely to be getting insurance for the flights.

Generations of Entrepreneurs.   Throughout the world, people age 40 and under are starting businesses at a record rate. Among the younger dot-coms, twice as many say they would prefer to own a business rather than be a top executive, and five times more would prefer to own a business rather than hold a key position in politics or government. Many of the companies they start will be in the hospitality industry. Expect a huge wave of new resorts, restaurants, tour operators, and other travel services in the next two decades.

End of Immigration.   Travel, and almost every land will open its arms to you. Threaten to stay, and you'll be as welcome as a two-cent tip. Throughout the industrialized world, native citizens complain that guest workers and other immigrants are taking jobs, soaking up public resources, and refusing to integrate into the local culture. And though many of those jobs are positions that no one else would willingly accept, there is enough truth in the other complaints to make this movement a powerful political force. Add post-9/11 security concerns, and it's all but inevitable. Under tomorrow's immigration policies, "your tired, your poor, your huddled masses yearning to breathe free" can darned well stay home.

2020

Faster Than a Speeding Bullet Train.   The world's fastest trains today operate at a paltry 200 mph or so, though magnetic levitation trains running on closed courses have topped 300 mph. By 2020, the first 500-mph maglev trains will finally carry tourists around Japan, from Los Angeles to Las Vegas, and along other flat, high-density routes. The technology should be available by 2010 or so, but economic and political problems will stall its use for years.

Build It, and They Will Come.   A host of tourist attractions have proved it in recent years. These include the sixty-story Burj Al Arab Hotel in Dubai, with a seafood restaurant submerged in the Red Sea; the fabulous new *Bibliotheque* in Alexandria; the ice hotels rebuilt each winter in Greenland and Swedish Lapland; and the spectacularly popular London Eye. By 2020, we expect to see at least sixty new destinations built. Most will have some unique appeal, but six of the world's major cities will erect their own versions of the London Eye. China already is developing thirteen tourist destinations outside the few—such as Beijing and the Great Wall—that Westerners are familiar with.

How do You Spell Kaopectate in Russian?   Point your camera at a sign or label, and it will tell you what is written there. IBM already is working on the technology to translate text written in Cyrillic, Arabic, Hebrew, and Chinese characters into Western languages. Suddenly, we won't have to speak the local language to identify the drugstore and find what we need. By 2010, automatic translators for written material, probably built into cameras and other digital hardware, will be standard cargo for well-equipped tourists.

Vacation Offer You Can't Refuse.   It's a way of life in Europe. Cities empty in the summer as workers head off for a month of R & R that is guaranteed by law. The day will come when American workers also enjoy shorter work weeks and mandatory vacations, despite the objections of politically influential employers. The reason: the jobs lost from manufacturing in recent years are just the beginning. Automation and global competition will continue to squeeze jobs from the American economy until, in the long run, it becomes impossible to create useful work for all who need it. The only answer will be to cut the work week, add time off, and open new jobs to fill in for vacationing workers. The result will be a burst of growth in tourism like nothing the industry has ever seen.

Note that this is the most "iffy" forecast in this report. A combination of dramatically reduced birthrates, limited immigration, much better public education, rapid economic growth, and other changes might conceivably forestall a job crisis indefinitely. Yet what we are experiencing is high immigration, unexpectedly high birthrates, generally ineffectual public education, and the threat that exploding government deficits could weaken our economy for years. And it seems likely that the day will come when few noncreative tasks still require human hands. At some point in the future, much-expanded leisure seems all but inevitable. The late 2020s are our best guess at when this will occur, but no more than a guess.

Advertising in 3D. Today, holographic videos are cutting-edge technology. Twenty years from now, they will be consumer products. For tour operators, hotels, and other segments of the hospitality industry, 3D videos—delivered either by mail or over the Internet—will be the ultimate advertising medium, showing potential visitors exactly what they will experience at their destinations. Of course, in a few years they will be supplanted by virtual reality systems that recreate the vacation experience even more vividly.

UN Uber Alles. America's go-it-alone foreign policy is an aberration that cannot last. A global economy calls for global institutions, and that means power will inevitably flow toward the United Nations, the International Court of Justice, and the few other bodies with worldwide jurisdiction. To provide broader representation in those bodies, India and one of the Scandinavian countries will finally be admitted to the U.N. Security Council. This will gradually provide much more uniform laws, regulations, and standards for the hospitality industry and other multinational businesses.

It's a Gas, Gas, Gas. Technologically, hydrogen-powered cars are just over the horizon. Economically and societally, they will not make the grade until some environmentally minded government mandates a change to hydrogen power. Once that happens, industry will ramp up hydrogen production and put fueling stations in every community. Then bigger things will happen. By 2025, ecotourists visiting the Arctic, Antarctic, and other pristine destinations will arrive by hydrogen-powered jets that emit only water as their exhaust and avoid contaminating sensitive environments.

Eco-Backlash. Yet having hundreds of tourists trampling the Arctic tundra and other fragile environments will not sit well with committed environmentalists, even if the vacationers do travel by eco-friendly aircraft. Global protests against this perceived despoiling of our common heritage will quickly give rise to stringent limits on the number of tourists who can visit what little true wilderness remains in the world.

2030

Beanstalk to the Stars.   The science fiction scenario that began this chapter contained one bit of future reality: the space elevator. First envisioned some forty years ago, the elevator will climb an enormous cable, like Jack up the beanstalk, to a terminal where passengers and cargo can board spacecraft for the trip further out. Until recently, this was just a fantasy; there were no materials strong enough to build the cable. Today, so-called carbon nanotubes up to twenty times stronger than steel are approaching mass production, and engineers say a space elevator could be completed within fifteen years. Unfortunately, economic and political factors probably will double that lead time. According to current estimates, the first space elevator could be built for about $10 billion. The cost for a trip to space would be $200 per pound or less, compared with $40,000 per pound for the Space Shuttle. At that price, the space elevator will make space tourism routine.

2040

Room Service?   Today, there is only one hotel under the sea, the two-bedroom Jules Underwater Resort in Key Largo, Florida, and just two restaurants. Four decades ahead, underwater hotels and restaurants will be almost common. Most will appear in shallow water, where sunlight penetrates to illuminate abundant life; the most spectacular will be located on Australia's Great Barrier Reef. However, at least one small, spartan, and incredibly expensive hotel will provide accommodations more than five miles down, where guests can see forests of giant tube worms, "volcanoes" of hot, mineral-rich water, and luminescent fish swimming past the tiny, foot-thick portholes.

Think It, and They May Not Come After All.   Scientists have dreamed for years of building computers that understand our thoughts and send data directly into our brains. But that means a kind of artificial telepathy. Think into your computer in San Francisco, and someone in Bangalore will "hear" the thought over the Internet. And that offers the ultimate virtual reality. If one person swims in the sea, walks on the moon, or runs a three-minute mile, the rest of us can share the experience from the comfort of our own living rooms. It brings up the obvious question, why leave home at all? One answer is snob appeal. Virtual reality will be good enough for many, but the rich will display their wealth by taking the time, and spending the money, to go in person.

You Too Can Be the Man in the Moon.   Or at least on it. The first permanent moon base is likely to appear in the 2030s. A decade later, it will be capable of accommodating up to 350 people, including 50 tourists. Thanks to a growing array of space elevators circling Earth's equator, a lunar jaunt will even be relatively affordable. As demand grows, a space elevator on the moon will bring the price within reach of solidly middle-class families.

2050

One World After All.   Five decades ahead, the dollar and euro will be supplanted by a single world monetary unit, ending exchange problems forever. Biometric identity cards will be issued soon after birth, and the data stored in banks accessible by any government. This will make it nearly impossible for terrorists and other criminals to move around undetected, but routine tracking of our daily movements will further erode what little is left of the old-fashioned concept of privacy.

Universal English.   Those automatic translators will be useful for only forty years or so. English already is the *de facto* language of business, as French once was the language of diplomacy. By 2050, 90 percent of the people in the world will speak English, at least as a second language. In major tourist destinations, the number will be even higher.

2060

Jobs Aplenty.   Today, an estimated 14 percent of the world's people work in the hospitality industry. Tomorrow, it will be 25 percent. In part, we will owe this dramatic growth to the explosion of leisure time when shorter work weeks and forced vacations spread from Europe to the rest of the world. But this also is in the nature of the industry. Sixty years from now, personal service could be the only job category that still requires human workers.

Meet and Greet.   With a global Internet, lifelike virtual reality, and even computerized telepathy available to all, who needs in-person meetings? Nearly everyone, as it turns out. Full-contact telecommunications will do for routine conversations, but to meet new business associates, conduct difficult negotiations, or just build relationships over a round of golf, people will need to "press the flesh" for many decades to come. The meetings and expositions segment will continue to struggle with economic, social, and technological issues as far into the future as the eye can see. But there will be more corporate and industry-wide meetings in 2060 than in 2006.

2075

Water, Water Everywhere.   At least in the low places of the world. At the rate things are going, global warming will raise the seas by two to three feet in the next 75 years. That will mean hard times for lands like Bangladesh and the Louisiana lowlands, which are barely above sea level even now and are sinking even as the water rises. It will also modify our travel habits, as temperatures and rainfall patterns change. Expect what is left of Florida to turn into baking jungle, while crops bloom in parts of Canada and Siberia that today hold little more than ice.

Atoms in Space.   Nuclear power is banned from space by international treaty. Nonetheless, by 2075 long-range space tugs powered by nuclear reactors will be ferrying cargo and very patient tourists out to Mars, the asteroid belt, and even beyond. Travel time: about 3 months each way for Mars, more than a year for Jupiter.

Oldies but Goodies.   Some of the hottest destinations tomorrow would probably be familiar to today's travel agents. As we have seen, fast, overwhelming technological change will bring a host of new options for tourism. However, it also will strengthen our taste for old, familiar things and our need to reconnect with the past. Crowds will still surround the Taj Mahal, the Great Wall of China, and the pyramids; visit the Grand Canyon and Old Faithful; tour the fjords, the Yangtze River dam, and the Amazon; and throng the halls of the Hermitage and the Acropolis.

Old Friends As Well.   Whatever other changes buffet the hospitality industry, it will still need the same fundamental services that all industries need: somewhere to gather to make contacts and win contracts, someone to provide job-related education, common standards, and certification. These are the province of industry associations, which can bring competitors together on common ground. In 2075, hospitality associations, many of them well known today, will be helping their members to manage one of the largest industries in the world.

Appendix A

52 Trends Now
Shaping the Future

For some four decades, Forecasting International has conducted an ongoing study of the forces changing our world. Over the last decade, our expectations have proved to be gratifyingly accurate. We believed that the economy of the developed world would be much more vibrant than most commentators imagined possible, and so it has been. We also foresaw many of the political and social problems brought about by the changing population. In all, no fewer than 95 percent of our projections have proved correct.

This new edition updates our 2001 report on the implications of 52 major trends now shaping the future. Whatever your concern, some of these trends will have a very direct impact upon it. Others will help to form the general environment in which we live and work. They all merit attention from anyone who must prepare for what lies ahead.

GENERAL LONG-TERM ECONOMIC AND SOCIETAL TRENDS

1. **The economy of the developed world will continue to grow for at least the next five years. Any interruptions will be relatively short-lived.**
   - The U.S. economy has been expanding continuously since the fourth quarter of 2001. In 2003, it grew by 3.1 percent, by 3.9 percent annually in the first three months of 2004, and by 2.8 percent in the second quarter. Growth in 2004 is expected to be near 4 percent, a level that economists believe can be sustained.
   - Factory orders were up 4.3 percent in March 2004, well above expectations. Shipments rose 3.8 percent in March, the largest one-month

increase on record. Orders shrank in April and May—by −1.1 percent and −0.3 percent, respectively—but preliminary figures showed solid growth again in June. In all, this is strong evidence that the economic expansion will continue.

- Real estate has proved to be extraordinarily resilient in the United States, thanks to the lowest mortgage rates in some forty years. In all, 1.848 million new homes were started in 2003, the most since 1978. Though housing starts appeared to be weakening on fears that interest rates could be about to rise, they were still predicting the construction of more than 1.9 million new homes in 2004. Starts actually ran at a rate of 2.011 million per year in March 2004 and maintained a rate of more than 1.8 million in June and nearly 1.98 million in July, despite a rise in mortgage rates. Record-breaking housing sales included many middle-income buyers, as well as large numbers from minority groups who traditionally have not participated strongly in this market.

- In spring 2004, new jobs finally started to appear in significant numbers—308,000 in March, 280,000 in April, and 248,000 the following month. Job creation dipped in June, but has remained positive through August. Sustained job growth would confirm the renewed health of the American economy.

- Inflation, however, is beginning to cause concern. Both the Consumer Price Index and the Producer Price Index were up 0.5 percent in March 2004, 0.7 percent in April, 0.6 percent in May, and 0.3 percent in June, or 6.3 percent per year. Virtually all of this and later increases have come from the energy and food sectors. Oil prices were expected to come down again in time for the U.S. elections in November.

- The Conference Board's Index of Leading Indicators, which foretells future economic growth, rose 0.1 percent in April 2004, its eighth increase in nine months. It finally dipped 0.2 percent in June and a bit more in July, its first losses since March 2003.

- Relaxation of borders within the European Union has brought new mobility to the labor force. This is making for a more efficient business environment on the continent. Expansion of the EU by ten more members in late April 2004 can only improve economic performance there in the years ahead.

- After prolonged recession, the French and German economies appeared to be stable or growing slightly in the first quarter of 2004, while the British economy never did fall into recession. In all, it appears that the European economy as a whole grew by 0.4 percent in 2003 and slightly more in 2004.

- According to the most recent figures, Japan's long-suffering economy is growing for the first time in years—by no less than 7 percent annually in the fourth quarter of 2003 and 6.1 percent in early 2004. Exports surged by 17.9 percent annualized, yet foreign demand added only 1.6 percentage points to fourth-quarter growth. The remainder came from domestic consumption and corporate capital spending. By August, the Conference Board's leading index for the country had been up almost continuously for 16 month's running. This would make Japan a much healthier trading partner for the West.

- China's economy grew by a spectacular 9.1 percent in 2003 and was accelerating toward year's end. Word that growth had slowed to "only" 9.2 percent in the second quarter of 2004, after reaching 10.7 percent in the first, actually came as good news; onlookers viewed it as evidence that China will achieve a "soft landing" and stabilize at sustainable growth rates, rather than falling into recession. Chinese exports grew by 50 percent in the five years ending in 2002 and are still growing by 20 percent annually. In the United States, cheap Chinese imports have reduced the price of consumer goods by several percent. At the same time, the cheap dollar helped American exports to China grow by nearly 27 percent in 2003, to $28.4 billion.

- New growth among all these trading partners should create a "benevolent cycle," in which the health of each partner helps to ensure the continued health of the rest for at least the next several years.

- Many nations of the former Soviet Union are bringing order to their economies, proving themselves viable markets for goods from western Europe. Recently, even Russia appears to be stabilizing its economy, long the weakest link in its region. The discovery of oil in Kazakhstan and new interest in the other "stans" as potential partners in the war on terrorism should further this process.

- Worldwide, improved manufacturing technology will continue to boost productivity and reduce the unit cost of goods. At the same time, workers who remain on the job longer will offset slow growth in the labor force, while the globalization of business will keep pressure on salaries in the developed countries. Thus, both prices and wages should remain under control.

Implications: The recent economic downturn is unlikely to return. The current round of new growth will spread throughout the developed world. It should continue for the remainder of this decade.

Economic unification is promoting all manner of trade within Europe. In the long run, the newly capitalist lands of the former Soviet Union should be among the fastest growing new markets. In the longer term, India will expand faster than any other market in the world.

Labor markets will remain tight, particularly in skilled fields. This calls for new creativity in recruiting, benefits, and perks, especially profit sharing. This hypercompetitive business environment demands new emphasis on rewarding speed, creativity, and innovation within the workforce.

The growing concentration of wealth among the elderly, who as a group already are comparatively well off, creates an equal deprivation among the young and the poorer old. This implies a loss of purchasing power among much of the population; in time, it could partially offset the forces promoting economic growth.

2. The world's population will grow to 9 billion by 2050.

- Early versions of this report said that the world's population would double by 2050. Since then, population growth has proceeded almost exactly "on schedule."
- The greatest fertility is found in those countries least able to support their existing populations. Countries with the largest population increases between 2000 and 2050 include Palestinian Territory (217 percent), Niger (205 percent), Yemen (168 percent), Angola (162 percent), the Democratic Republic of Congo (161 percent), and Uganda (133 percent).
- Even these estimates may be much too low. According to the Center for Strategic and International Studies (CSIS), most official projections underestimate both fertility and future gains in longevity.
- In contrast to the developing world, many industrialized countries will see fertility rates below the replacement level and hence significant declines in populations, excluding the effects of immigration. This means that the population of the developed nations will fall from 23 percent of the total world population in 1950 and about 14 percent in 2000 to only 10 percent in 2050.
- In ten years or so, the workforce in Japan and much of Europe will be shrinking by 1 percent per year. By the 2030s, it will contract by 1.5 percent annually.

Implications: Rapid population growth will reinforce American domination of the global economy, as the European Union falls to third place behind the United States and China.

To meet human nutritional needs over the next forty years, global agriculture will have to supply as much food as has been produced during all of human history.

Unless fertility in the developed lands climbs dramatically, either would-be retirees will have to remain on the job, or the industrialized nations will have to encourage even more immigration from the developing world. The third alternative is a sharp economic contraction and loss of living standards.

Barring enactment of strict immigration controls, rapid migration will continue from the southern hemisphere to the north, and especially from former colonies to Europe. A growing percentage of job applicants in the United States and Europe will be recent immigrants from developing countries.

Culture clashes between natives and immigrants are likely to destabilize societies throughout the developed world. Germany, Britain, and other lands traditionally welcoming to refugees and other migrants already are experiencing strong backlashes against asylum-seekers

3. The population of the developed world is living longer.

- Each generation lives longer and remains healthier than the last. Since the beginning of the twentieth century, every generation in the United States has lived three years longer than the previous one. An 80-year-old in 1950 could expect 6.5 more years of life; today's 80-year-olds are likely to survive 8.5 more years.
- Life expectancy in Australia, Japan, and Switzerland is now over 75 years for males and over 80 for females.
- A major reason is the development of new pharmaceuticals and medical technologies, which are making it possible to prevent or cure diseases that would have been fatal to earlier generations. In many developed countries, credit also goes to government health programs, which have made these treatments available to many or all residents. In the developing lands, a primary cause is the availability of generic drugs, which cut the cost of care and make health affordable even for the poor.
- These figures are much too conservative because they assume that life expectancy will grow more slowly in the future, argues the Center for Strategic and International Studies (CSIS).
- Medical advances that slow the fundamental process of aging now seem to be within reach. They could well help today's middle-aged baby boomers to live far longer than even CSIS anticipates today.
- Any practical extension of the human life span will prolong health as well and will reduce the incidence of late-life disorders such as cancer, heart disease, arthritis, and possibly Alzheimer's disease.

Implications: Global demand for products and services aimed at the elderly can only grow quickly in the coming decades.

Developed countries may face social instability as a result of competition for resources between retirement-age boomers and their working-age children and grandchildren. In the United States and other developed countries, public spending on retirement benefits could grow to one-fourth of GDP by 2050, even as the number of workers available to support each retiree declines sharply, according to (CSIS).

Barring dramatic advances in geriatric medicine, the cost of health care is destined to skyrocket throughout the developed lands. This could create the long-expected crisis in health-care financing and delivery.

However, dramatic advances in geriatric medicine are all but inevitable. Paying the high cost of new drugs and technologies will reduce the cost of caring for patients who would have suffered from disorders eliminated or ameliorated by new therapies. In the end, cost increases and reductions should just about balance out, leaving the average American health-care bill nearly unchanged.

4. **The elderly population is growing dramatically throughout the world.**
   - People over age 65 made up only 8 percent of the population in the developed world in 1950, but 15 percent in 2000, and will grow to 27 percent of the population in the next half-century, according to CSIS.
   - Throughout the developed world, population growth is fastest among the elderly. In Europe, the United States, and Japan, the aged also form the wealthiest segment of society.
   - The world's elderly population, age 60 and older, will reach 1 billion by 2020, 13.3 percent of the projected world total population. Three-fourths will be in developing countries, principally China, India, Brazil, Indonesia, and Pakistan.
   - In Germany, the retirement-age population will climb from under 16 percent of the population in 2000 to nearly 19 percent in 2010 and 31 percent in 2050.
   - By 2050, one in three Italians will be over age 65, nearly double the proportion today.
   - Japan's over-65 population made up 17 percent of the total in 2000 and is projected to rise to 22 percent in 2010 and nearly 37 percent in 2050.

Implications: Not counting immigration, the ratio of working-age people to retirees needing their support will drop dramatically in the United States, Germany, Italy, Russia, and Japan by 2050. This represents a burden on national economies that will be difficult to sustain under current medical and social security systems.

The United States in particular will need more doctors specializing in diseases of the elderly—at least double the 9,000 now available. Yet by 2030 the number of certified American geriatric specialists is expected to decline dramatically.

The nursing shortage is another problem that is severe today and will grow much worse as the senior population expands. In all, the United States will be short 515,000 nurses by 2020, just as senior baby boomers begin to flood the health-care system. State health-care agencies will be forced to take the lead in recruiting new workers to this critical field.

5. **The growth of the information industries is creating a knowledge-dependent global society.**
   - Information is the primary commodity of more and more industries.
   - By 2007, 83 percent of American management personnel will be knowledge workers. Europe and Japan are not far behind.
   - The number of telecommuters in the United States grew 63.2 percent between 1999 and 2003. The number of telecommuters working for the federal government more than doubled—to only 106,000—between 2001 and 2003. By 2005, 80 percent of companies worldwide expect to have employees who work at home, up from 54 percent in 2003.
   - The Internet makes it possible for small businesses throughout the world to compete for market share on an even footing with industry leaders.
   - In the United States, the "digital divide" seems to be disappearing. In early 2000, a poll found that where half of white households owned computers, so did fully 43 percent of African American households, and their numbers were growing rapidly. Hispanic households continued to lag behind, but their rate of computer ownership was expanding as well.
   - By 2005, the average PC workstation will include a computer, a fax, a picture phone, and a duplicator—possibly in one unit—for less than $2,500 (in 1995 dollars). By 2006 or so, these systems will include a flat screen of 20 by 30 inches and real-time voice translation, so that conversations originating in one of seven or eight common languages can be heard in any of the others.
   - Computer competence will approach 100 percent in U.S. urban areas by 2005. Cities in Europe and Japan will achieve universal computer "literacy" shortly thereafter.

Implications: Knowledge workers are generally better paid than less-skilled workers, and their proliferation is raising overall prosperity.

Even entry-level workers and those in formerly unskilled positions require a growing level of education. For a good career in almost any field, computer competence is mandatory. This is one major trend raising the level of education required for a productive role in today's workforce. For many workers, the opportunity for training is becoming one of the most desirable benefits any job can offer.

New technologies create new industries, jobs, and career paths, which can bring new income to developing countries. An example is the transfer of functions such as technical support in the computer industry to Asian divisions and service firms.

For some developing countries, computer skills are making it faster and easier to create wealth than a traditional manufacturing economy ever could. India, for example, is rapidly growing a middle class, largely on the strength of its computer and telecom industries. Many other lands will follow its example.

6. **Mass migration is redistributing the world's population.**
   - Immigration is quickly changing the ethnic composition of the American population. In 2000, Latinos made up 12.6 percent of the U.S. population, up from only 6 percent in 1980. By 2010, they will account for 15.5 percent of all Americans, and 24.5 percent—103 million people—by 2050. There were some 11.2 million Asians in the United States in 2000. Their numbers will reach an estimated 19.6 million by 2020 and 33 million—8 percent of the population—by 2050.
   - This trend is accelerated by the relatively high fertility of the Latino population. As of 2002, women in the United States produced about two children during their lives, just enough to maintain the population. Among Hispanics, the average was more than 2.7 births per woman. Among Mexican immigrants, it was nearly 2.9.
   - Immigration to Western Europe from Eastern Europe, North Africa, the Middle East, and the Indian subcontinent continues.
   - More than 400,000 legal immigrants from Central Europe now live and work in Western Europe. Between 3 million and 4 million more migrants are expected to join them in the next twenty-five years.
   - In China, 98 million people have moved from rural areas to cities in recent years, without ever leaving the country.
   - There are about 80 million international migrant workers in the world, according to the United Nations. About half settle in Europe; the rest are divided evenly between North America and Asia.

Implications: Impoverished migrants will place a growing strain on Social Security systems in the industrialized countries of Europe and North America. Similar problems will afflict the urban infrastructures of China and India.

Remittances from migrants to their native countries are helping to relieve poverty in many developing countries. These payments are expected to exceed $100 billion in 2004.

Significant backlashes against foreign migrants, such as the skinhead movement in Europe, will be seen more frequently in the years ahead.

Backlashes will be seen even in the most peaceful lands. For example, in Scandinavia, resentment against foreign workers is strong, in part because they can return to their native lands after three years of employment and collect a pension equal to the minimum wage for the rest of their lives.

7. **Growing acceptance of cultural diversity, aided by the unifying effect of mass media, is promoting the growth of a truly integrated global society. However, this is subject to local interruptions and reversals.**
   - Migration is mixing disparate peoples and forcing them to find ways to coexist peacefully and productively.
   - Information technologies promote long-distance communication as people hook up with the same commercial databases and computer networks, and above all with the Internet.
   - Television is even more homogenizing, as it encourages the spread of standard accents and language patterns, particularly in the United States.
   - Within the United States and Europe, regional differences, attitudes, incomes, and lifestyles are blurring as business carries people from one area to another.
   - Intermarriage also continues to mix cultures geographically, ethnically, socially, and economically.
   - Minorities are beginning to exert more influence over national agendas as the growing number of African Americans, Hispanics, and Asians in the United States is mirrored by the expanding population of refugees and former "guest workers" throughout Europe.
   - In the United Kingdom, 21 percent of young adults answering a recent poll viewed themselves as primarily European, rather than British. Some 31 percent of French Gen Xers, 36 percent of Germans, and 42 percent of Italians also said they thought of themselves as primarily European.
   - However, in many countries there are powerful reactions against these changes. The growth of the German neo-Nazi movement is one obvious example.

Implications: Over the next half-century, growing cultural exchanges at the personal level will help to reduce some of the conflict that plagued the twentieth century. However, this is likely to produce a violent backlash in societies where xenophobia is common. Some of the most fervent "culturist" movements will continue to spring from religious fundamentalism. Would-be dictators and strongmen will use these movements to promote their own interests, ensuring that ethnic, sectarian, and regional violence will remain common. Terrorism especially will be a continuing problem.

Companies will hire ever more minority workers and will be expected to adapt to their values and needs. Much of the burden of accommodating foreign-born residents will continue to fall on employers, who must make room for their languages and cultures in the workplace.

However, the greatest responsibility will continue to fall on two public institutions, schools and libraries. Primary concerns for schools include providing all students with a solid grounding in English, our only common language, and finding ways to recruit and reward the best teachers and weed out the least effective. Public libraries act as sites for after-hours learning, reference facilities, sources of Net access for those who do not have it at home and bad-weather shelters for the homeless. They, too, require greater support.

8. The global economy is growing more integrated.

- Rather than paying salaries and benefits for activities that do not contribute directly to the bottom line, companies are farming out secondary function to suppliers, service firms, and consultants, which increasingly are located in other countries.
- They also are "outsourcing" management and service jobs to low-wage countries. An estimated 3.3 million American jobs are expected to migrate to India and China by 2015. Jobs from Western Europe are migrating to Eastern Europe, the former Soviet Union, and the English- and French-speaking former colonies of Africa. Even India has begun to ship jobs to even lower-cost countries in Africa.
- In the European Union, relaxation of border and capital controls and the adoption of a common currency and uniform product standards are making it still easier for companies to distribute products and support functions throughout the continent.
- Standardization of product standards throughout Europe is even more beneficial.
- NAFTA has had a similar, though much less sweeping, effect in the Americas.
- The Internet and cable-TV home shopping channels have brought retailers and manufacturers closer to distant customers, who had been out of reach. This is reshaping distribution patterns in many retail industries.
- New procurement regulations and standards promise to open the government market to suppliers who previously found the bidding process too difficult, costly, or just confusing.

Implications: The growth of commerce on the Internet makes it possible to shop globally for raw materials and supplies, thus reducing the cost of doing business. In niche markets, the Internet also makes it possible for small companies to compete with giants worldwide with relatively little investment.

Demand for personnel in distant countries will increase the need for foreign-language training, employee incentives suited to other cultures, aid to executives going overseas, and the many other aspects of doing business in other countries. As eastern Europe integrates more fully with the European Union, a major investment in personnel development will be needed over the next few years.

Western companies may have to accept that proprietary information will be shared, not just with their immediate partners in Asian joint ventures, but with other members of the partners' trading conglomerates. In high technology and aerospace, that may expose companies to extra scrutiny, due to national-security concerns.

9. **Militant Islam is spreading and gaining power.**
   - It has been clear for years that the Muslim lands face major problems with religious extremists dedicated to advancing their political, social, and doctrinal views by any means necessary. Those problems often have spilled over into the rest of the world. They will do so again.
   - In a 1994 terrorism study for the Department of Defense and other government clients, Forecasting International predicted that by 2020 a strong majority of the world's twenty-five or so most important Muslim lands could be in the hands of extremist religious governments. At the time, only Iran was ruled by such a regime; Afghanistan's Taliban movement gained power two years later, and Sudan has since followed.
   - Most of the Muslim lands are overcrowded and short of resources. Many are poor, save for the oil-rich states of the Middle East. Virtually all have large populations of young men, often unemployed, who are frequently attracted to violent extremist movements.
   - The United States massively fortified the Muslim extremist infrastructure by supplying it with money, arms, and above all training during its proxy war with the Soviet Union in Afghanistan.
   - American support for Israel has also made the United States a target for the hatred of Muslim extremists. If the deteriorating situation in Palestine leads to more active conflict, or if Israel renounces any attempt to make peace with its neighbors, American interests will be targeted by a new wave of terrorism.
   - The invasion of Iraq has done more than any other single action to reinforce extremist hatred of the United States. It also has provided a training ground for a new generation of terrorists.

Implications: Virtually all of the Muslim lands face an uncertain, and very possibly bleak, future of political instability and growing violence. The exceptions are the oil states, where money can still buy relative peace, at least for now.

Saudi Arabia is likely to be taken over by a fundamentalist regime on the death of King Fahd.

The necessary overthrow of the Taliban in Afghanistan, and the ouster of Saddam Hussein in Iraq, have inflamed extremist passions throughout the Muslim world. This may make future fundamentalist revolutions more likely, rather than less so.

The West, and particularly the United States, is likely to face more and more violent, acts of terrorism for at least the next twenty years.

Both Europe and the United States ultimately may face home-grown Muslim extremist movements. Thanks largely to waves of immigration since the 1980s, Islam is the fastest growing religion in both regions. There are credible reports that extremist clerics in Europe are successfully recruiting young Muslims to the cause of *jihad* against their adopted homes.

Western interests also will be vulnerable in many countries outside the Muslim core. The strong international ties formed among Islamic militants during the anti-Soviet war in Afghanistan have produced an extremist infrastructure that can support terrorist activities almost anywhere in the world.

This development must be taken even more seriously, because for the first time a Muslim country, Pakistan, has nuclear weapons, which Muslim extremists view as an "Islamic bomb," available to promote their cause. As the world has learned, some high-ranking Pakistanis have been willing to donate nuclear technology to other Muslims. From here on out, the possibility of nuclear terrorism is a realistic threat.

TRENDS IN VALUES, CONCERNS, AND LIFESTYLES

10. **Societal values are changing rapidly.**
    - Industrialization raises educational levels, changes attitudes toward authority, reduces fertility, alters gender roles, and encourages broader political participation. This process is just beginning throughout the developing world. Witness the increases in literacy, decreases in fertility, and broad voter turnout seen in India over the last five years.
    - Developed societies will increasingly take their cue from Generations X and Dot-com, rather than the baby boomers who have dominated its

thinking for most of four decades. This will tend to homogenize basic attitudes throughout the world, because Gen Xers and especially Dot-coms around the globe have more in common with each other than with their parents.

- In the future, both self-reliance and cooperation will be valued— self-reliance because we will no longer be able to fall back on Social Security, pensions, and other benefits; cooperation because group action often is the best way to optimize the use of scarce resources, such as retirement savings.

- Post-September 11 worry over terrorist attacks have led Americans to accept almost without comment security measures that their vaunted love of privacy once would have made intolerable. This continues a long-established tendency in the United States to prefer a greater sense of safety at the cost of increased government surveillance and intervention in their lives.

- Once national security issues lose their immediacy, family issues will again dominate American society, at least through 2008: long-term health care, day care, early childhood education, antidrug campaigns, and the environment.

- Narrow, extremist views of either the left or the right will slowly lose their popularity. Moderate Republicans and conservative Democrats will lead their respective parties. This trend has been reinforced by the experience of recent presidential elections in which third-party candidates siphoned votes from less-extreme main-party candidates. Many voters, feeling that a vote for an alternative candidate is tantamount to a vote for the major opposition, are likely to accept less doctrinal purity in their party's representatives.

Implications: The highly polarized political environment that has increasingly plagued the United States in the 1980s and 1990s will slowly moderate as results-oriented Generations X and Dot-com begin to dominate the national dialogue.

Current accounting reforms are just the leading edge of a wave of stockholder protection laws and regulations that can be expected within the next five years.

The demand for greater accountability and transparency in business will be crucial, not only in the United States business community, but also for countries that wish to attract international investors.

Reaction against changing values is one of the prime motives of cultural extremism, particularly in the Muslim world and in parts of India.

11. **Young people place increasing importance on economic success, which they have come to expect.**
    - Throughout the 1990s—effectively, their entire adult lives—Generations X and Dot-com knew only good economic times, and the recent economic downturn seemed to them a confusing aberration, rather than a predictable part of the business cycle. Most expect to see hardship on a national level, but they both want and expect prosperity for themselves.
    - Growing numbers of people now become entrepreneurs. Generations X and Dot-com are the most entrepreneurial generations in history.
    - In the United States especially, most young people have high aspirations, but many lack the means to achieve them. Only one in three high-school graduates goes on to receive a college degree. Many of the rest wish to go, but cannot afford the high cost of further schooling.
    - Without higher education, expectations may never be met: The real income of high school graduates has declined steadily for more than 50 years. In addition, more young people report no earnings—up from 7 percent of all 20- to 24-year-old men in 1973 to a relatively constant 12 percent since 1984.

    Implications: This will prove to be a global trend, as members of Generations X and Dot-com tend to share values throughout the world. Gen X and Dot-com entrepreneurs are largely responsible for the current economic growth in India and China, where they are becoming a major force in the Communist party. In India, the younger generations dress and think like their American counterparts, not their parents. In China, the democratic fervor that spawned Tienanmin Square has been replaced by capitalist entrepreneurialism.

    If younger-generation workers find their ambitions thwarted, they will create growing pressure for economic reform and deregulation. If reforms do not come fast enough in the developing world, disappointed expectations will raise the number of young people who emigrate to the developed lands.

    Disappointment also will drive underemployed young men in the developing world into fringe political and religious movements. This could cause a new wave of terrorism and instability, with profound effects on the cultures and economies of the United States and other target countries.

12. **Tourism, vacationing, and travel (especially international) will continue to grow in the next decade, as they did throughout the 1990s.**
    - People today have more disposable income, especially in two-earner families.

- The number of Americans traveling to foreign countries (excluding Canada and Mexico) increased at 5 percent per year from 1981 through 1996. Once current worries over the threat of terrorism recede, that growth will resume and will continue for the foreseeable future.
- In the United States, 2004 forecasts call for a rise in travel and tourism revenues to about $568 billion, nearing the $570.5 billion seen four years ago.
- Globally, the World Travel & Tourism Council (WTTC) predicts that all components of the travel market will turn out to have grown in 2004. Spending on travel and tourism, they estimate, will be up by 5.9 percent over 2003, to $5.5 trillion.
- The industry will create 3.3 million jobs worldwide.
- Over the next ten years, travel and tourism are expected to grow by an average of 4.5 percent annually. By 2014, that will amount to a market of more than $9.5 trillion, adding nearly $7 trillion to the world's GDP.
- Direct employment will not grow quite as quickly, but it will be up 1.7 percent annually, to nearly 87.5 million jobs, while indirect employment will account for some 260 million jobs around the world.
- Chinese spending for international travel will reach $100 billion by 2008. By 2020, according to the World Trade Organization, an army of 100 million Chinese will fan out across the globe, replacing Americans, Japanese, and Germans as the world's most numerous travelers.
- China soon will be the world's most popular destination as well, with 130 million arrivals in 2020.
- By 2020, 50 million Indians are expected to tour overseas.
- Tourism will benefit as Internet "virtual" tours replace printed brochures in promoting vacation destinations. Web sites cover not only popular attractions, but also provide current, detailed information on accommodations, climate, culture, currency, language, immunization, and passport requirements.
- Multiple, shorter vacations spread throughout the year will continue to replace the traditional two-week vacation.
- More retirees will travel off-season, spreading travel evenly throughout the year and eliminating the cyclical peaks and valleys typical of the industry.

Implications: The hospitality industry will grow at a rate of at least 5 percent per year for the foreseeable future, and perhaps a bit more. Tourism offers growing opportunities for out-of-the-way destinations that have not yet cashed in on the boom. This will make it an important industry for still more developing countries.

The number of people whose jobs depend on tourism will approach 14 percent of the global workforce.

Cruise ships such as the giant, 2,600-passenger *Queen Mary 2* will continue to grow larger.

13. **The physical-culture and personal-health movements will remain strong, but far from universal.**
   - Emphasis on preventive medicine continues to grow. In recent years, most insurance carriers in the United States have expanded coverage or reduced premiums for policyholders with healthy lifestyles. By 2007, 90 percent of insurers will offer such benefits.
   - A 2001 Harris Poll showed that about one-third of Americans ate at fast-food restaurants less often than a year before, citing health reasons.
   - In another 2001 poll, 75 percent of Canadians reported having changed their diets in the previous year in order to improve or maintain their health. Some 20 percent had reduced fat consumption, 18 percent had cut back on sweets, and 11 percent had trimmed red meat.
   - The low-carb weight-loss fad trumps other health concerns. Though Japan and Korea closed their doors to American beef after one case of mad cow disease was discovered in December 2003, demand in the United States never faltered. Carb-crazed dieters kept beef prices near record highs well into 2004.
   - This trend has not yet had a similar impact on Europe, and people in many countries of the developing world still worry more about eating enough than eating well.
   - U.S. consumers are purchasing less distilled liquor. Exception: Younger generations have revived the once passe taste for mixed drinks, but have proved to be uncommonly responsible drinkers. Most limit themselves to one or two drinks with a meal, and designated drivers are standard practice.
   - Smoking also is in general decline in the United States. Only 21 percent of Americans smoked cigarettes as of January 2000, down from 30 percent in 1983. Financial disincentives such as higher taxes on cigarettes should produce further declines of 10 percent.
   - It appears that the antismoking movement is finally making its way to Europe. Ireland banned smoking from its pubs in April 2004.

Implications: Better health in later life will make us still more conscious of our appearance and physical condition. Thus, health clubs will continue to boom, and some will specialize in the needs of older fitness buffs. Diet, fitness, stress control, and wellness programs will prosper.

Like tobacco companies, producers of snack foods, liquor, and other medically dubious products will increasingly target markets in developing countries, where this trend has yet to be felt.

The cost of health care for U.S. baby boomers and their children could be much lower in later life than is now believed. However, Asia faces an epidemic of cancer, heart disease, emphysema, and other chronic and fatal illnesses related to health habits.

As the nutrition and wellness movements spread, they will further improve the health of the elderly. The market for cosmetic surgery and Botox treatments—which may be more about *appearing* than *being* healthy—will continue to expand quickly.

14. Consumerism is still growing rapidly.

- A networked society facilitates a consumerist society. Shoppers increasingly have access to information about pricing, services, delivery time, and customer reviews on the Internet. Marketers, of course, can also check the competition's offerings. This may gradually halt the decline of prices and shift competition increasingly to improvements in service and salesmanship.
- Consumer advocacy agencies and organizations will continue to proliferate, promoting better information—unit pricing, improved content labels, warning notices, nutrition data, and the like—on packaging, TV, and the Internet.
- Discount stores such as Home Depot and Wal-Mart, factory outlets, and food clubs will continue to grow in the United States, a trend that has just begun to spread to Europe and Japan.

Implications: In the next twenty years, Europe and Japan can expect to undergo the same revolution in marketing that has replaced America's neighborhood stores with cost-cutting warehouse operations and "category killers." This will inspire social unrest in countries where farmers and owners of small shops have strong cultural or political positions.

This trend also will spread to China, though it will run several years behind developments in Europe and Japan.

As prices fall to commodity levels and online stores can list virtually every product and brand in their industry without significant overhead, service is the only field left in which marketers on and off the Net can compete effectively.

Branded items with good reputations are even more important for developing repeat business.

15. **The women's equality movement is beginning to lose its significance, thanks largely to past successes.**
    * Generations X and Dot-com are virtually gender-blind in the workplace, compared with older generations. This is true even in societies such as India and Japan, which have long been male-dominated, though not yet in conservative Muslim lands.
    * Fully 57 percent of American college students are women. Among minorities, the number is even higher: 60 percent of Hispanic and two-thirds of African American college students are women.
    * Women's increasing entrepreneurialism will allow the formation of entrenched "old girl" networks comparable to the men's relationships that once dominated business.
    * An infrastructure is evolving that allows women to make more decisions and to exercise political power, especially where both spouses work. One indication of growing dependence on the wife: Life insurance companies are selling more policies to women than to men.
    * More women are entering the professions, politics, and the judiciary. As we have seen in Iraq, they also are finding roles as combat soldiers.

Implications: Whatever careers remain relatively closed to women will open wide in the years ahead.

Demand for child care and other family-oriented services will continue to grow, particularly in the United States, where national services have yet to develop. Over the next twenty years, this may force American companies to compete on a more even footing with their counterparts in Europe, whose taxes pay for national daycare programs and other social services the United States lacks.

In the long run, the need to work with female executives from the developed countries will begin to erode the restrictions placed on women's careers in some developing regions.

16. **Family structures are becoming more diverse.**
    * In periods of economic difficulty, children and grandchildren move back in with parents and grandparents to save on living expenses. In the United States, one-third of Gen Xers have returned home at some point in their early lives.
    * Growing numbers of grandparents are raising their grandchildren, because drugs and AIDS have left the middle generation either unable or

unavailable to care for their children. This trend is strongest in Africa, where AIDS has orphaned some 12 million children, half between the ages of 10 and 14. In Botswana, Lesotho, Swaziland, and Zimbabwe, more than one in five children will be orphaned by 2010 according to UNICEF. Of these, about 80 percent will have lost at least one parent to AIDS. In the seven African countries most affected by AIDS, life expectancy at birth has now dropped below age 40.

- Among the poor, grandparents also provide live-in daycare for the children of single mothers trying to gain an education or build a career.
- Vermont's first-in-the-country law granting partners in same-sex relationships most of the legal rights formerly reserved to married couples took effect in 2000. As of mid-2002, California legislators were considering a civil-union law. And in 2004, the Massachusetts Supreme Court ruled that the state's ban on gay marriage was unconstitutional. Germany, the Netherlands, and parts of Canada all have such laws, and similar proposals have wide support in Britain.
- Yet the nuclear family also is rebounding, as baby boom and Gen X parents focus on their children and grandparents retain more independence and mobility.

Implications: Tax and welfare policies need adjustment to cope with families in which heads of households are retired or unable to work.

Policies also need to be adjusted for those who receive Social Security and are forced to work to support an extended family.

In the United States, the debates over homosexuality and the "decline of the family"—temporarily displaced from attention by the antiterrorist campaign—will regain their status as hot-button issues for at least two more election cycles.

Concern for other "family values" will return as well, but this time the debate will be shaped by the real-world needs of diverse families rather than the agendas of religious conservatives.

ENERGY TRENDS

17. **Despite all the calls to develop alternative sources of energy, oil consumption is still rising rapidly.**
    - The world used only 57 million barrels of oil per day in 1973, when the first major price shock hit. By 2004, it was using nearly 82 million barrels daily, according to the International Energy Agency. Consumption is expected to reach 110 million barrels daily by 2020.

- However, oil's share of world energy consumption has begun to decline: It is expected to drop from 40 percent in 1999 to about 37 percent in 2020.
- The United States consumed 19.7 million barrels of oil daily in 2000, of which 10.4 million barrels came from net imports—up from 6.3 million barrels in net imports in 1973. In 2004, about 55 percent of the petroleum used in the United States still is imported. Domestic oil production is expected to disappear by about 2055, even if reserves are tapped in the Arctic National Wildlife Refuge.
- In the first quarter of 2004, China consumed about 6.14 million barrels of oil, up 18 percent over the same period in 2003. In February 2004, it imported 3.182 million barrels per day, mostly from the Middle East.

Implications: Low oil prices in the mid- to late-1990s slowed development of fields outside the Middle East. It costs $10,000 to increase oil production by one barrel per day in most of the world, but only $5,500 for the OPEC lands.

It would take a prolonged surge in oil prices, to levels like those seen in 2000, to provide an incentive to develop new fields, such as the Arctic National Wildlife Refuge. (Such sites could benefit from new drilling techniques that make it possible to extract oil with less damage to the environment.)

18. **Contrary to popular belief, the world is not about to run out of oil.**
    - As a result of intensive exploration, the world's proven oil reserves climbed from about 660 billion barrels in 1980 to more than 1 trillion barrels in 1990. Despite consumption, they have hovered over 1 trillion barrels ever since. Natural gas reserves stand at about 5.15 trillion cubic feet.
    - OPEC officials claim that the eleven member countries can provide for the world's energy needs for roughly the next eighty years. OPEC currently supplies about 40 percent of the world's oil and holds 60 percent of the oil available internationally. It will continue to supply most of the oil used by the developed world. According to the U.S. Department of Energy, OPEC oil production will nearly double to about 57 million barrels of oil per day by 2020.
    - OPEC will continue to supply most of the world's oil, with Russia the second-largest producer. According to the U.S. Department of Energy, OPEC oil production will grow by some 24 million barrels of oil per day by 2020, to about 55 million barrels per day. This is nearly two-thirds of the world's total projected increase in production.
    - Oil production outside the OPEC nations has not yet peaked. By 2010, China, Russia, and Kazakhstan will be major suppliers, if the necessary

pipelines can be completed and political uncertainties in Russia and Kazakhstan do not block investment by Western oil companies. Russia alone is expected to become the world's second-largest oil producer by 2010.

- Exploitation of oil in Venezuela has barely begun. Reserves there may be even larger than those in Saudi Arabia, according to some estimates. However, it is more expensive to refine and use, because it contains much higher levels of sulfur than the Middle Eastern oil currently in production.

- India also is believed to own substantial reserves of oil in deposits beneath the Indian Ocean.

- Recent reports that the world's oil reserves may be up to 20 percent smaller than previously believed are not credible, in part because they originate with an odd coalition of the American Petroleum Institute and alternative energy proponents—two groups with a vested interest in keeping oil prices high. In any event, 80 percent of OPEC's estimated supply would still be oil enough to supply the world for the next 64 years.

Implications: If the price of oil rises significantly beyond current levels, new methods of recovering oil from old wells will become cost-effective. Technologies already developed could add nearly 50 percent to the world's recoverable oil supply.

However, proposed construction of ethanol plants to supplement oil supplies would be a wasted effort. Until oil prices rise significantly more than they are likely to in the near future, ethanol simply is not cost-effective. This has been amply demonstrated by the history of Brazil's ambitious program to replace oil with ethanol, which has proved an abject failure.

Other alternative energy sources face similar problems with economic viability. Barring substantial incentives, this will inhibit efforts to stem global warming for the foreseeable future.

There is reason to wonder whether OPEC oil will be available to the United States. Saudi Arabia is likely to be taken over by a fundamentalist Islamic government similar to that of Iran; if, upon the death of King Fahd, Osama bin Laden or one of his deputies seizes power, the new regime could be reluctant to provide oil to the United States.

19. Oil prices are stable at; $25 to $28 per barrel; they rise above that range only in times of trouble.
- Prices above $45 per barrel seen in 2004 result from uncertainty in Iraq, the Yukos conflict in Russia, and other short-term problems.

- Despite claims that OPEC would prefer to keep crude affordable, the organization's current aim is to hold the price of oil no lower than $30 per barrel. Yet doing so requires a unity of purpose that member countries have never been able to sustain for very long.
- The vulnerability of oil prices was reinforced in the months after September 11, when they fell to just $19.88 despite severe worries about possible instability in the Middle East.
- New oil supplies coming on line in the former Soviet Union, China, and other parts of the world will make it even more difficult to sustain prices at artificially high levels.
- The twenty most industrialized countries all have at least three-month supplies of oil in tankers and underground storage. Most have another three months' worth in "strategic reserves." In times of high oil prices, customer nations can afford to stop buying until the costs come down.

Implications: High oil prices cannot be sustained. They are likely to fall below $30 per barrel by 2006 as non-OPEC oil sources come on line and American refineries expand their capacity.

In response to high (by American standards) gas prices, the U.S. government will probably boost domestic oil production and refining to increase the reserve of gasoline and heating oil. This stockpile would be ready for immediate use in case of future price hikes, as in the winter 2000 release from strategic reserves. This will make it easier to negotiate with OPEC.

The United States almost certainly will drill for oil in the Arctic National Wildlife Reserve. To minimize environmental damage, drilling will take place only in the winter, when the tundra is rock hard, slant drilling will be used to minimize the number of wells required, and the oil will be shipped through a double-walled pipeline.

One upward pressure on the price of American gasoline: the Environmental Protection Agency's "Tier 2" regulations, which aim to reduce dramatically emissions of sulfur and nitrogen oxides and particulates, are scheduled to take effect between 2004 and 2006. Production of super-low sulfur fuels mandated under the plan is expected to add about 4 cents per gallon to the cost of gas and 6 cents per gallon to the price of diesel fuel.

The one development that could change this scenario is the establishment of a Muslim extremist government in Saudi Arabia following the death of King Fahd, leading to a ban on oil sales to the United States and its allies. A religious takeover of Saudi Arabia is highly likely. An oil boycott against the U.S. seems less so, as the new rulers will need the income as urgently as the Saud monarchy did.

20. **Growing competition from other energy sources also will help to limit the price of oil.**

   - Solar, geothermal, wind, and wave energy will ease power problems where these resources are most readily available, though they will supply only a very small fraction of the world's energy in the foreseeable future.

   - Global energy production from renewable sources such as geothermal wells, wind turbines, and solar generators grew from 151.64 billion kWh in 1990 to 274.04 billion kWh in 2002.

   - During the same period, nuclear electric output grew from 648.89 billion kWh to 860.29 kWh, while hydroelectric power generation declined from 606.46 billion kWh to 595.06 billion kWh, having peaked at 727.62 billion kWh in 1996.

   - Worldwide wind-power generating capacity grew by 6,500 megawatts in 2001 alone, the fastest rate of growth yet recorded and 50 percent more than the previous year. Photovoltaic solar energy production has been growing at a steady 25 percent per year since 1980.

   - Natural gas burns cleanly, and there is enough of it available to supply the world's total energy demand for the next 200 years. Consumption of natural gas is growing by 3.3 percent annually, compared with 1.8 percent for oil.

   - According to the Energy Information Agency at the U.S. Department of Energy, shifting 20 percent of America's energy supply to renewable resources by 2020 would have almost no impact on the total cost of power. At present, less than 5 percent of the energy used in the United States comes from renewable resources.

   - A new technique called muon-catalyzed fusion reportedly could produce commercially useful quantities of energy by 2020.

Implications: Though oil will remain the world's most important energy resource for years to come, two or three decades forward it should be less of a choke point in the global economy.

   Declining reliance on oil eventually could help to reduce air and water pollution, at least in the developed world. By 2060, a costly but pollution-free hydrogen economy may at last become practical.

   In the interim, nuclear power will supply a growing portion of the world's energy needs. Nuclear plants will supply 16 percent of the energy in Russia and Eastern Europe by 2010. In early 2004, China had only nine operating nuclear power plants. It plans to build 30 more by 2020, bringing nuclear energy consumption from 16 billion kWh in 2000 to 66 billion kWh in 2010 and 142 billion kWh in 2020. By 2020, Russia will consume 129 billion kWh of nuclear energy per year, while Canada will use 118 billion kWh.

ENVIRONMENTAL TRENDS

21. People around the world are becoming increasingly sensitive to environmental issues such as air pollution as the consequences of neglect, indifference, and ignorance become ever more apparent.

- Soot and other particulates are coming under greater scrutiny as threats more dangerous to human health than sulfur dioxide and other gaseous pollutants. In the United States alone, medical researchers estimate that some 64,000 people each year die from cardiopulmonary disease as a result of breathing particulates. In sub-Saharan Africa, the toll is between 300,000 and 500,000 deaths per year, and in Asia, between 500,000 and 1 million people annually die of particulate exposure.

- A 2004 report for the U.S. Environmental Protection Administration estimated that pollution by American power plants causes 23,600 needless deaths per year.

- In all, the World Health Organization estimates that 3 million people die each year from the effects of air pollution, about 5 percent of the total deaths annually.

- The European Parliament estimates that 70 percent of the continent's drinking water contains dangerous concentrations of nitrate pollution. In the United States, there is growing concern that pollutants such as perchlorate, the gasoline additive MTBE, and even the chlorine used to kill water-borne pathogens may represent significant health concerns.

- Though some debate remains about the cause, the fact of global warming has become undeniable. At Palmer Station on Anvers Island, Antarctica, for example, the average annual temperature has risen by 3 to 4 degrees since the 1940s, and by an amazing 7 to 9 degrees in June—early winter in that hemisphere. Recent analyses say there is a 90 percent chance that the planet's average annual temperature will rise between 3 and 9 degrees over the next century.

- Governments are taking more active measures to protect the environment. For instance, after years of ineffective gestures, Costa Rica has incorporated about 25 percent of its land into protected areas, such as national parks. Cambodia has protected a million-acre forest. Gabon, in Africa, has set aside 10 percent of its land for parks. And Liberia is protecting 155,000 acres of forest in an effort to safeguard endangered western chimpanzees.

- An estimated 80 percent of logging in the Amazon basin is illegal. In 1999, Brazil raised the maximum fine for illegal logging to more than $27 million and changed legal procedures so that the fines can actually be imposed.
- In an effort to promote cleaner energy technologies and to slow global warming, most European nations now tax carbon emissions or fossil fuels. In Germany, a carbon tax raises the cost of gasoline by nearly 11 cents per gallon.
- In India, government policies consistently rate industrial development more important than the environment. Yet in an effort to reduce air pollution, India's Supreme Court has limited sales of new cars in New Delhi to 18,000 per year, less than one-fourth of the average previously sold.
- Nonetheless, none of India's 23 million-plus cities meets WHO air quality standards. Indoor smoke from cooking fires kills an estimated 500,000 people in India each year, mostly women and children.
- Pollution-related respiratory diseases kill about 1.4 million people yearly in China and Southeast Asia.
- Anticipating a three-foot rise in sea levels, the Netherlands is spending $1 billion to build new dikes.

Implications: If air pollution were halted instantly, it would take an estimated 200 years for carbon dioxide and other greenhouse gasses to return to preindustrial levels.

Environmental policies will provoke a political backlash wherever they conflict with entrenched interests, as they have long done in the American West. However, the cost of not protecting the environment is too obvious to be ignored. Throughout most of the world, polluters and private beneficiaries of public assets will increasingly confront restrictive regulations designed to serve the interests of the community at large.

22. Water shortages will be a continuing problem for much of the world.

- One-third of the population of Africa and most of the major cities in the developing world will face water shortages, according to the United Nations.
- The northern half of China, home to perhaps half a billion people, already is short of water. The water table under Beijing has fallen nearly 200 feet since 1965. It declined by 8 feet in 1999 alone.
- Water usage is causing other problems as well. For example, irrigation water evaporates, leaving minerals in the soil. By 2020, 30 percent of the world's arable land will be salty; by 2050, 50 percent. Salinization already is cutting crop yields in India, Pakistan, Egypt, Mexico, Australia, and parts of the United States.

- Pollution further reduces the supply of safe drinking water. In India, an estimated 300 million people lack access to safe drinking water, due to widespread pollution of rivers and groundwater.
- Water quality is a growing problem even in the developed lands. In the United States, cities such as Atlanta, where the delivery system is a century old and poorly maintained, suffer frequent water-main breaks, which suck dirt, debris, bacteria, and pollutants into the water supply. There are an estimated 237,600 such breaks each year in the United States.
- Many ecologists believe that global warming will make drought much more frequent—even the norm—west of the Mississippi.
- Contaminated water is implicated in 80 percent of the world's health problems. An estimated 40,000 people around the world die each day of diseases directly caused by contaminated water—that's more than 14 million per year.

Implications: By 2040, at least 3.5 billion people will run short of water, almost ten times as many as in 1995. By 2050, fully two-thirds of the world's population could be living in regions with chronic, widespread shortages of water.

Water wars, predicted for more than a decade, are an imminent threat in places like the Kashmir: Much of Pakistan's supply comes from areas of Kashmir now controlled by India. Such problems as periodic famine and desertification also can be expected to grow more frequent and severe in coming decades.

Other present and future water conflicts involve Turkey, Syria, and Iraq over the Tigris and Euphrates; Israel, Jordan, Syria, and Palestine over water from the Jordan River and the aquifers under the Golan Heights; India and Bangladesh, over the Ganges and Brahmaputra; China, Indochina, and Thailand, over the Mekong; Kyrghyzstan, Tajikistan, and Uzbekistan over the Oxus and Jaxartes rivers; and Ethiopia, Sudan, and at least six East African countries, including Egypt, which share the Nile.

Impurities in water will become an even greater problem as the population ages and becomes more susceptible to infectious diseases.

In the United States, repair of decayed water systems is likely to be a major priority for older cities such as New York, Boston, and Atlanta. Cost estimates for necessary replacement and repair of water mains range up to $1 trillion.

Water providers in the United States will face more new regulations in the next five years than have been adopted since the Safe Drinking Water Act was signed in 1974.

23. **Recycling has delayed the "garbage glut" that threatened to overflow the world's landfills, but the threat has not passed simply because it has not yet arrived.**
    - Americans now produce about 4.4 pounds of trash per person per day, twice as much as they threw away a generation ago.
    - In June 2002, New York City abandoned its 14-year-old recycling effort for glass, plastic, and beverage cartons, which city authorities held was not cost-effective. This cut recycling from about 21 percent of waste to an estimated 10 percent and sent an extra 1,200 tons of litter to landfills each day. By contrast, Seattle recycles about half of its solid waste.
    - Seventy percent of U.S. landfills will be full by 2025, according to the EPA.
    - In London and the surrounding region, landfills will run out of room by 2012. For household trash, landfill space will be exhausted by 2007.
    - In some other regions, simply collecting the trash is a major problem. Brazil produces an estimated 240,000 tons of garbage daily, but only 70 percent reaches landfills. The rest accumulates in city streets, where it helps to spread disease.
    - Recycling and waste-to-energy plants are a viable alternative to simply dumping garbage. The United States has more than 2,200 landfills. Europe, where recycling and energy conversion are much more common, gets by with 175.

    Implications: Expect a wave of new regulations, recycling, waste-to-energy projects, and waste management programs in an effort to stem the tide of trash. It will, of course, begin in California.

    Existing regulations will be tightened and disposal prices raised in Pennsylvania, South Carolina, Louisiana, and other places that accept much of the trash from major garbage producers such as New York.

24. **Industrial development trumps environmental concerns in many parts of the world.**
    - In 1999, *Samachar,* an Internet newspaper from India, asked its readers what significant problems face their country. Despite rampant deforestation, widespread air and water pollution, loss of biodiversity, and many other such problems, environmental degradation came in next to last among ten issues, cited by only 1 percent of the respondents.
    - "A deep and abiding distrust of environmental imperatives has been cultivated in large segments of South Africa's population," due to years of apartheid-era restrictions that were often justified as environmental measures, according to a study of environmental business opportunities by Industry Canada.

- Some 70 percent of the energy used in China comes from coal-burning power plants, few of which are equipped with pollution controls. Scientists estimate that by 2025 China will emit more carbon dioxide and sulfur dioxide than the United States, Japan, and Canada combined.
- Acid rain like that afflicting the United States and Canada will appear wherever designers of new power plants and factories neglect emission controls. A 1995 study of 77 Chinese cities found that 81 percent suffered from acid rain. In India, an area the size of the United States is covered by a haze of sulfates and other chemicals associated with acid rain. Look for this problem to appear in most other industrializing countries as well.

Implications: Broad regions of the planet will be subject to pollution, deforestation, and other environmental ills in the coming decades.

Diseases related to air and water pollution will spread dramatically in the years ahead. Already, chronic obstructive pulmonary disease is five times more common in China than in the United States. As citizens of the developing countries grow to expect modern health care, this will create a growing burden on their economies.

This is just a taste of future problems, and perhaps not the most troublesome. Even the U.S. government now admits that global warming is a result of human activities that produce greenhouse gases. It now seems that China and India soon will produce even more of them than the major industrialized nations. Helping the developing lands to raise their standards of living without causing wholesale pollution will require much more aid and diplomacy than the developed world has ever been willing to devote to this cause.

25. **Though species extinction may not be so rapid as once believed, loss of biodiversity will be a growing worry for decades to come.**
    - Just twenty-five so-called "hot spots" covering 11 percent of the world's surface have lost 70 percent of their original vegetation. What is left, about 2 percent of the planet's surface, is home to 44 percent of all plant species and 35 percent of all vertebrates other than fish. The hot spots also are home to 1.2 billion people, or one-fifth of the world's population.
    - An estimated 50,000 species disappear each year, up to 1,000 times the natural rate of extinction, according to the United Nations Environmental Program.
    - Eleven percent of birds, 25 percent of mammals, and 20 percent to 30 percent of all plants are estimated to be nearing extinction.
    - By 2100, as many as half of all species could disappear.

- Throughout the world, amphibian populations are in decline, for reasons that, after more than a decade of intensive research, remain poorly understood.
- Coral reefs throughout the world are dying rapidly, again for reasons that are not entirely clear.
- The chief cause for species loss, according to University of Colorado scientists, is the destruction of natural habitats by logging, agriculture, and urbanization. Some 30 million acres of rainforest are destroyed each year.
- Though commercial fishing is not known to have exterminated any species—largely because the last few members of a species are too costly to catch—it is turning out to be another important cause of species depletion. Stocks of cod, tuna, swordfish, marlin, and sharks are down 90 percent since modern industrialized fishing got its start forty years ago.

Implications: Species loss has a powerful negative impact on human well-being. Half of all drugs used in medicine are derived from natural sources, including 55 of the top 100 drugs prescribed in the United States. About 40 percent of all pharmaceuticals are derived from the sap of vascular plants. So far, only 2 percent of the 300,000 known sap-containing plants have been assayed for potential drugs.

In Indonesia, home to one-eighth of the world's coral reefs, more than 70 percent of the reefs are dead or dying. The Indonesian economy loses an estimated $500,000 to $800,000 annually per square mile of dead or damaged reef.

Researchers from the United Kingdom's National Environmental Research Council Centre for Population Biology report that diverse ecosystems absorb more carbon dioxide than those with fewer species. Loss of biodiversity thus is a potential cause of global warming.

26. **Continuing urbanization will aggravate most environmental and social problems.**
    - In 2000, some 2.8 billion people were urbanites, about 47 percent of the total world population. By 2030, 60 percent of the global population will live in cities.
    - Between 2000 and 2030, the global population will grow by an estimated 2.2 billion. Of this, 2.1 billion people will be added to the world's cities.
    - In the past, urbanization has proceeded fastest in the countries now industrialized. In the more developed countries, 76 percent of the population lives in cities; in the developing lands, only 40 percent

are urbanites. Today, cities are growing fastest in the developing world.

- The big are getting bigger. In 1950, there were just eight megacities, with populations over 5 million, in the world. By 2015, there will be 59 megacities, 48 of them in less developed countries. Of these, 23 will have populations over 10 million, all but four in the developing lands.
- Natural increase now accounts for more than half of population increase in the cities; at most, little more than one-third of urban growth results from migration.
- In many areas of the developing world, natural increase is producing population densities formerly seen only in the largest cities.
- Up to 1 billion city dwellers lack adequate shelter, clean water, toilets, or electricity. The United Nations estimates that these problems cause 10 million needless deaths annually.
- According to the Worldwatch Institute, fuels burned in cities account for 75 percent of global carbon emissions from human activity.
- NASA scientists point out that urbanization also tends to put buildings and blacktop on the most fertile land, eliminating significant quantities of carbon-absorbing plants.
- Urbanization also deprives surrounding areas of water: Instead of sinking into the ground, rain is collected, piped to the city, used, treated as gray water, and then discarded into the ocean. In some regions, such as near Atlanta, water levels in local aquifers are declining rapidly because the water that once replenished them now is lost.
- The United States is the one major counterexample to this trend. This automobile-reliant society built one of the best highway systems in the world and has relatively little mass transit, so more Americans live in the suburbs than in the cities.

Implications: Cities' contribution to global warming can only increase in the years ahead.

As the world's supply of potable water declines, people are concentrating in those areas where it is hardest to obtain and is used least efficiently.

Deaths due to shortages of shelter, water, and sanitation can only grow. Epidemics will become still more common as overcrowding spreads HIV and other communicable diseases more rapidly.

Since the growth is now due more to natural increase than to migration, programs designed to encourage rural populations to remain in the countryside may be misplaced. Education and family planning seem more likely to rein in the growth of cities.

TECHNOLOGY TRENDS

27. Technology increasingly dominates both the economy and society.

- In all fields, the previous state of the art is being replaced by new high-tech developments at an ever faster rate.
- Computers are fast becoming part of our environment, rather than just tools we use for specific tasks. With wireless modems, portable computers give us access to networked data wherever we go.
- Mundane commercial and service jobs, environmentally dangerous jobs, and assembly and repair of inaccessible equipment such as undersea cables and space-station components in orbit increasingly will be done by robots, as NASA proposes to do in refueling the Hubble Space Telescope. Personal robots will appear in the home by 2010.
- Global sales of packaged software are growing at a rate of more than 15 percent per year.
- Wireless links such as satellite-based telephone systems and Internet connections will simplify relocation of personnel, minimize delays in completing new installations, and let terminals travel with the user instead of forcing the user to seek out the terminal.
- By 2010, artificial intelligence, data mining, and virtual reality will help most companies and government agencies to assimilate data and solve problems beyond the range of today's computers. AI's uses include robotics, machine vision, voice recognition, speech synthesis, electronic data processing, health and human services, administration, and airline pilot assistance.
- Superconductors operating at commercially viable temperatures will be in commercial use soon after 2015. Products eventually will include supercomputers the size of a three-pound coffee can, electric motors 75 percent smaller and lighter than those in use today, practical hydrogen-fusion power plants, electrical storage facilities with no heat loss, and noninvasive analyzers that can chart the interaction of individual brain cells.

Implications: New technologies should continue to improve the efficiency of many industries, helping to keep costs under control. However, this increased productivity retarded U.S. job creation from 2002 through early 2004. Other developed countries are likely to feel the same effect in the future.

New technologies often require a higher level of education and training to use them effectively. They also provide dozens of new opportunities to create businesses and jobs.

Automation will continue to cut the cost of many services and products, making it possible to reduce prices while still improving profits. This will be critical to business survival as the Internet continues to push the price of many products to the commodity level.

New technology also will make it easier for industry to minimize and capture its effluent. This will be a crucial ability in the environmentally conscious future.

28. Research and development plays a growing role in the economy.

- Throughout the 1990s, R & D outlays rose steadily, at rates ranging between 2.4 percent and 2.7 percent of U.S. GDP, and future increases will pace the growth of GDP.
- R & D outlays in Japan have risen almost continuously, to nearly 3 percent of GDP.
- China has taken third place in the world's R & D spending, with a budget totaling about $60 billion in 2001, the most recent year for which the figure is available. The United States spent $282 billion on research that year, while Japan spent $104 billion. Germany, in fourth place, spent $54 billion.
- In the European Union overall, they amount to 1.99 percent of the EU GDP. R & D spending in individual countries ranges from 4.27 percent of GDP in Sweden to just 1.8 percent in Britain, where it has declined steadily for more than ten years.
- In Russia, R & D budgets fell from about 2 percent of GDP in 1990 to under 1 percent in 1997; they are believed to have recovered to about 1.1 percent by 2003.
- In the United States, federal funding for basic research has almost disappeared, as Washington focuses on military research and engineering. Despite official claims that R & D spending would rise sharply in the FY 2004 budget, most research programs have suffered cuts. Even at the Department of Defense science and technology research is down 8 percent from the previous year.
- Corporate R & D in the United States also has shifted in the post-9/11 period, with less emphasis on pharmaceuticals and computer-related fields and more focus on biotechnology, nanotechnology, and security technologies.
- Western corporations are beginning to outsource R & D to foreign contractors, just as they do other functions. Russian laboratories, which are technologically sophisticated but have been hard-pressed to survive budget cuts for more than a decade, are taking on much of this work.

- Jobs created by high-tech exports are more than replacing those lost to competition under the North American Free Trade Agreement and similar agreements, providing a net gain in employment in the United States. Some 2.9 million American jobs are now supported by exports to NAFTA countries, more than double the number of jobs believed to have been lost from low-tech manufacturing industries. Canada and Mexico report proportionally greater gains.

Implications: The demand for scientists, engineers, and technicians will continue to grow, particularly in fields where research promises an immediate business payoff.

Low-wage countries such as China will continue to take low-wage jobs from advanced industrialized countries such as the United States, but those jobs will be replaced by higher-paid jobs in technology and service industries.

Countries like India, China, and Russia may continue to suffer a "brain drain" as those with high-tech skills emigrate to high-demand, high-wage destinations. However, there is evidence that growing numbers of technology students and professionals are spending time in the West to learn cutting-edge skills, and then returning to their native lands to work, start companies, and teach. This trend may promote the growth of some developing countries while reducing the competitive advantages of the developed world.

By inhibiting stem-cell research, the United States has made itself a less attractive place for cutting-edge biomedical scientists. The United Kingdom is capitalizing on this to become the world's leader in stem-cell research. In the process, it is reversing the "brain drain" that once deprived it of top scientists.

Washington's neglect of basic science is being felt in the declining fraction of patents, Nobel prizes, and other awards going to American scientists. As other countries become more skilled in critical high-tech fields, the United States is fast losing its edge. If this trend is not reversed, it will begin to undermine the American economy and shift both economic and political power to other lands.

29. **Advances in transportation technology will make travel and shipping faster, cheaper, and safer by land, sea, and air.**
    - By 2010, New York, Tokyo, and Frankfurt will emerge as transfer points for passengers of high-speed, large-capacity supersonic planes.
    - Airline crashes will decline, and will involve fewer fatalities, thanks to such technical advances as safer seat design and flash-resistant fuels.
    - Following European practice, the U.S. airline industry will begin to replace the spokes of its existing hub-and-spokes system with high-speed trains for journeys of 100 to 150 miles.

- There are more than 500 million cars in the world, and the number is growing quickly.
- The average life of a car in the United States is approaching 22 years.
- Advances in automobile technology such as road-condition sensors, continuously variable transmissions, automated traffic management systems, night-vision systems, and smart seats that tailor airbag inflation to the passenger's weight will all be in common use by 2010.
- The first commercial hybrid gas-electric cars are available already. New models will begin to win market share from traditional gas guzzlers between 2005 and 2010.
- To reduce the number and severity of traffic accidents, trucks on the most heavily used highways will be exiled to car-free lanes, and the separation will be enforced.

Implications: One of the fastest growing transport industries is trucking, in part because computers encourage "just-in-time" inventory management. Deliveries for Internet-based companies are an expanding market for shipping. This field will grow more efficient as GPS-based truck tracking and other new technologies spread through the industry.

More efficient vehicles, especially with hybrid power trains, should begin to reduce the demand for oil by 2008, easing one of the few remaining sources of inflation.

By 2010, "smart car" technologies will begin to reduce deaths due to auto accidents in Europe and, slightly later, the United States.

Cities increasingly will struggle to reduce auto congestion, either by limiting the use of private automobiles—as in Munich, Vienna, and Mexico City—or by encouraging the development and use of mass transit, as in Copenhagen and Curitiba, Brazil.

Technology may offer other alternatives. One proposal is "dual-mode transportation," in which private cars would be used normally on short hauls but would run on automated guideways for long-distance travel.

30. **The pace of technological change accelerates with each new generation of discoveries and applications.**
    - The design and marketing cycle—idea, invention, innovation, imitation— is shrinking steadily. Thus, products must capture their market quickly, before the competition can copy them. As late as the 1940s, the product cycle stretched to thirty or forty years. Today, it seldom lasts thirty or forty weeks.

- Computer-aided design in the automobile and other industries shortens the lag time between idea and finished design.
- Eighty percent of the scientists, engineers, and doctors who ever lived are alive today—and exchanging ideas in real time on the Internet.
- All the technical knowledge we work with today will represent only 1 percent of the knowledge that will be available in 2050.

Implications: Industries will face much tighter competition based on new technologies. Those who adopt state-of-the-art methods first will prosper. Those who ignore them eventually will fail.

Lifelong learning is a necessity for anyone who works in a technical field, and for growing numbers who do not.

31. Important medical advances will continue to appear almost daily.
- Medical knowledge is doubling every eight years.
- Half of what students learn in their freshman year about the cutting edge of science and technology is obsolete, revised, or taken for granted by their senior year.
- The Human Genome Project has already begun to yield promising new treatments for genetic disease. Early results include possible cures for hemophilia, cystic fibrosis, familial hypercholesterolemia, a number of cancers, and AIDS. Eventually, some 4,000 hereditary disorders may be prevented or cured through genetic intervention. As many as 300 such treatments are expected to enter clinical testing by 2005.
- The discovery that human chorionic gonadotropin, or hCG, appears in all cancer cells tested thus far, and (among adults) only in cancer cells, seems to promise the development of a generalized "cure for cancer." If early tests pan out, by 2010 tumors could be treated routinely and successfully with simple injections in the family doctor's office.
- Our growing knowledge of biochemistry, aided by advanced computer modeling, has made it possible to design drugs to fit specific receptors in the cell. Drugs created through this technology often are much more effective than natural derivatives or the products of "synthesize, scan, and hope" methods, and they are much less likely to cause adverse side effects.
- By 2005, artificial blood will begin to stretch the blood supply, which is expected to fall short of demand by 4 million units per year for the next thirty years.

- Memory-enhancing drugs should reach clinical use by 2010.
- New computer-based diagnostic tools are providing unprecedented images of soft and hard tissues inside the body, eliminating much exploratory surgery.
- "Magic bullet" drug delivery systems will make it possible to direct enormous doses of medication exactly where they are needed, sparing the rest of the body from possible side effects. This will improve therapeutic results in cancers and many other conditions that require the use of powerful drugs.
- Laparoscopic and endoscopic surgeries are providing similar benefits for a growing number of conditions.
- Brain-cell and nerve-tissue transplants to aid victims of retardation, head trauma, and other neurological disorders will enter clinical use by 2007. Heart repairs using muscles from other parts of the body will arrive soon after. Transplanted animal organs will find their way into common use. Laboratory-grown bone, muscle, and blood cells also will be employed in transplants.
- Other transplanted tissues will come from cloning and related technologies used to grow stem cells. Radical new treatments for diabetes, Parkinson's disease, perhaps Alzheimer's, and many other refractory disorders can be expected to arrive within the next five to ten years. Whether American physicians will be allowed to use them is still being debated. Forecasting International believes that cloning and related methods will be accepted for the treatment of disease.
- Surgeons working via the Internet will routinely operate on patients in remote areas using robot manipulators.
- In the next ten years, we expect to see more and better bionic limbs, hearts, and other organs; drugs that prevent disease rather than merely treating symptoms; and body monitors that warn of impending trouble. These all will reduce hospital stays.
- "Foodaceuticals" and "nutraceuticals"—foods and nutritional supplements containing drugs and pharmacologically useful substances—are earning interest among researchers. So far, most are being considered as new and improved sources of phytochemicals and antioxidants known to fight disorders from heart disease to Parkinson's, but other uses are under study. For example, scientists at Cornell, Tulane, and the University of Rochester created a strain of genetically engineered potatoes that produce a vaccine against human papilloma virus, a common sexually transmitted disease that causes nearly all cases of cervical cancer. Edible vaccines for a variety of other viruses are in the works.

- By 2025, the first nanotechnology-based medical therapies should reach clinical use. Microscopic machines will monitor our internal processes, remove cholesterol plaques from artery walls, and destroy cancer cells before they have a chance to form a tumor.
- The latest research suggests that aging itself originates as genetic deterioration in the mitochondria, the cell's energy-producing organelles, and might be slowed, or even reversed, within the lives of today's adults.

Implications: Even without dramatic advances in life extension, baby boomers are likely to live much longer, and in better health, than anyone now expects. This will reduce the cost of health care well below most current projections, but is likely to raise dramatically the cost of Social Security, Medicare, and the few remaining fixed-benefit pension plans.

A growing movement to remove barriers to stem-cell research in the United States could speed progress in this critical field. This could be expected to produce new treatments for neurological disorders such as Parkinson's and Alzheimer's disease and many other illnesses now incurable, and often untreatable.

High development and production costs for designer pharmaceuticals, computerized monitors, and artificial organs will continue to push up the cost of health care far more rapidly than the general inflation rate. Much of these expenses will be passed on to Medicare and other third-party payers.

Severe personnel shortages can be expected in high-tech medical specialties, in addition to the continuing deficit of nurses.

Widespread sex selection is producing many more male than female children in countries such as China (120/100), India (as high as 156/100, though the official figures say 113/100), and Saudi Arabia (125/100). The resulting population of unattached young men could act to destabilize the affected countries. (See Trend 49.)

32. The Internet is growing logarithmically and globally.
- In spring 2004, Net users numbered around 945 million worldwide. Just two years earlier, forecasts said there would be between 709 million and 946 million Net users by 2005.
- The world's population of Net users is expected to grow to 1.1 billion by 2005, 1.28 billion by 2006, and 1.46 billion by 2007.
- One reason for this fast growth is the rapid expansion of Net connectivity in some developing lands. India had only 170,000 Net subscribers in 1998; by 2004, it had 39 million, more than half as many as had been predicted just two years earlier.

- In early 2003, China's population of Net users amounted to more than 95 million.
- Over 80 percent of Japanese households were online by early 2003. Almost 78 million people—over 60 percent of Japan's population—access the Internet via computers, cell phones, and other devices.
- American consumers are finally adopting broadband. Some 8.3 million homes and businesses signed up for broadband service in 2003, bringing the total to 28.2 million lines.
- Most Internet communication is commercial, business-to-business rather than personal e-mail.
- Internet-based commerce is growing rapidly. Total e-commerce revenue is expected to be about $2.7 trillion in 2004, $1 trillion in the United States alone. Business-to-business sales passed $1 trillion by the end of 2003. Online retail sales in the United States grew by 51 percent in 2003 and are expected to grow another 27 percent in 2004.
- Not long ago, the Internet was predominately English-speaking. By 2004, there were an estimated 280 million Net users in countries where English is the dominant language, but 680 million in non-English-speaking countries. (This is a bit more than the total cyber-population because some Net users access the Internet in more than one language.)

Implications: Americans made up 42 percent of the total Net-using population in 2000, dropping to less than 20 percent in May 2004.

B2B sales on the Internet are dramatically reducing business expenses throughout the Net-connected world, while giving suppliers access to customers they could never have reached by traditional means.

Internet-based operations require more sophisticated, knowledgeable workers. People with the right technical training will find a ready market for their services for at least the next fifteen years, as major businesses compete to hire them. However, the specialties required in any given country will change as some skills are outsourced abroad.

Cultural, political, and social isolation has become almost impossible for countries interested in economic development. Even China's attempts to filter the Internet and shield its population from outside influences have proved relatively ineffective, as "hackers" elsewhere provide ways to penetrate the barrier.

However, isolationism is still possible for those who are not concerned with trade. The number of Net users in Iran has fallen from an estimated 1 million to about 420,000 since the mullahs shut down the country's cybercafes.

TRENDS IN LABOR FORCE AND WORK

33. Education and training are expanding throughout society.
- Approximately 130,000 additional K–12 teachers will be needed in the United States between 2000 and 2010, according to the National Center for Educational Statistics.
- Also needed: An annual $10 billion increase in federal spending for programs such as Head Start, aid for disadvantaged children, the Job Corps, and the Job Training Partnership Act.
- Starting salaries for teachers (as a ratio of per capita GDP) declined in most OECD countries throughout the 1990s; exceptions were the Netherlands and New Zealand.
- The half-life of an engineer's knowledge today is only five years; in ten years, 90 percent of what an engineer knows will be available on the computer. In electronics, fully half of what a student learns as a freshman is obsolete by his senior year.
- Eighty-five percent of the information in National Institutes of Health computers is upgraded in five years.
- Rapid changes in the job market and work-related technologies will necessitate increased training for virtually every worker.
- In the next ten years, close to 10 million jobs will open up for professionals, executives, and technicians in the highly skilled service occupations.
- A substantial portion of the labor force will be in job retraining programs at any moment. Much of this will be carried out by current employers, who have come to view employee training as a good investment.
- Schools will train both children and adults around the clock. The academic day will stretch to seven hours for children; adults use much of their remaining free time to prepare for their next job.
- We already are seeing a trend toward more adult education. One reason is the need to train for new careers as old ones are displaced or boomers grow bored with them. The other reason is the need for healthy, energetic people to keep active during retirement.
- In the United States, education is moving rapidly to the Internet, as small, rural grammar and high schools supplement their curricula with material from larger institutions, while universities increasingly market their programs to distant students.

Implications: Even small businesses must learn to see employee training as an investment rather than as an expense. Motorola estimates that it reaps $30 in profits for each dollar it spends on training.

Both management and employees must get used to the idea of lifelong learning. It will become a significant part of work life at all levels.

As the digital divide is erased and minority and low-income households buy computers and log onto the Internet, groups now disadvantaged will be increasingly able to educate and train themselves for high-tech careers.

34. Specialization is spreading throughout industry and the professions.

- For doctors, lawyers, engineers, and other professionals, the size of the body of knowledge required to excel in any one area precludes excellence across all areas.
- The same principle applies to artisans. Witness the rise of post-and-beam homebuilders, old-house restorers, automobile electronics technicians, and mechanics trained to work on only one brand of car.
- The information-based organization depends on its teams of task-focused specialists.
- Globalization of the economy calls for the more independent specialists. For hundreds of tasks, corporations will turn to consultants and contractors who specialize more and more narrowly as markets globalize and technologies differentiate.

Implications: This trend creates endless new niche markets to be served by small businesses. It also brings more career choices, as old specialties quickly become obsolete, but new ones appear even more rapidly.

35. Services are the fastest growing sector of the global economy.

- Retail sales in the United States grew by about 12 percent between 1999 and 2002, according to the Census Bureau, while revenues in selected service industries rose by 14.4 percent. Similar trends are seen in other industrialized countries.
- Service industries accounted for 83 percent of private nonfarm employment in the United States in 2000, the most recent year for which figures are available, up from only 70 percent in 1990. In the decade ending 2010, services are expected to account for virtually the entire net gain in U.S. employment.
- The U.S. health-care budget will more than double from $1.3 trillion in 2000 to $2.8 trillion by 2011, predicts the Centers for Medicare and Medicaid Services.
- Service jobs have replaced many of the well-paid positions lost in manufacturing, transportation, and agriculture. These new jobs, often part time, pay half the wages of manufacturing jobs. On the other hand,

computer-related service jobs pay much more than the minimum for those with sound education and training.

- Some of the fastest growth is in some of the least-skilled occupations, such as cashiers and retail salespersons.

Implications: Services are now beginning to compete globally, just as manufacturing industries have done over the last twenty years. By creating competitive pressure on wages in the industrialized lands, this trend will help to keep inflation in check.

The growth of international business will act as a stabilizing force in world affairs, as most countries find that conflict is unacceptably hard on the bottom line.

36. Women's salaries are approaching equality with men's—but very slowly.

- Women's salaries have been rising faster than men's since 1975. However, there still is a long way to go. Nationally, average earnings for a man employed full time and year-round reported in the 2000 Census was about $8,000—$10,000 more than for a woman working a comparable job. Women doctors make only 58 percent as much as their male colleagues.
- On average, American men make $38,000 per year in a full-time, year-round job; for similar jobs, women average only $28,000.
- Women's salaries have reached parity with men's in only five fields, nearly all of them areas where women have broken into trades long dominated by men: hazardous material removal workers, telecommunications line installers and repairers, meeting and convention planners, dining room or cafeteria workers, and construction trade helpers.
- Similar statistics are found elsewhere. In the United Kingdom, government statistics report that women earn 19 percent less than men for comparable jobs. PayFinder.com, a Web site specializing in salary comparisons, says the gap is actually 24 percent and, in some regions, rising.
- However, women's average income could exceed men's within a generation. College graduates enjoy a significant advantage in earnings over peers whose education ended with high school. Today, some 64 percent of young American women enroll in college, compared with only 60 percent of young men.
- To the extent that experience translates as prestige and corporate value, older women should find it easier to reach upper-management positions. They will strengthen the nascent "old-girl" networks, which will help to raise the pay scale of women still climbing the corporate ladder.

Implications: The fact that women's salaries are lagging despite higher academic achievement than men suggests that many college-educated women may be underemployed.

More new hires will be women, and they will expect both pay and opportunities equal to those of men.

Competition for top executive positions, once effectively limited to men, will intensify even as the corporate ladder loses many of its rungs.

The glass ceiling has been broken. One-fourth of upper executives today, and nearly 20 percent of corporate board members, are women. While this is still too few, it is far more than in any previous generation, and their numbers can only grow. Generations X and Dot-com are gender-blind in the workplace, and there are more women than men among college graduates. As more women reach decision-making levels in business and government, being a "sister" could become a career advantage.

37. Workers are retiring later as life expectancy stretches.
- OECD data show that people are retiring earlier in the developed world, but this is only part of the picture. Americans often return to work and delay complete retirement for several years. This trend will spread to other industrialized countries as the retirement-age population grows and the number of active workers to support them declines.
- People increasingly will work at one career, "retire" for a while (perhaps to travel) when they can afford it, return to school, begin another career, and so on in endless variations. True retirement, a permanent end to work, will be delayed until very late in life.
- In the long run, it may prove impossible to maintain the tradition of retirement, except through personal savings and investment.
- By 2010, we expect the average retirement age in the United States to be delayed well into the 70s. Benefits may also continue their decline, and they will be given based on need rather than as an entitlement.

Implications: Since the penalty on earnings of Social Security recipients was rescinded, more American retirees will return to work, and those not yet retired will be more likely to remain on the job.

Older workers will partially make up for the shortage of entry-level employees. The chance to remain in the workplace will reduce the risk of poverty for many elderly people who otherwise would have had to depend on Social Security to get by.

Retirees will act as technical aides to teachers, especially in the sciences.

38. Unions are losing their power.

- In the United States, unions enrolled 23 percent of employed wage and salary workers in 1980, but only 13 percent by 2003. By 2005, despite several recent successes in organizing, contract negotiations, and strikes, it will fall under 12 percent.
- In South Korea, where organized labor once was invincible, the government has increasingly stood up to strikes by doctors, electrical workers, car makers, and other trade groups.
- In Britain, where the Thatcher government broke union power in the 1980s, labor has recovered little of its former strength.
- One reason for this decline is that jobs now are free to move around the globe from heavily unionized areas to regions where unions are less well established. Companies also contract out a growing proportion of business activities to nonunion firms.
- Another reason is that the increased use of robots, CAD/CAM, and flexible manufacturing complexes can cut a company's workforce by up to one-third. The surviving workers tend to be technicians and other comparatively well-educated semiprofessionals, who always have tended to resist union membership. The growing industrial use of artificial intelligence will further this trend.
- A third reason is the high cost of strikes. The once-wealthy Teamsters Union spent an estimated $15 million on its strike against UPS in 1997, leaving only $700,000 in its coffers—this after substantial borrowing from the AFL-CIO. In 2002, they settled without a strike.

Implications: For large companies, this promises greater stability in employee wages and benefits.

Unions eager to regain their membership will target any substantial company with less-skilled employees to organize. This could raise labor costs for companies that unions once would have considered too small to organize.

In ten to fifteen years, American labor unions will compete with AARP to lead the battle for the rights of late-life workers and for secure retirement benefits. They face an inherent conflict between the interests of workers in what once would have been the retirement years and those of younger members, who rightly see the elderly as having saddled them with the cost of whatever benefits older generations enjoy.

Democrats have been losing support from unions as organized labor declines. However, the three groups replacing unions in the power bloc—the AARP, Hispanics, and African Americans—also have tended to vote Democratic.

The old paradigm of unions versus corporations is obsolete. In today's economy, workers negotiate alongside management, winning shared bonuses.

39. Second and third careers are becoming common, as more people make midlife changes in occupation.
- The fast pace of technological change makes old careers obsolete, even as new ones open up to replace them.
- People change careers every ten years, on average.
- A recent Louis Harris poll found that only 39 percent of workers say they intend to hold the same job five years from now; 31 percent say they plan to leave their current work; 29 percent do not know.
- Boomers and their children will have not just two or three careers, but five or six, as dying industries are replaced by new opportunities.

Implications: "Earn while you learn" takes on new meaning: Most people will have to study for their next occupation, even as they pursue their current career.

In many two-earner couples, one member or the other will often take a sabbatical to prepare for a new career.

Self-employment is becoming an increasingly attractive option, as being your own boss makes it easier to set aside time for career development. This is especially true for Generations X and Dot-com.

Retirement plans must be revised so that workers can transfer medical and pension benefits from one career to the next—a change that has long been needed.

40. The work ethic is vanishing.
- Tardiness is increasing; sick-leave abuse is common.
- Job security and high pay are not the motivators they once were, because social mobility is high and people seek job fulfillment. Some 48 percent of those responding in a recent Louis Harris poll said they work because it "gives a feeling of real accomplishment."
- This is not wholly the workers' fault, as job security is increasingly hard to come by. Gen Xers watched their parents remain loyal to their employers, only to be downsized out of work. As a result, they have no corporate loyalty at all. Many will quit their job at even the hint of a better position.
- For Generation X, the post–Baby Boom generation, work is only a means to their ends: money, fun, and leisure.
- Fifty-five percent of the top executives interviewed in the poll say that erosion of the work ethic will have a major negative effect on corporate performance in the future.

- Ethics at the top are no better: Enron, WorldCom, Tyco International, Adelphia Cable, and ImClone just begin the list of companies under investigation for deceptive accounting practices, looting of corporate assets, and other misdeeds with dire implications for stock values.
- Seeking the root of such problems, a Zogby International poll of college seniors found that 97 percent said that their studies had prepared them to act ethically in the future. However, 73 percent said that professors had taught them that right and wrong are not susceptible to uniform standards, but depend on individual values and cultural norms.

Implications: The new generation of workers cannot simply be hired and ignored. They must be nurtured, paid well, and made to feel appreciated. Training is crucial. Without the opportunity to learn new skills, young people will quickly find a job that will help them to prepare for the rest of their career.

41. Two-income couples are becoming the norm.
- In 75 percent of U.S. households, both partners will work full time by 2005, up from 63 percent in 1992.
- The percentage of working-age women who are employed has grown steadily throughout the industrialized world. In the United States, it has grown from 46 percent in 1970 to 68.8 percent in 2000. The lowest are Italy, Spain, and Mexico, with just 40 percent of working-age women employed, according to the Organization for Economic Cooperation and Development (OECD).
- This emphasis on work is one big reason the richest 25 percent to 50 percent of the U.S. population has reached zero population growth. They have no time for children and little interest in having large families.
- The number of working mothers with young children is actually declining. Only 58 percent of married women with children under 3 held jobs in 2002, compared with 61 percent in 1997. At the same time, the number of married working women with children under a year old fell from 59 percent to 53 percent.

Implications: Demand for on-the-job childcare, extended parental leave, and other family-oriented benefits can only grow. In the long run, this could erode the profitability of some American companies, unless it is matched by an equal growth in productivity.

Two-career couples can afford to eat out often, take frequent short vacations, and buy new cars and other such goods. And they feel they deserve whatever time-savers and outright luxuries they can afford. This is quickly expanding the market for consumer goods and services, travel, and leisure activities.

This also promotes self-employment and entrepreneurialism, as one family member's salary can tide them over while the other works to establish a new business.

Look for families that usually have two incomes, but have frequent intervals in which one member takes a sabbatical or goes back to school to prepare for another career. As information technologies render former occupations obsolete, this will become the new norm.

42. Generations X and Dot-com will have major effects in the future.

- Members of Generation X—roughly, the 30-plus cohort—and especially of Generation Dot-com, now in their 20s, have more in common with their peers throughout the world than with their parents' generation.
- There are approximately 50 million people in Europe between the ages of 15 and 24; 30 million more are between 25 and 29. The under-30 cohort represents about 22 percent of the European population.
- The under-20 cohort is remaining in school longer and taking longer to enter the workforce than before.
- Generation X should be renamed "Generation E," for entrepreneurial. Throughout the world, they are starting new businesses at an unprecedented rate.
- The younger Dot-com generation is proving to be even more business-oriented, caring for little but the bottom line. Twice as many say they would prefer to own a business rather than be a top executive. Five times more would prefer to own a business rather than hold a key position in politics or government.
- Many in Generation X are economically conservative. On average, those who can do so begin saving much earlier in life than their parents did in order to protect themselves against unexpected adversity. They made money in the stock market boom of the 1990s, then lost it in the "dot-bomb" contraction, but have left their money in the market. For Generations X and Dot-com, time is still on their side.

Implications: Employers will have to adjust virtually all of their policies and practices to the values of these new and different generations, including finding new ways to motivate and reward them. Generations X and Dot-com thrive on challenge, opportunity, and training—whatever will best prepare them for their next career move. Cash is just the beginning of what they expect.

For these generations, lifelong learning is nothing new; it's just the way life is. Companies that can provide diverse, cutting-edge training will have a strong recruiting advantage over competitors that offer fewer opportunities to improve their skills and knowledge base.

Generations X and Dot-com are well equipped for work in an increasingly high-tech world, but have little interest in their employers' needs. They also have a powerful urge to do things their way.

As both customers and employees, they will demand even more advanced telecommunications and Net-based transactions.

43. Time is becoming the world's most precious commodity.

- Computers, electronic communications, the Internet, and other technologies are making national and international economies much more competitive.
- In the United States, workers spend about 10 percent more time on the job than they did a decade ago. European executives and nonunionized workers face the same trend.
- In this high-pressure environment, single workers and two-income couples are increasingly desperate for any product that offers to simplify their lives or grant them a taste of luxury—and they can afford to buy it.

Implications: Stress-related problems affecting employee morale and wellness will continue to grow. Companies must help employees balance their time at work with their family lives and need for leisure. This may reduce short-term profits but will aid profitability in the long run.

As time for shopping continues to evaporate, Internet and mail-order marketers will have a growing advantage over traditional stores.

MANAGEMENT TRENDS

44. More entrepreneurs start new businesses every year.

- Workers under age 30 would prefer to start their own company rather than advance through the corporate ranks. Some 10 percent are actively trying to start their own businesses, three times as many as in previous generations.
- A large majority simply distrust large institutions. Most believe that jobs cannot provide a secure economic future in a time of rapid technological change. Examples of Silicon Valley start-ups that turned their founders

into billionaires "overnight" dramatically advanced this change of values. This attitude seems to have been moderated only slightly by the failure of many dot-com companies.

- By 2006, the number of self-employed people in the United States will rise to 10.2 million, according to the Bureau of Labor Statistics. However, Forecasting International believes that figure to be too low: Expect closer to 12 million self-employed Americans in 2006.

- More women also are starting small businesses. Many are leaving traditional jobs to go home and open businesses, even as they begin a family. In 1980, only 26 percent of nonfarm sole proprietorships were owned by women. By 2000, the number had grown to 35 percent. An estimated 10.6 million privately held firms in the United States are at least 50 percent owned by women; they employ 19.1 million people and generate $2.46 trillion in sales annually.

- Since the 1970s, small businesses started by entrepreneurs have accounted for nearly all of the new jobs created. For much of this period, giant corporations have actually cut employment. In 1995, small entrepreneurial businesses produced 1 million new full-time jobs versus barely 100,000 among larger companies.

- By 2005, 80 percent of the labor force will be working for firms employing fewer than 200 people.

Implications: This is a self-perpetuating trend, as all those new service firms need other companies to handle chores outside their core business.

It is driven as well by the attitudes and values of Generations X and Dot-com and by the rapid developments in technology, which create endless opportunities for new business development.

Specialty boutiques will continue to spring up on the Internet for at least the next 20 years.

This trend will help to ease the poverty of many developing countries, as it already is doing in India and China.

45. Information-based organizations are quickly displacing the old command-and-control model of management.

- The typical large business is struggling to reshape itself. Soon, it will be composed of specialists who rely on information from colleagues, customers, and headquarters to guide their actions.

- Management styles will change as upper executives learn to consult these skilled workers on a wide variety of issues. Employees will gain new power with the authority to make decisions based on the data they develop.

- Information-based organizations require more specialists, who will be found in operations, not at corporate headquarters. R & D, manufacturing, and marketing specialists will work together as a team on all stages of product development rather than keeping each stage separate and distinct.
- Upper management is giving fewer detailed orders to subordinates. Instead, it sets performance expectations for the organization, its parts, and its specialists and supplies the feedback necessary to determine whether results have met expectations.

Implications: This is a well-established trend. At this point, many large corporations have restructured their operations for greater flexibility. However, many others still have a long way to go.

Downsizing has spread from manufacturing industries to the service economy. Again, this process encourages the entrepreneurial trend, both to provide services for companies outsourcing their secondary functions and to provide jobs for displaced employees.

Many older workers have been displaced in this process, depriving companies of their corporate memory. Companies have replaced them with younger workers, whose experience of hard times is limited to the relatively mild recession since 2000. Many firms may discover that they need to recruit older workers to help them adapt to adversity.

46. A typical large business in 2010 will have fewer than half the management levels of its counterpart in 1990, and about one-third the number of managers.
- Computers and information management systems have stretched the manager's effective span of control from six to twenty-one subordinates. Information now flows from front-line workers to higher management for analysis. Thus, fewer mid-level managers are needed, flattening the corporate pyramid.
- Downsizing, restructuring, reorganization, and cutbacks of white-collar workers will continue through 2006. Outsourcing will continue to grow until at least 2010.
- However, many companies are finding it necessary to bring back older workers, so as to preserve an effective corporate memory.
- Opportunities for advancement will be few because they will come within the narrow specialty. By 2001, only one person for every fifty was promoted, compared with one for every twenty in 1987.
- Information-based organizations will have to make a special effort to prepare professional specialists to become business executives and leaders.

Implications: Top managers will have to be computer-literate to retain their jobs and must make sure they achieve the increased span of control that computers make possible.

Finding top managers with the broad experience needed to run a major business already has become difficult and can only grow more so as the demand for specialization grows.

Executives increasingly will start their own companies rather than trusting the old-fashioned corporate career path to provide advancement.

47. Government regulations will continue to take up a growing portion of the manager's time and effort.
- In 1996, the U.S. Congress passed regulatory reform laws intended to slow the proliferation of government regulations. Nonetheless, by 2001 more than 14,000 new regulations have been enacted. Not one proposed regulation was rejected during this period. The Federal Register, where proposed and enacted regulations are published, was 37 percent larger in 1999 than it had been 10 years earlier—73,880 pages in all. In 2001, that number fell for the first time in more than a decade, to 64,431 pages. However, it was back up to 75,606 pages in 2002, and 75,795 in 2003.
- This is not solely an American trend. The Brussels bureaucrats of the European Union are churning out regulations at an even faster rate, overlaying a standard regulatory structure on all the national systems of the member countries.
- The growth of regulations is not necessarily all bad. A study by the U.S. Congressional Office of Management and Budget estimated that the annual cost of major federal regulations enacted between October 1992 and September 2002 amounted to between $38 billion and $44 billion per year. However, the estimated benefits of those regulations added up to between $135 billion and $218 billion annually.

Implications: Regulations are both necessary and unavoidable, and often beneficial. Yet it is difficult not to see them as a kind of friction that slows both current business and future economic growth.

The proliferation of regulations in the developed world could give a competitive advantage to countries such as India and China, where regulations that impede investment and capital flow are being stripped away, while health, occupational safety, and environmental codes are still rudimentary or absent.

Other lands, such as Russia, will remain at a competitive disadvantage until they can pass and enforce the regulations needed to ensure a stable, fair business environment.

INSTITUTIONAL TRENDS

48. Multinational corporations are uniting the world, and growing more exposed to its risks.
- By 2005, parts for well over half of the products built in the United States will originate in other countries.
- Multinational corporations that rely on indigenous workers may be hindered by the increasing number of AIDS cases in Africa and around the world. Up to 90 percent of the population in parts of sub-Saharan Africa reportedly tests positive for the HIV virus in some surveys. Thailand is equally stricken, and many other parts of Asia show signs that the AIDS epidemic is spreading among their populations.
- The continuing fragmentation of the post-Cold War world has reduced the stability of some lands where government formerly could guarantee a favorable—or at least predictable—business environment. The current unrest in Indonesia is one example.
- One risk now declining is the threat of currency fluctuations. In Europe, at least, the adoption of the euro is making for a more stable economic environment.

Implications: It is becoming ever more difficult for business to be confident that decisions about plant location, marketing, and other critical issues will continue to appear wise even five years into the future. All long-term plans must include an even greater margin for risk management. This will encourage outsourcing rather than investment in offshore facilities that could be endangered by sudden changes in business conditions.

Countries that can demonstrate a significant likelihood of stability will enjoy a strong competitive advantage over neighbors that cannot. Witness the rapid growth of investment in India now that deregulation and privatization have general political support, compared with other Asian lands where conditions are less predictable.

Major corporations also can help to moderate some risks in unstable countries, such as by threatening to take their business elsewhere.

49. International exposure includes a greater risk of terrorist attack.
- State-sponsored terrorism appears to be on the decline, as tougher sanctions make it more trouble than it is worth. However, some rogue states may still provide logistical or technological support for independent terrorist organizations when opportunities present themselves.
- Until recently, attacks on American companies were limited to rock-throwing at the local McDonald's, occasional bombings of bank

branches and of American-owned pipelines in South America, and kidnappings. Since 9/11, American-owned hotel chains have experienced several major bombings, in part because American government facilities overseas have been effectively hardened against terrorist assault.

- Nothing will prevent small, local political organizations and special-interest groups from using terror to promote their causes.
- However, as the United States has been forced to recognize, the most dangerous terrorist groups are no longer motivated by specific political goals, but by generalized, virulent hatred based on religion and culture.
- On balance, the amount of terrorist activity in the world is likely to go up, not down, in the next ten years. This was seen in corrections to the State Department's April 2004 report on terrorism, which originally seemed to show a sharp decline in terrorist incidents and was used to claim success for the Bush administration's tactics in the "war on terror." In fact, the State Department's corrections in June 2004 showed that terrorist attacks have risen sharply since the invasion of Iraq, both in number and in severity.
- Risks of terrorism are greatest in countries with repressive governments and large numbers of unemployed, educated young men.

Implications: Western corporations may have to devote more of their resources to self-defense, while accepting smaller-than-expected profits from operations in the developing countries.

Like the attacks on the World Trade Center and Pentagon, and the American embassies in Kenya and Tanzania before them, any attacks on major corporate facilities are likely to be designed for maximum destruction and casualties. Bloodshed for bloodshed's sake has become a characteristic of modern terrorism.

Where terrorism is most common, countries will find it impossible to attract foreign investment, no matter how attractive their resources.

Though Islamic terrorists form only a tiny part of the Muslim community, they have a large potential for disruption throughout the region from Turkey to the Philippines.

The economies of the industrialized nations could be thrown into recession at any time by another terrorist event on the scale of September 11. This is particularly true of the United States. The impact would be greatest if the attack discouraged travel, as the hijacking of airliners to attack the World Trade Center and Pentagon did in 2001 and 2002.

The U.S. economy is being affected already by American antiterrorism measures. Since Washington began to photograph incoming travelers and required more extensive identification from them, tourism to America is off by some 30 percent. The number of foreign students coming to American universities has declined by a similar amount.

50. Consumers increasingly demand social responsibility from companies and each other.

- Companies increasingly will be judged on how they treat the environment. For example, nuclear power plant controversies are now seen in the light of the Chernobyl nuclear accident.
- Safety testing of children's products also enforces corporate responsibility. One company recently was forced to recall 7 million child car seats. Another recalled more than 440,000 pairs of children's sneakers with metal eyelets that could become detached and pose a choking hazard.
- Government intervention will supplant deregulation in the airline industry (in the interest of safety and services), financial services (to control instability and costs), electric utilities (nuclear problems), and the chemical industry (toxic wastes).
- With 5 percent of the world's population and 66 percent of the lawyers on the planet, American citizens will not hesitate to litigate if their demands are not met.

Implications: For industry, this represents one more powerful pressure to adopt environmentally friendly technologies, to work with area schools and community groups, and to participate in other local activities. It also represents an opportunity to market to environmentally concerned consumers.

As the Internet spreads Western attitudes throughout the world, environmental activists in other regions will find ways to use local court systems to promote their goals. Litigation is likely to become a global risk for companies that do not make the environment a priority.

51. On average, institutions are growing more transparent in their operations, and more accountable for their misdeeds.

- China, rated by PricewaterhouseCooper as the most opaque of the major nations, was forced to open many of its records as a precondition for joining the World Trade Organization.
- In India, a country generally regarded as one of the world's most corrupt, the Central Vigilance Commission has opened the country's banking system to more effective oversight.
- In the United States, powerful forces are inspiring demands for greater transparency and accountability in large institutions. These include both

the current wave of business scandals and the controversy over child abuse within the Catholic Church.

- The wave of support for government since the September 11 terrorist attacks has made Americans willing to accept greater transparency—that is, less privacy—in their personal lives.
- At the same time, the nationalist response to September 11 temporarily muted most demands for transparency in the American government. In mid-2004, this reluctance to question Washington appears to be evaporating in the wake of the torture scandal in Iraq.
- Wars against terrorism, drug trafficking, and money laundering are opening the world's money conduits to greater scrutiny. It is also opening up the operations of nongovernmental organizations that function primarily as charitable and social service agencies but are linked to terrorism as well.

Implications: Countries with high levels of transparency tend to be much more stable than more opaque lands.

They also tend to be much more prosperous, in part because they find it easier to attract foreign investment.

Greater transparency seems likely to reduce the operational effectiveness of the world's drug traffickers and terrorist organizations.

52. **Institutions are undergoing a bimodal distribution: The big get bigger, the small survive, and the midsized are squeezed out.**
    - By 2005, 20 major automakers around the world will hold market shares ranging from 18 percent (GM) to 1 percent (BMW). Daimler Chrysler already owns Mercedes Benz, Dodge, Jeep, Smart, Maybach, Vauxhall, and part of Mitsubishi. GM owns Hummer, Opel, Saab, two-thirds of Daewoo, and parts of Fiat and Isuzu, in addition to its traditional product lines. Ford owns Volvo, Jaguar, Land Rover, and Aston Martin.
    - By 2010, there will be only five giant automobile firms. Production and assembly will be centered in Korea, Italy, and Latin America.
    - By 2005, just three major corporations will make up the computer hardware industry: IBM, Compaq, and Dell.
    - Seven domestic airlines in the United States today control 80 percent of the market, leaving the smaller domestic carriers with only 20 percent. The most recent consolidation is the alliance between Continental and Northwest. By 2005 there will be only three major domestic carriers.
    - Where local regulations allow, mergers and acquisitions are an international game. Witness the takeovers of the United States' MCI by WorldCom in the United Kingdom and of Chrysler by Daimler-Benz.

The continuing removal of trade barriers among EU nations will keep this trend active for at least the next decade.

- Manufacturers often sell directly to the dealer, skipping the wholesaler or distributor.
- We are now in the second decade of the micro-segmentation trend, as more and more highly specialized businesses and entrepreneurs search for narrower niches. These small firms will prosper, even as midsized, "plain vanilla" competitors die out. This trend extends to nearly every endeavor, from retail to agriculture.
- "Boutique" businesses that provide entertainment, financial planning, and preventive medical care for aging baby boomers will be among the fastest-growing segments of the U.S. economy.

Implications: Thus far, industries dominated by small, regional, often family-owned companies have been relatively exempt from the consolidation now transforming many other businesses. Takeovers are likely even in these industries in the next decade.

This consolidation will extend increasingly to Internet-based businesses, where well-financed companies are trying to absorb or outcompete tiny online startups, much as they have done in the brick-and-mortar world.

This trend leads us to believe that AT&T may be reconsolidated by 2010.

No company is too large to be a takeover target if it dominates a profitable market or has other features attractive to profit-hungry investors.

Appendix B

Vital Signs of National Stability

SOCIOPOLITICAL INDICATORS

- Population of men between ages 15 and 30
  - Young men are the most prone to violence.
- Unemployment rate among young males
  - Young men are most volatile, and most likely to adopt violent causes if they are unemployed and without hope.
  - A sudden, permanent loss of job opportunities, as when a war is lost, heightens the possibility of terrorism.
- Educational status of young males
  - Young men are most susceptible to terrorist causes if they have been educated for a middle-class life that is no longer available to them.
- Percentage of ethnic minorities
  - Ethnic divisions reduce national stability, particularly in regions with traditional tribal animosity. However, division among many ethnic groups can produce relative peace, so long as power and prosperity are shared.
- Political power of ethnic minorities
  - An effective political voice promotes stability among minority populations and reduces the likelihood of terrorist activity.
  - States dominated by an ethnic minority may be even less stable and more prone to terrorism than those in which the minority is persecuted.
- Percentage of religious minorities
  - The effects of religious divisions mirror those of ethnic divisions, but may be even more vicious and intractable.
- Prevalence of political corruption
  - Widespread political corruption undermines the legitimacy of governments and tends to promote the growth of dissident and terrorist movements.

- Prevalence of police corruption
    - Police corruption is equivalent to political corruption at the local level. It can be even more damaging to social stability, and more conducive to terrorism, because the police have both weapons and a coherent management structure to use them.
- Length of visa lines outside embassies
    - Eagerness to leave the country reveals instability; any sudden change in this indicator is particularly important.
- Hoarding of food, medical supplies, and gasoline
    - These all suggest a general expectation of hard times to come and a decline in national stability.
- Number of foreign students in the United States in technical, business, and liberal arts courses
    - American colleges are a traditional haven for the younger members of wealthy families in unstable lands.
- Percent of homes with indoor plumbing
    - A low number indicates widespread poverty and a population with little investment in the existing regime.
- Degree of religious freedom
    - Great religious freedom indicates a nation with little to fear from social differences.
- Degree of press freedom
    - The press can be free, monitored, or controlled; the greater the freedom, the more confident the government is likely to be in the acceptance of its power.
- Consolidation of wealth in the hands of political leaders and their families, of military leaders, and of political cronies of the head of government
    - The more wealth is consolidated within any elite, the less stable any nation will be.
- Subsidies for food, housing, and medicine or medical care
    - These indicate that the nation's underlying economy is not adequately providing for all its citizens and when they become a major source of income for a large fraction of its citizens, suggest that social and political stability are low.
- Changes in subsidies to the poor
    - Sudden increases in subsidies often are an attempt to buy the loyalty of a population that is no longer willing to grant it.
- Percent of the population below the poverty line
    - Social and political stability is inversely related to poverty rates.
- Number of AIDS patients
    - In extreme cases, such as in Central Africa and Thailand, high rates of AIDS can undermine entire economies and cause instability.

- Rates of morbidity and mortality
  - High rates indicate that the society has not been able to deliver basic social services to its population, which will have little loyalty to the existing government.
- Life expectancy
  - This extends the previous indicator.
- Sharing data and information on technology, politics, economics, social conditions, criminal activity, military intelligence, and terrorism
  - Governments unwilling to share basic information often are uncertain of their hold on power.

ECONOMIC INDICATORS

- Percentage of home ownership
  - A high rate of home ownership suggests that wealth is being distributed relatively fairly and indicates that much of the population has a stake in the country's continued stability and prosperity.
- Percentage of imports
  - In the absence of some balancing factor, the need to import an unusually high fraction of a nation's goods suggests the absence of a native manufacturing base, and perhaps the existence of widespread poverty.
- Percentage of exports
  - Strong exports of manufactured goods suggest a prosperous economy, and therefore a stable nation; an export economy based on raw materials suggests the reverse.
  - Oil-based economies will be vulnerable to unrest so long as petroleum remains relatively cheap.
- Difference in income and wealth between the richest and poorest deciles of the population
  - A wide gap between the rich and poor is one of the most reliable warnings of social and political instability.
  - Developed by Forecasting International many years ago, this indicator has recently been adopted by the Central Intelligence Agency for the country reports presented in the *CIA World Factbook,* which is available on the Internet.
- Transfer of wealth to other countries
  - In the absence of other investment incentives, this may suggest strong doubts about political stability among those well positioned to make such a judgment.

- Movement of cash to the United States
  - This is one measure of the previous indicator.
- Investment in U.S. stocks or bonds
  - And yet another.
- Increased sales of diamonds
  - This may reveal conversion of wealth to easily portable form, a traditional sign of instability.
- Increased numbers of expensive homes on the market
  - Another harbinger of impending flight by the wealthy.
- Growing investment in homes or real estate in the United States or Canada by the wealthy elite, by high-ranking military officers, and by politicians
  - This strongly confirms the previous indicator.
- Form in which workers are paid
  - Payment in goods or credit—in any form other than a regular salary—indicates a severely unhealthy economy in which unrest is likely.
  - For a time, Russian teachers were paid in vodka, which is easily sold and resisted inflation better than rubles. They had refused to accept payment in toilet paper or credit toward funeral costs.
- Access to drug funds
  - Drug money represents a convenient and lucrative way both to support terrorist activity and to make it pay.

TECHNOLOGY INDICATORS

- Number of automobiles
  - A high rate of automobile ownership suggests at least moderate general prosperity and the existence of a well-developed infrastructure to maintain and supply the cars and roads; both these implications suggest political and economic stability.
- Availability of modern communications facilities
  - General access to information-related technologies suggests the existence of a high-tech infrastructure to manufacture, operate, and maintain the equipment; a population both sufficiently well educated to have use for telephones, computers, and the like and wealthy enough to buy them; and a government that trusts its citizens with information and with access to the world at large. Specific indicators include:
    - __ Number of cell phones per capita
    - __ Number of regular telephones per capita
    - __ Number of computers per capita
    - __ Number of printers per capita

___ Number of copiers per capita
___ Number of fax machines per capita
___ Number of shortwave radio receivers per capita
___ Number of satellite receivers per capita
___ Number of Internet users per capita

MILITARY INDICATORS

- Percentage of military
  - In a stable country, the military usually employs a small fraction of the population and forms a minor segment of the economy.
- Military salaries
  - Military pay scales substantially above those of the population at large may indicate a nation with little social cohesion.
- Numbers of palace guard or "elite" guard
  - The existence of a strong elite guard indicates that leaders cannot trust even their own military.
- Changes in salary of palace guard per year
  - A sudden, substantial pay raise for an elite guard is often an attempt to buy loyalty where none is otherwise available and is a clear sign of impending unrest.
  - This was one of the most important symptoms of social and political instability in Iran in the years before the fundamentalist revolution in 1980. More than any other single factor, it allowed Forecasting International to warn its clients of impending trouble fully two years before the event.
- Role of military in politics
  - Relatively few governments remain stable for long unless the military is subservient to civilian rule.
- Nuclear, biological, and chemical weapons capabilities
  - There is little impetus for nations to develop weapons of mass destruction in the face of international sanctions unless they perceive some imminent threat to their sovereignty or are planning future aggression.
- Use of underground tunnels or laboratories
  - The felt need to hide weapons development and other such military preparations are a clear warning that war is contemplated.

Appendix C

Hospitality Associations and Publications

LISTING OF ASSOCIATIONS

American Correctional Foodservice Association
304 West Liberty Street, Suite 301
Louisville, KY 40202
Tel: 502-583-3783
Fax: 502-589-3502
Website: www.acfsa.com

American Culinary Federation
P.O. Box 3466
St. Augustine, FL 32085
Tel: 904-824-4468
Fax: 904-825-4758
Website: www.acfchefs.org

American Dietetic Association
216 West Jackson Boulevard, Suite 800
Chicago, IL 60606-6995
Tel: 312-899-0040
Fax: 312-899-1758
Website: www.eatright.org

American Hotel & Lodging Association
1201 New York Avenue NW, #600
Washington, DC 20005-3931
Tel: 202-289-3100
Fax: 202-289-3199
Website: www.ahma.com

American Hotel & Lodging Association Educational Institute
800 North Magnolia Avenue, Suite 1800
Orlando, FL 32803
Tel: 407-999-8100; 800-752-4567
Fax: 407-236-7848
Website: www.ei-ahla.org

American School Food Service Association
1600 Duke Street, 7th Floor
Alexandria, VA 22314-3436
Tel: 800-877-8822
Fax: 703-739-3915
Website: www.ahma.com

American Society for Hospital Food Service Administrators
840 North Lake Shore Drive
Chicago, IL 60611
Tel: 312-280-6416
Fax: 312-280-4152
Website: www.ashfsa.org

Club Managers Association of America
1733 King Street
Alexandria, VA 22314
Tel: 703-739-9500
Fax: 703-739-0124
Website: www.cmaa.org

Council on Hotel, Restaurant and Institutional Education
1200W 17th Street NW
Washington, DC 20036-3097
Tel: 202-331-5990
Fax: 202-331-2429
Website: www.chrie.org

Council on Hotel and Restaurant Trainers
11515 Orchid Avenue
Fountain, CA 92708
Tel: 714-531-8263
Fax: 714-839-0465
Website: www.chart.org

Cruise Lines International Association
80 Broad Street, Suite 1800
New York, NY 10004

Tel: 212-921-0066
Fax: 212-921-0549
Website: www.cruising.org

Dietary Managers Association
400 East 22nd Street
Lombard, IL 60148
Tel: 708-932-1444
Fax: 708-932-1482
Website: www.dmaonline.org

Education Foundation of the National Restaurant Association
250 South Wacker Drive, Suite 1400
Chicago, IL 60606
Tel: 312-715-1010
Fax: 312-715-0807
Website: www.rcfws.com

Foodservice Consultants Society International
304 West Liberty Street, Suite 301
Louisville, KY 40202
Fax: 502-589-3602
Website: www.fcsi.org

Healthcare Food Service Management Association
204 E Street NE
Washington, DC 20002
Tel: 202-546-7236
Fax: 202-547-3648
Website: www.hfm.org

Inflight Foodservice Association
304 West Liberty Street, Suite 301
Louisville, KY 40202
Tel: 502-583-3783
Fax: 502-589-3602
Website: www.ifsanet.com

International Association of Amusement Parks and Attractions
1448 Duke Street
Alexandria, VA 22314
Tel: 703-836-4800
Fax: 703-836-4801
Website: www.iaapa.org

International Association of Culinary Professionals
304 West Liberty Street, Suite 301
Louisville, KY 40202
Tel: 502-583-3783
Fax: 502-589-3602
Website: www.iacp.com

International Council on Hotel, Restaurant and Institutional Education
2613 North Parham Road, 2nd Floor
Richmond, VA 23294
Tel: 804-346-4800
Fax: 804-346-5009
Website: www.chrie.org

International Foodservice Distributors Association
201 Park Washington Court
Falls Church, VA 22046
Tel: 703-832-9400
Fax: 703-583-4673
Website: www.ifdaonline.org

International Foodservice Executives Association
1100 State Road 7, #103
Margate, FL 22068
Tel: 305-977-0767
Fax: 305-977-0874
Website: www.ifsea.org

International Foodservice Manufacturers Association
334 North Clark Street, Suite 2900
Chicago, IL 60610
Tel: 312-644-8989
Fax: 312-644-8185
Website: www.ifmaworld.com

MICROS Systems, Inc.
7031 Columbia Gateway Drive
Columbia, MD 21046-2289
Tel: 443-285-6000
Website: www.micros.com

National Association of Black Hospitality Professionals, Inc.
P.O. Box 5443
Plainfield, NJ 07060

Tel: 908-354-5117
Fax: 908-354-8804

National Association of College University Foodservice
Michigan State University
1405 South Harrison Road, Suite 103
East Lansing, MI 48824
Tel: 517-332-2494
Fax: 517-332-8144
Website: www.nacufs.org

National Association of Concessionaires
35 East Wacker Drive, Suite 1545
Chicago, IL 60601
Tel: 312-236-3585
Fax: 312-236-7807
Website: www.naconline.org

National Association of Food Equipment Manufacturers
401 North Michigan Avenue
Chicago, IL 60611
Tel: 312-644-6610
Fax: 312-321-6869
Website: www.nafem.org

National Automatic Merchandising Association
20 North Wacker Drive, Suite 3500
Chicago, IL 60606-3102
Tel: 312-346-0370
Fax: 312-704-4140
Website: www.vending.org

National Club Association
3050 K Street N, Suite 330
Washington, DC 20007
Tel: 202-625-2080
Fax: 202-625-9044
Website: www.natlclub.org

National Restaurant Association
1200 17th Street NW
Washington, DC 20036-3097
Tel: 800-424-5156
Fax: 202-289-3199
Website: www.restaurant.org

The Professional Convention Management Association
2301 South Lakeshore Drive, Suite 1001
Chicago, IL 60616-1419
McCormick Place-Lakeside Center
Tel: 312-423-7262
Fax: 312-423-7222
Website: www.pcma.org

Research and Development Associates for Military Food
  and Packaging Systems, Inc.
16607 Blanco Road, Suite 305
San Antonio, TX 78232
Tel: 210-493-8024
Website: www.militaryfood.org

Roundtable for Women in Foodservice
425 Central Park West, 2A
New York, NY 10025
Tel: 212-865-8100
Fax: 212-688-6457

Society for the Advancement of Foodservice Research
Conrad N. Hilton College of Hotel
  and Restaurant Management
University of Houston
Houston, TX 77204-3902
Tel: 713-743-2560
Fax: 713-743-2482
Website: www.hrm.uh.edu

Society for Foodservice Management
304 West Liberty Street, Suite 201
Louisville, KY 40202
Tel: 502-583-3783
Fax: 502-589-3602
Website: www.sfm-online.org

Technomic, Inc.
300 South Riverside Plaza, Suite 1940 South
Chicago, IL 60606
Tel: 312-876-0004
Fax: 312-876-1158
Website: www.technomic.com

Travel Industry Association of America
1100 New York Avenue NW, Suite 450
Washington, DC 20005-3934
Tel: 202-408-8422
Fax: 202-408-1255
Website: www.tia.org

PUBLICATIONS AND JOURNAL PUBLISHERS

*Activities Report and Minutes of Work Groups and Sub-Work Groups
    of the R&D Associates*
R&D Associates
16607 Blanco Road, Suite 305
San Antonio, TX 78232
Tel: 210-493-8024
Fax: 210-493-8036

Club Director
National Club Association
3050 K Street NW, Suite 330
Washington, DC 20007
Tel: 202-625-2080
Website: www.nationalclubassociation.org

Club Managers Association of America
1733 King Street
Alexandria, VA 22314
Tel: 703-739-9500
Fax: 703-739-0124
Website: www.cmaa.org

Club Management
Financial Publishing Company
8730 Big Bend Boulevard
St. Louis, MO 63119
Tel: 314-961-6644
Website: www.nationalclubassociation.org

Cornell Hotel & Restaurant Administration Quarterly
Elsevier Science Publishers
P.O. Box 882, Madison Square Station
New York, NY 10159
Tel: 212-633-3950
Website: www.hotelschool.cornell.edu/publications/hraq/

Food Executive
International Food Service Executive Association
1100 South State Road 7 #103
Margate, FL 33068
Tel: 305-977-0767
Website: www.ifsea.org

Food Institute
One Broadway
Elmwood Park, NJ 07407
Tel: (201) 791-5570
Fax: (201) 791-5222
Website: www.foodinstitute.com

Food Management
Penton Publishing
1100 Superior Avenue
Cleveland, OH 44114
Tel: 800-659-5251

Food Technology
Institute of Food Technologists
Subscription Department
221 North LaSalle Street, Suite 300
Chicago, IL 60601
Tel: 312-782-8424
Website: www.ift.org

Foodservice Consultants Society International
304 West Liberty Street, Suite 301
Louisville, KY 40202
Tel: 502-583-3783
Website: www.fcsi.org

Foodservice Research International
Food and Nutrition Press
6527 Main Street
Trumbull, CT 06611
Tel: 203-261-8587
Fax: 203-261-9724
Website: www.foodscipress.com

Foodservice Director
Bill Communications, Inc.
355 Park Avenue South
New York, NY 10010
Tel: 212-592-6530

Health Care Management Review
Aspen Publishers, Inc.
7201 McKinney Circle
Frederick, MD 21701
Tel: 800-234-1660

HOTELS
2000 Clearwater Drive
Oak Brook, IL 60544-8809
Tel: 630-288-8260
Fax: 630-288-8265
Website: www.hotelsmag.com

Journal of the American Dietetic Association
American Dietetic Association
216 West Jackson Boulevard, Suite 800
Chicago, IL 60606-6995
Tel: 312-899-0040
Website: www.eatright.org

Journal of Child Nutrition and Management (online)
School Nutrition Association
    (formerly ASFSA)
700 South Washington Street, Suite 300
Alexandria, VA 22314
Tel: 800-877-8822
Fax: 703-739-3915
Website: www.schoolnutrition.org

Journal of Food Protection
Margaret Marble
502 East Lincoln Way
Ames, IA 50010-6666
Tel: 515-232-6699
Website: www.foodprotection.org

Journal of Food Science
Institute of Food Technologists
Subscription Dept.
221 North LaSalle Street, Suite 300
Chicago, IL 60601
Tel: 312-782-8424
Website: www.ift.org

Journal of Hospitality & Tourism Research
Sage Publications
2455 Teller Road
Thousand Oaks, CA 91320
Tel: 805-499-9774 or 800-818-7243
Fax: 805-499-0871 or 800-583-2665
Website: www.sagepub.com

Journal of Nutrition Education
Williams & Wilkins
428 East Preston Street
Baltimore, MD 21202
Tel: 800-638-6423
Website: www.jneb.org

Lodging Magazine
385 Oxford Valley Road, Suite 420
Yardley, PA 19067
Tel: 215-321-9662
Fax: 215-321-5124
Website: www.lodgingmagazine.com

National Restaurant News
Lebhar Freidman, Inc.
425 Park Avenue
New York, NY 10022
Tel: 800-447-7133
Website: www.nrn.com

Restaurant Hospitality
Penton Media, Inc.
1300 East 9th Street
Cleveland, OH 44114
Tel: 216-696-7000
Fax: 216-696-1752
Website: www.restaurant-hospitality.com

Restaurants and Institutions
Reed Business Information
2000 Clearwater Drive
Oak Brook, IL 60523
Tel: 630-288-8242
Fax: 630-288-8225
Website: www.rirrag.com

Restaurants USA
National Restaurant Association
1200 17th Street NW
Washington, DC 20036-3097
Tel: 202-331-5900
Website: www.restaurant.org

Smith Travel Research
735 East Main Street
Hendersonville, TN 37075
Tel: 615-824-8664
Fax: 615-824-3848
Website: www.smithtravelresearch.com

Training and Development
American Society for Training and Development
1640 King Street, P.O. Box 1443
Alexandria, VA 22313-2043
Tel: 703-683-8129
Website: www.astd.org

Appendix D

College Programs in Hospitality

Academie Internationale de Management (AIM)—Hotel Management—Paris, France
http://www.academy.fr

Academy of Travel and Tourism—New York, NY
http://www.naf.org/theacademies/travel

Alexandria Technical College—Hotel & Restaurant Management Program—Alexandria, MN
http://www.alextech.org/hotelrestaurant

Arkansas Tech University—Hospitality Administration—Russellville, AR
http://www.atu.edu

Art Institutes International Minnesota—Culinary Arts—Minneapolis, MN
http://www.aim.artinstitutes.edu

Asheville-Buncombe Technical Community College—Dept. of Hospitality Education—Asheville, NC
http://www.asheville.cc.nc.us/bh/hospitality/Default.asp

Blue Mountains Hotel School—Tourism & Hospitality Management—Leura, Australia
http://www.hotelschool.com.au

Borough of Manhattan Community College—New York, NY
http://www.bmcc.cuny.edu

Boston University—School of Hospitality Administration—Boston, MA
http://www.bu.edu/hospitality/

Canadian Tourism College—College of Tourism & Hospitality Management—
Vancouver, BC, Canada
http://www.tourismcollege.com

Cecil B. Day School of Hospitality Administration—Georgia State University—
Atlanta, GA
http://robinson.gsu.edu/hospitality

Champlain College—Hospitality Industry Management Program—Burlington, VT
http://www.champlain.edu/majors/hospitality

Chemeketa Community College—Hospitality Systems Management Program—
Salem, OR
http://www.hsm.org

College of Charleston—Hospitality & Tourism Management—Charleston, SC
http://www.cofc.edu/~baecon/tourism.htm

Columbus State Community College—Hospitality Management—Columbus, OH
http://www.cscc.edu/hospitality

Conrad N. Hilton College of Hotel and Restaurant Management Program—
Houston, TX
http://www.MHMOnLine.uh.edu

Cornell University—School of Hotel Administration—Ithaca, NY
http://www.hotelschool.cornell.edu

Culinary Institute Of America (CIA)—Hyde Park, NY
http://www.ciachef.edu

Culinary School of the Rockies—Professional Culinary Arts Programs—
Boulder, CO
http://www.culinaryschoolrockies.com

Dedman School of Hospitality—Tallahassee, FL
http://www.cob.fsu.edu/ha

Delaware State University—Hospitality & Tourism Management—Dover, DE
http://www.crmdsc.com

Douglas College—Hotel and Restaurant Management Diploma Program—
Coquitlam, BC, Canada
http://www.douglas.bc.ca

East Carolina University—Dept. of Nutrition & Hospitality Management—
Greenville, NC
http://www.ecu.edu/hes/nuhm/NUHMhome.htm

Eastern Michigan University—Hotel and Restaurant Management—Ypsilanti, MI
http://www.emich.edu/public/hecr

Emirates Academy of Hospitality Management—Dubai, United Arab Emirates
http://www.emiratesacademy.edu

ESHOTEL—Ecole Supérieure de Gestion Hôtelière et de Tourisme—Paris/Lille,
France
http://www.eshotel.fr

Fairleigh Dickinson University—International School of Hospitality & Tourism
Management—Teaneck, NJ
http://www.fdu.edu

Florida Gulf Coast University—Resort & Hospitality Management (RHM)—
Fort Myers, FL
http://cps.fgcu.edu/resort

Florida International University—Hospitality/Tourism Management—North
Miami, FL
http://hospitality.fiu.edu

Foothill College—Travel Careers Program—Los Altos Hills, CA
http://bss.foothill.fhda.edu/tc

Fort Lewis College—School of Business Administration—Durango, CO
http://www.fortlewis.edu

Frederick Community College—Culinary & Hospitality Institute—Frederick, MD
http://www.frederick.edu

George Washington Univ.—Dept. of Tourism and Hospitality Management—
Washington, DC
http://www.gwutourism.org

Griffith University—School of Tourism and Hotel Management—Queensland,
Australia
http://www.gu.edu.au/school/thm

Hesser College—Assoc. of Business Science Degree: Travel & Tourism—Manchester, NH
http://www.hesser.edu

Highline Community College—Hotel & Tourism Management—Seattle, WA
http://flightline.highline.edu/hoteltourism

Hong Kong Polytechnic University's School of Hotel and Tourism Management (HTM)
http://www.polyu.edu.hk/~htm

Hotel School—Sydney, Australia
http://www.scu.edu.au/schools/tourism/hotel

Humber College—School of Hospitality, Recreation & Tourism—Toronto, Ontario, Canada
http://www.hrtalliance.com

Imperial Hotel Management College—Hotel Management School—Vancouver, BC, Canada
http://www.ihmc.ca

Indiana University-Purdue University (IPFW)—Hospitality & Tourism Management—Fort Wayne, IN
http://www.ipfw.edu/cfs/dinner1.htm

International College of Tourism & Hotel Management—Manly (Sydney), Australia
http://www.icthm.edu.au

International Hotel Management Institute and International Tourism Institute—Switzerland
http://www.imi-luzern.com

Iowa Lakes Community College—Travel and Tourism Management—Emmetsburg, IA
http://www.ilcc.cc.ia.us/ProgramsStudy/Technical/Hotel.htm
http://www.ilcc.cc.ia.us/ProgramsStudy/CareerOptions/Travel.htm

IUPUI—Department of Tourism, Conventions and Event Management—Indianapolis, IN
http://petm.iupui.edu

J. Sargeant Reynolds Community College—School of Hospitality and Tourism—Richmond, VA
http://old.jsr.cc.va.us/dtcbusdiv/hospitality

Johnson State College, Hospitality & Tourism Management—Johnson, VT
http://www.johnsonstatecollege.edu/academics/257.html

Johnson & Wales University—Hospitality College—North Miami, FL
http://www.jwu.edu/florida

Kemmons Wilson School of Hospitality & Resort Management—University of Memphis—Memphis, TN
http://memphis.edu/hospitality

Kendall College—Hospitality & Restaurant Management—Evanston, IL
http:www.kendall.edu

Lester E. Kabacoff School of Hotel, Restaurant & Tourism Administration—
University of New Orleans, LA
http://www.uno.edu/~hrt

Lexington College—Hospitality Management—Chicago, IL
http://www.lexingtoncollege.edu

Lincoln University—Hotel & Institutional Management—Lincoln (Canterbury),
New Zealand
http://www.lincoln.ac.nz/study/areas/him.htm

Mercyhurst College—Hotel, Restaurant & Institutional Management Dept.
(HRIM)—Erie, PA
http://www.mercyhurst.edu

Metro Community College—Tourism Career Programs—Edmonton, Alberta,
Canada
http://www.metrocommunitycollege.ca

Miami Dade Community College—Hospitality Management Program—
Miami, FL
http://www.mdcc.edu

Michigan Licensed Beverage Association—National Hospitality Institute—East
Lansing, MI
http://www.mlba.org

Michigan State University—The School of Hospitality Business—East Lansing, MI
http://www.bus.msu.edu/shb

Montclair State University—Commercial Recreation, Tourism & Hospitality
Management—Upper Montclair, NJ
http://www.montclair.edu

National Schools—National Culinary & Bakery School—La Mesa, CA
http://www.nationalschools.com

New England Culinary Institute (NECI)—Hospitality Education Programs—
Montpelier, VT
http://www.neculinary.com

New York University, Tisch Center for Hospitality, Tourism & Travel Administration—New York, NY
http://www.scps.nyu.edu/dyncon/hosp

Niagara University—College of Hospitality and Tourism Management—
Niagara Falls, NY
http://www.niagara.edu/hospitality

Normandale Community College—Tourism & Hospitality Management—
Bloomington, MN
http://www.normandale.edu

North Carolina Central University—Hospitality and Tourism Program—
Durham, NC
http://www.nccu.edu/Academics/More_Services/ewsp.shtml

Northeastern State University—Meetings and Destination Management—
Tahlequah, OK
http://arapaho.nsuok.edu/~mdm

Northern Alberta Institute of Technology (NAIT)—Hospitality Management—
Alberta, Canada
http://www.nait.ab.ca/schools/hospitality

Northern Arizona University—School of Hotel & Restaurant Management—
Flagstaff, AZ
http://www.nau.edu/hrm

Northwestern Business College—Chicago, IL
http://www.northwesternbc.edu/cf-
dbm/careeropps/careeroppspages.cfm?page=hospitality

Oklahoma State University—School of Hotel and Restaurant Administration—
Stillwater, OK
http://www.osuhrad.com

Penn State—School of Hotel, Restaurant, and Recreation Management—
University Park, PA
http://www.hrrm.psu.edu

Professional Development Institute of Tourism (PDIT)—Parksville, BC, Canada
http://www.pdit.ca

Purdue University—Department of Hospitality and Tourism Management—
West Lafayette, IN
http://www.cfs.purdue.edu/htm

Red Deer College—Hospitality & Tourism Program—Red Deer, Alberta, Canada
http://www2.rdc.ab.ca/hospitality

Richland College—Travel, Exposition and Meeting Management Program—
Dallas, TX
http://www.rlc.dcccd.edu/HAD/temmhome/temmhome.html

Robert Morris University—Hospitality and Tourism Programs—Pittsburgh, PA
http://www.rmu.edu

Rochester Institute of Technology—School of Hospitality & Service Management—Rochester, NY
http://www.rit.edu

Roosevelt University—Steinfeld School of Hospitality & Tourism Management—Chicago, IL
http://www.roosevelt.edu/academics/etsuc/hosm.htm

Rosen School of Hospitality Management—University of Central Florida—Orlando, FL
http://www.hospitality.ucf.edu

San Diego State University, Hospitality and Tourism Management Program—San Diego, CA
http://www.sdsu.edu/business/htm

Schiller International University—Hotel Management University—Engelberg, Switzerland
http://www.schiller-university.ch

Seneca College—Centre for Tourism and Leisure Studies—King City, Ontario, Canada
http://www.senecac.on.ca/tourism

Seton Hill University—Bachelor of Science in Hospitality and Tourism—Greensburg, PA
http://www.setonhill.edu

Sinclair Community College—Hospitality Programs—Dayton, OH
http://www.sinclair.edu

Southern Cross University—New South Wales, Australia
http://www.scu.edu.au/schools/tourism/

Southern Illinois University Carbondale—Hospitality and Tourism—Carbondale, IL
http://siu.edu/departments/coagr/animal/ht

St. Cloud State University—Travel and Tourism Program—St. Cloud, MN
http://www.condor.stcloudstate.edu/~geog/

Sullivan County Community College—Division of Business & Culinary—Loch Sheldrake, NY
http://www.sullivan.suny.edu

Sullivan University—National Center For Hospitality Studies—Louisville, KY
http://www.sullivan.edu/nchs

SUNY College of Agriculture/Technology—Culinary Arts, Hospitality & Tourism—Cobleskill, NY
http://www.cobleskill.edu

SUNY College of Technology at Delhi—Hospitality Programs (inc. F&B)—Delhi, NY
http://www.delhi.edu

Temple University—School of Tourism & Hospitality Management (STHM)—Philadelphia, PA
http://www.temple.edu/sthm

Texas Tech University—Restaurant, Hotel & Institutional Management—Lubbock, TX
http://www.hs.ttu.edu/enrhm/rhim

Travelcampus—Education Systems—Salt Lake City, UT
http://www.travelcampus.com

University of Arkansas, Fayetteville—Hospitality & Restaurant Management—Fayetteville, AR
http://www.uark.edu/depts/hesweb/fdnh/hosprest.html

University of Calgary—World Tourism Education and Research Centre—Calgary, Alberta, Canada
http://www.haskayne.ucalgary.ca/tourism

University of Colorado at Boulder—Tourism Management Program—Boulder, CO
http://www.sustainabletourism.org

University of Delaware "HRIM"—Newark, DE
http://www.udel.edu/HRIM/home.html

University of Denver—School of Hotel, Restaurant and Tourism Management—Denver, CO
http://www.daniels.du.edu/hrtm

University of Guelph—School of Hospitality & Tourism Management—Guelph, Ontario, Canada
http://www.htm.uoguelph.ca

University of Hawaii–Manoa—School of Travel Industry Management—Honolulu, Hawaii
http://www.tim.hawaii.edu

University of Massachusetts—Department of Hospitality & Tourism Management—Amherst, MA
http://www.umass.edu/hrta

University of Missouri–Columbia—Hotel & Restaurant Management—Columbia, MO
http://www.fse.missouri.edu/hrm

University of Nebraska at Kearney—Travel & Tourism—Kearney, NE
http://www.unk.edu/acad/hperls/travel.html

University of Nevada, Las Vegas—Harrah College of Hotel Administration—Las Vegas, NV
http://hotel.unlv.edu

University of New Brunswick—Bachelor of Applied Management in Hospitality/Tourism—New Brunswick, Canada
http://business.unbsj.ca/bamht/welcome.html

University of New Hampshire—Department of Hospitality Management—Durham, NH
http://orbit.unh.edu/dhm

University of New Mexico—Travel & Tourism Management—Albuquerque, NM
http://traveltourism.mgt.unm.edu

University of North Texas—Hospitality Management—Denton, TX
http://www.smhm.unt.edu

University of San Francisco—Hospitality Management Program—San Francisco, CA
http://www.usfca.edu/sobam/under/hosp/hospitality.html

University of South Florida/Sarasota–Manatee—B/S in Hospitality Management—Sarasota, FL
http://www.sarasota.usf.edu

University of Tennessee—Consumer and Industry Services Management—Knoxville, TN
http://trcs.he.utk.edu

University of Wisconsin–Stout—Hotel, Restaurant & Tourism Management—Menomonie, WI
http://www.uwstout.edu

Virginia State University—Hospitality Management Program—Petersburg, VA
http://www.vsu.edu

Virginia Tech—Hospitality and Tourism Management—Blacksburg, VA
http://www.cob.vt.edu/htm

Washburne Culinary Institute—Culinary Arts—Chicago, IL
http://www.ccc.edu/washburne

Washington State University—School of Hospitality Business Management—
Pullman, WA
http://www.cbe.wsu.edu/departments/hra

Widener University—School of Hospitality Management—Chester, PA
http://www.widener.edu/soh

William Rainey Harper College—Hospitality Management—Palatine, IL
http://www.harpercollege.edu/academics/career/hm.htm

Appendix E

Annotated Bibliography

AIRLINES

Markus, F. "Competition between network carriers and low-cost carriers—retreat battle or breakthrough to a new level of efficiency?" *Journal of Air Transport Management*, 10.1 (2004), 15–21.

<http://www.sciencedirect.com/science?_ob=MImg&_imagekey=B6VGP-4B4RRNS-2-F&_cdi=6044&_orig=search&_coverDate=01%2F31%2F2004&_sk=999899998&view=c&wchp=dGLbVzz-zSkzk&_acct=C000015498&_version=1&_userid=260508&md5=6f9506afbd5ca2d5722edc3b1eef86c3&ie=f.pdf>.

In the authors' view, the crisis of the global aviation industry grew out of a temporary revenue "bubble" after the first Iraq war, leading to historically high airline profits and major capacity expansions. After the end of the 1990s, an economic downturn and a fear of terrorism resulted in massive overcapacities, with yields returning to long-term decline. This article analyzes the key drivers of the current transition and outlines a vision of advanced airline business models that might lead to a new era of equilibrium.

CRUISE LINES

Carnival News. Carnival Launches New On-Line Embarkation Portal. *Carnival News*. 23 December 2003

<http://www.carnival.com/CCLNews/NewsDesk.asp?page=2&type=cclnews>.

To comply with the new data-gathering requirements by the U.S. Department of Homeland Security (DHS), Carnival Cruise Lines has established a new online embarkation portal that enables guests to submit the required information for their upcoming "Fun Ship" cruise. The new system was launched November 25, 2003, and was in effect for all Carnival departures beginning December 15, 2003.

Doidge, Jennifer. "Expedia Charts Cruising Trends and Unique Customer Stories at Sea During 'Wave Period'." PR Newswire. 1 April 2004.

This article looks at some new trends in the cruise industry, where cruises to the Caribbean, Europe, and Alaska all are regaining customer interest.

Marti, B.E. "Trends in world and extended-length cruising (1985–2002)." *Marine Policy*, in press. 19 November 2003

<http://www.sciencedirect.com/science?_ob=QuickSearchListURL&_me thod=list&_aset=W-WA-A-A-EV-MsSAYWA-UUW-AUDVDUVWYY-AEZU DWWYA-EV-U&_sort=d&view=c&_st=13&_acct=C000015498&_ version=1&_userid=260508&md5=bf6923ef34a74f73f8f55cb507c53ee2>.

A comparative empirical analysis identifies and reviews the status and trends of the world and extended-cruise markets. It also tests and supports three broad hypotheses regarding cruise ship attributes and cruise characteristics.

Stieghorst, T., & Ridder, K. "Hotels Outpacing Airlines and Cruises with Internet Bookings." *Hotel Online*.

<http://www.hotel-online.com/News/PR2003_3rd/Jul03_Internet BookingStats.html>.

Credit Suisse First Boston predicts that by 2006, the share of cruises sold by travel agents will fall from 90 percent to 60 percent. The report forecasts that one-fourth of cruises will be sold directly over the phone or online by the cruise companies, while 15 percent will come from online travel agencies.

Wood, R.E. "Caribbean cruise tourism: Globalization at sea." *Annals of Tourism Research*, 27.2 (2000), 345–370.

<http://www.sciencedirect.com/science?_ob=MImg&_imagekey=B6V7Y-3Y6H0P7-5-1&_cdi=5855&_orig=search&_coverDate=04%2F30%2F 2000&_sk=999729997&view=c&wchp=dGLbVtz-zSkWz&_acct= C000015498&_version=1&_userid=260508&md5=a6b61bec72ceffdec23 1d81e344788d9&ie=f.pdf>.

After documenting the rapid expansion of Caribbean cruise tourism, the paper explores manifestations of globalization at work in this industry.

The author asserts that "globalization at sea" illustrates the contradictions, ambiguities, and uncharted course of contemporary globalization processes.

GENERAL TRENDS

Blair, A.R., Nachtmann, R., Saaty, T.L., & Whitaker, R. "Forecasting the resurgence of the US economy in 2001: An expert judgment approach." *Socio-Economic Planning Sciences,* 36.2, (2002), 77–91.

<http://www.sciencedirect.com/science?_ob=MImg&_imagekey=B6V6Y-44B2232-3-3&_cdi=5827&_orig=search&_coverDate=06%2F30%2F2002&_sk=999639997&view=c&wchp=dGLbVzz-zSkzk&_acct=C000015498&_version=1&_userid=260508&md5=600a67fa94a93f6d9fe252d994805a24&ie=f.pdf>.

This paper, written early in 2001, describes a forecast of the date for the resumption of growth of the U.S. economy. It uses an expert judgment approach within the framework of decision theory, the Analytic Hierarchy Process, as well as its generalization to dependence and feedback, the Analytic Network Process. Though its conclusions were invalidated by the terrorist attacks of September 11, 2001, the study provides a valuable example of the forecasting techniques.

"Bush Deficit Reduction Plan Criticized." Associated Press. 18 December 2003 <http://www.foxnews.com/story/0,2933,106122,00.html>.

President Bush's goal of halving 2003's projected $500 billion deficit by 2009 distracts from the more serious crunch the government faces later as the huge Baby Boom generation ages, critics say.

Mohammad, A. "Urbanization by implosion." *Habitat International,* 28.1 (2004), 1–12.

<http://www.sciencedirect.com/science?_ob=MImg&_imagekey=B6V9H-49DFBKH-1-7&_cdi=5899&_orig=search&_coverDate=03%2F31%2F2004&_sk=999719998&view=c&wchp=dGLbVlb-zSkWb&_acct=C000015498&_version=1&_userid=260508&md5=e5b11d3cecf8846ba3c4a823f1b6d623&ie=f.pdf>.

Rural parts of the Third World are becoming urbanized through in-place growth of population producing densities that equal or surpass the urban threshold of 400 persons per km^2. This level of density may or may not bring about social, economic, or local government institutions associated with the urban living, but it surely recasts settlement patterns, land tenure systems, and demand for facilities and services in urban modes. This spatial urbanization is building up another urban crisis that remains unnoticed. It is another frontier opening up for urban planning in the twenty-first century.

Murray, A. "Mortgage rates hit 40-year low." Eagle-Tribune Publishing. 27 September 2002.

<http://www.eagletribune.com/news/stories/20020927/FP_001.htm>.

The average interest rate on a 30-year mortgage has dropped below 6 percent for the first time in 40 years, triggering a torrent of refinancing applications from local homeowners seeking to reduce their mortgage payments.

Ommeren, J., Rietveld, P., & Nijkamp, P. "A model of workplace and residence choice in two-worker households." *Regional Science and Urban Economics,* 27.1 (2002), 30–40.

<http://www.sciencedirect.com/science?_ob=MImg&_imagekey=B6VCT-44SHF9C-8-4F&_cdi=5963&_orig=search&_coverDate=03%2F16%2F2002&_sk=998629996&view=c&wchp=dGLbVzz-zSkWA&_acct=C000015498&_version=1&_userid=260508&md5=6af7af2f58f48fd2fafac62564812626&ie=f.pdf>.

Evidence from five cities shows that women's earnings opportunities and commuting burdens influence not only the wife's choice of workplace but the husband's job site and the household residence as well. Where strong downtown economies offer attractive earnings opportunities for professional women, wives' uninterrupted professional careers encourage the choice of central jobs for both spouses and a central residence.

United States Census Bureau. *Population Profile of the United States.* 23 December 2003

http://www.census.gov/population/pop-profile/2000/chap02.pdf

This article provides data on population distribution and composition across the United States in 2000.

Vincent, M. "Scientists prove humans are living longer." *The World Today.* 29 September 2000

<http://www.abc.net.au/worldtoday/s193207.htm>.

Among a group of people born every year in Sweden, the oldest age for the group is increasing, thanks to better treatment of chronic disease in old age and the reduction of death rates earlier in life.

Zhou, W., & Sornette, D. "2000–2003 real estate bubble in the UK but not in the USA." *Physica A: Statistical Mechanics and its Applications,* 329.1-2 (2003), 249–263.

<http://www.sciencedirect.com/science?_ob=MImg&_imagekey=B6TVG-492W066-8-39&_cdi=5534&_orig=search&_coverDate=11%2F01%2F2003&_sk=996709998&view=c&wchp=dGLbVzb-zSkWb&_acct=C000015498&_version=1&_userid=260508&md5=0ba2c4a5d2c226175f997e6eb17734d8&ie=f.pdf>.

There is growing concern that historically low interest rates in the United States are creating a bubble in real estate, as strong housing demand is fuelled by historically low mortgage rates. The authors rule out this possibility for the United States but find evidence of a strong, unsustainable bubble in Britain.

TECHNOLOGY

Ayres, R.U., & Williams, E. "The digital economy: Where do we stand?" *Technological Forecasting and Social Change,* in press. 14 January 2004

<http://www.sciencedirect.com/science?_ob=MImg&_imagekey=B6V71-4BFVRP7-1-1&_cdi=5829&_orig=search&_coverDate=01%2F14%2F2004&_sk=999999999&view=c&wchp=dGLbVlb-zSkzV&_acct=C000015498&_version=1&_userid=260508&md5=de389c8436bdea25b2b7c74d1a964e5d&ie=f.pdf>.

This article surveys the converging innovations that produced the digital economy and looks ahead to the new "killer apps" that could stimulate a new round of growth. Possibilities include interactive video-on-demand and telecalls/teleconferencing. However, providing such high-bandwidth services will probably require new networking protocols and changes in the economic model of information transfer via the Net.

Credé, M., & Sniezek, J.A. "Group judgment processes and outcomes in video-conferencing versus face-to-face groups." *International Journal of Human–Computer Studies,* 59.6 (2003), 875–897.

<http://www.sciencedirect.com/science?_ob=MImg&_imagekey=B6WGR-49RCDPY-2-2K&_cdi=6829&_orig=search&_coverDate=12%2F31%2F2003&_sk=999409993&view=c&wchp=dGLbVzz-zSkWW&_acct=C000015498&_version=1&_userid=260508&md5=ea37b4e16cb6889650789711fdddf775&ie=f.pdf>.

A sizable experiment found that small-group decisions made by video-conferencing were objectively as good as those made in face-to-face discussions, but left the participants feeling less confident about them. Implications for the design and application of advanced systems for decision-making support and research are discussed.

"E-procurement in the Hospitality Industry." December 2003. Accessed 14 March 2004.

<ftp://ftp.software.ibm.com/software/retail/marketing/fs/eprocurement_fsu_dec2003.pdf>.

E-procurement is a new phase in the inventory management of the food and beverage industry. While facilitating ordering and receiving, e-procurement is the new hot wave in getting business done. Better communication and greater control are the reasons behind this new trend.

Liu, Z. "Internet Tourism Marketing: Potential and Constraints." *Hotel Online.*

<http://www.hotel-online.com/Trends/ChiangMaiJun00/Internet Constraints.html>.

This paper examines the Internet as a marketing tool and the characteristics of the tourism industry, suggesting that the Internet is ideal for marketing tourism. The author concludes with a brief discussion of the major strategic issues in the implementation of Internet tourism marketing.

Long, R.L. "e-business—from the inside." *Hospitality Upgrade Magazine.* Summer 2000. 23 December 2003

<http://www.hospitalityupgrade.com/client/hu/articles.nsf/(Article Listings)/BEA6FB1ADFF1A40885256900006B6E47?OpenDocument &Flag=Hide&Selection=Article&Issue=Summer-2000>.

Republished by *Hotel Online.*

<http://www.hotel-online.com/News/PressReleases2000_3rd/Sept00 _EbusinessInside.html>.

Most companies in the hospitality industry have implemented intranets, but have not realized their true potential in terms of cost savings, employee productivity, and business effectiveness. This article explores internally focused initiatives by taking a look at "e-business from the inside."

"Over 39 Million Americans Booked Travel Using the Internet in 2002; Up 25% Over Last Year." *Hotel Online.*

<http://www.hotel-online.com/News/PR2002_4th/Dec02_Online Bookings.html>.

According to the Travel Industry Association of America's latest Travelers' Use of the Internet study, some 96 million travelers are currently using the Internet, while 64 million Americans used the Internet for actual travel planning in 2002. The rate of growth in the online travel planning market has slowed considerably, due to slower growth of "wired" households in the United States.

Wilde, S.J., Kelly, S.J., & Scott, D. "An exploratory investigation into e-tail image attributes important to repeat, Internet savvy customers." *Journal of Retailing and Consumer Services,* in press. 19 June 2003

<http://www.sciencedirect.com/science?_ob=MImg&_imagekey=B6VGN -48WB666-1-1&_cdi=6043&_orig=search&_coverDate= 06%2F19%2F2003&_sk=999999999&view=c&wchp=dGLbVtb-zSkWA& _acct=C000015498&_version=1&_userid=260508&md5=45dd0f8f9f3ed 9b5c86458a44c9e2f55&ie=f.pdf>.

This paper offers results from a study investigating e-tail store image attributes important to repeat, Internet savvy customers of a major Australian grocery e-tailer. Three components incorporating traditional and e-tail specific attributes were identified: core demands, institutional factors, and information.

HOTEL MANAGEMENT

Badinelli, R.D. "An optimal, dynamic policy for hotel yield management." *European Journal of Operational Research,* 121.3 (16 March 2000), 476–503.

<http://www.sciencedirect.com/science?_ob=MImg&_imagekey=B6VCT- 3YB4CWB-3-1&_cdi=5963&_orig=search&_coverDate=03%2F16%2 F2000&_sk=998789996&view=c&wchp=dGLbVlz-zSkWb&_acct= C000015498&_version=1&_userid=260508&md5=1d4f7345c898cc318a 3745a1d21e89c4&ie=f.pdf>.

Most research into the yield management problem has been based on simplifying assumptions about the demand process and heuristic decision rules. This paper gives a dynamic programming formulation of the problem that allows for general demand patterns and a policy that is based on time and the number of vacancies. Furthermore, this policy incorporates both revealed-price and hidden-price market behavior. This formulation has a simple, closed-form solution that can be efficiently computed. This model was developed specifically for small hotels.

Donaghy, K., McMahon, U., & McDowell, D. "Yield management: an overview." *International Journal of Hospitality Management,* 14.2 (1995), 139–150.

<http://www.sciencedirect.com/science?_ob=MImg&_imagekey=B6VBH -3Y45T3X-P-1&_cdi=5927&_orig=search&_coverDate=06%2F30%2 F1995&_sk=999859997&view=c&wchp=dGLbVtz-zSkWz&_acct= C000015498&_version=1&_userid=260508&md5=35721a88d3eb329118 3ec1cfa2c2fbb0&ie=f.pdf>.

The concept of yield management is reviewed, and the authors present a comprehensive structured operational framework for management in the hospitality industry, focusing on ten key areas. The article concludes with a look at the future of yield management and some areas for further research.

Luciani, S. "Implementing yield management in small and medium sized hotels: An investigation of obstacles and success factors in Florence hotels." *International Journal of Hospitality Management,* 18.2 (June 1999), 129–142.

<http://www.sciencedirect.com/science?_ob=MImg&_imagekey=B6VBH
-3WSMRP8-4-1&_cdi=5927&_orig=search&_coverDate=06%2
F30%2F1999&_sk=999819997&view=c&wchp=dGLbVlz-zSkWb&_acct
=C000015498&_version=1&_userid=260508&md5=5262eae1ba38e23cb
4b305667546a61d&ie=f.pdf>.

Where most authors deal with yield management for large businesses, this paper explains this technique as it applies to small- and medium-size hotels, whose managers are concerned primarily with surviving in a changing market. This article focuses on the situation in Florence, a city with characteristics that can be found in many other European cities.

O'Neill, J.W., & Lloyd-Jones, A.R. "Hotel values: In the aftermath of September 11, 2001." *The Cornell Hotel and Restaurant Administration Quarterly,* 42.6 (2001), 10–21.

<http://www.sciencedirect.com/science?_ob=MImg&_imagekey=B6V60-
45WG12K-4-1&_cdi=5800&_orig=search&_coverDate=12%2
F31%2F2001&_sk=999579993&view=c&wchp=dGLbVzb-zSkWb&
_acct=C000015498&_version=1&_userid=260508&md5=a6090ffb447ac
4246be051bfdc75d7ab&ie=f.pdf>.

This model of hotel values demonstrates the importance of maintaining solid fundamentals, such as occupancy percentage and average daily rate.

Sheldon, P.J. "The impact of technology on the hotel industry." *Tourism Management,* 4.4 (1983), 269–278.

<http://www.sciencedirect.com/science?_ob=ArticleURL&_aset=W-WA-
A-A-W-MsSAYVW-UUA-AUDWBDCWDE-AZWZEYBWZ-W-U&_rdoc=
2&_fmt=summary&_udi=B6V9R-45P18SD-MN&_coverDate=12%2
F31%2F1983&_cdi=5905&_orig=search&_st=13&_sort=d&view=
c&_acct=C000015498&_version=1&_urlVersion=0&_userid=
260508&md5=973a44e779bc1c67a86c392b28ec08df>.

This article discusses the use of front-office information-processing systems, telecommunications and teleconferencing, energy management, security systems, and other technologies in the lodging industry.

Sturman, M.C. "The hospitality industry one year since September 11, 2001: An introduction to this special-focus issue." *The Cornell Hotel and Restaurant Administration Quarterly*, 43.5 (2002), 7–10.

<http://www.sciencedirect.com/science?_ob=MImg&_imagekey=B6V60-47HJXT0-4-1&_cdi=5800&_orig=search&_coverDate=10%2F31%2F2002&_sk=999569994&view=c&wchp=dGLbVlz-zSkWb&_acct=C000015498&_version=1&_userid=260508&md5=337c7c50cde7bd3c4f3d5efe4b14c950&ie=f.pdf>.

The effects of 9/11 extend from personal experiences and reactions to distortions in the industry's business patterns, company policies, and government statutes.

RESTAURANTS

"Acting casual." *Prepared Foods*, 172.11 (November 2003), 22(1).

This article describes the growing segment of fast, casual restaurants that provide fresh foods.

Alison, A. "At Area Restaurants, Change is on the Menu." *Boston Globe*. 4 February 2004, Third Edition: E1.

This article looks at the trend of "reinventing" the menu to attract guests. It looks at what many big restaurants in the Boston area have done to reposition themselves in that market, changing the name, menu, and even décor of an entire restaurant.

Arnst, C. "Let Them Eat Cake—If They Want To." *Business Week*, 23 February (2004), 110.

The World Health Organization has made several proposals for governments to help them solve their citizens' weight problem, which include restriction on advertising and increased taxes on junk food. However, the U.S. views obesity as a personal responsibility.

"Beefing up foodservice: Despite flat foodservice sales in recent years, beef is poised for future growth." *Business and Industry*, 217.10 (October 2003), 34.

This article looks at why beef consumption may increase greatly in the future: It is a low-carb item high in protein and a healthy part of a regular diet if eaten in moderation.

Bindon, B.M., & Jones N.M. "Cattle supply, production systems and markets for Australian beef." *Australian Journal of Experimental Agriculture*, 41.7 (25 October 2003), 861(17).

The authors examine the effects of globalization and the increasing problem of diseases such as hoof and mouth and mad cow in markets such as Europe and the United States. They suggest that Australia will have an advantage in supplying these markets.

Britton, I. "Wining and dining." *Leisure Management,* 20.1 (2000), 50–52.

This article examines how current eating-out trends are likely to affect the future of restaurants. Trends are reported by frequency, by region, by food type, and by type of visit, whether during the evening or during the day.

Brumback, N. "Orient Express: Asian fast-casual in on the fast track, with more new players jumping on board." *Restaurant Business,* 15 January 2004, 42–43.

The Asian/noodle subsegment is growing twice as fast as the total fast-casual category—about 20 percent annually for the next three years, compared with 10 percent annual growth for all fast-casual. This article introduces several big Asian chain restaurants that are building their own brand and working hard on brand strategies.

Cadji, M. "The power of one: Miriam Cadji finds out how restaurant and bar chains have reacted since the public began to lose its appetite for brazen branding." *Design Week,* 18.23 (June 5, 2003), 16.

The author states that designers are being asked to walk a tightrope between maintaining a certain degree of familiarity in a tried and tested formula and avoiding a soulless, bland, branded look. Designers must find subtler ways of conveying the values their client aims to communicate.

"Chain Restaurant Trends—Chocolate Cake." DessertExperts.com. Accessed 14 March 2004.

<http://www.dessertexperts.com/trend.asp?ID=7>.

This article reports that chocolate cake has gained new popularity in the top 200 restaurant chains, defying the weight-conscious, low-carb trend.

Childs, N., & Maher, J. "Gender in food advertising to children: Boys eat first." *British Food Journal,* 105.7 (2003), 408–419.

Although food products are most often gender-neutral, a sample of food advertisements to children exhibits greater gender preference in presentation than a comparison sample of nonfood advertisements to children.

Cole, W. "Sweet Priorities." *Time,* 161.8 (24 February 2003), 67.

In a minor trend, a number of restaurants across the United States focus primarily on dessert.

Cortese, A. "An Ancient Drink, Newly Exalted." *Business Week,* 1 March 2004, 122.

Exotic teas are appearing in restaurants and shops, in part because of its reputation as an elixir. The tannins and vitamin in tea are believed to have potent antioxidant and antibacterial properties that can help combat cancer, heart disease, and many other diseases.

Cullen, L.T., "Have It Your Way." *Time,* 1 March 2004, 63.

This article states that "cook-it-yourself restaurants" are booming, as heartland diners discover its fun to play with food.

Dalin, S. "Are We There Yet?" *St. Louis Post-Dispatch,* 26 February 2004 C1

A restaurant in Missouri lets parents rent a portable DVD player that their children can use. The article also takes a brief look at some other "toys" that assist parents with having a nice, quiet meal, a trend that is becoming more and more common in the restaurant industry.

Daniel, J. "Do Fondue and Cigars Still Swing?" *Everyday Magazine,* 8 February 2004, E1.

This article profiles The Melting Pot, where this apparently dead trend is now coming to the forefront. It also briefly talks about the trend of cigars.

Dombkowski, D. "More diners today are eating fast slowly; Trend in fast food is making dining casual." *Sunday Telegram* (Worcester, MA), 21 December 2003.

This article examines "fast-casual" dining restaurants that are being segmented off from bigger chains. It looks in depth at Panera and what they are doing to attract people away from the other QSRs.

Druce, C., Wood, J., & Sims, F. "Trends in high places; Future trends in food, wine and restaurants? We asked the experts what they thought." *Restaurants & Institutions,* 19 February 2004, 36.

This article looks at trends for the future of new food items, wines, and organic foods for the restaurant, bar, and pub.

Eade, R. "What's hot (and not): We ask prominent chefs for their take on exciting food trends this year." *The Ottawa Citizen,* 7 January 2004, B4.

This article looks into trends being found in the Canadian restaurant industry that might easily be applied in the U.S. market. It talks about fresh ingredients such as herbs, poultry, beef, lamb, etc.

Ebbin, R. "Restaurateurs Cope With Tight Labor Market." *Restaurants USA.* September 2002.

The labor market has been the most pressing operational challenge for the restaurant industry for several years. Although the recent economic downturn pushed the unemployment rate up, the industry continues to experience a labor shortage.

ElBoghdady, D. "Takeout: They Take Out to You; More Casual-Dining Restaurants Begin Offering Curbside Service." *The Washington Post,* 13 September 2003, E01.

This article looks at the relatively new trend of curbside pickup from major chain restaurants such as Outback Steakhouse, Applebees, and Ruby Tuesday.

"Flavor trends in foodservice." *Food Beat,* 171.12 (December 2002), 20.

This article looks at many new trends that are occurring in the food service industry, from dips and appetizers to main course entrees. It also examines the burger versus vegetarian debate.

Godinez, V. "Chains tailor dishes to suit followers of latest diet trend." *Dallas Morning News,* 13 February 2004.

Many big chains are now adopting low-carb and other specialty requests/diets.

Josiam, B.M., & Monteiro, P.A. "Tandoori tastes: perceptions of Indian restaurants in America." *International Journal of Contemporary Hospitality Management,* 16.1 (2004), 18–26.

This article examines perceptions of the food and service in Indian restaurants and finds universal likes/dislikes as well as differential perceptions between ethnic groups. The authors discuss implications for researchers and operators of Indian restaurants.

Hochwald, Lambeth. "Dining out, eating organic a new trend in restaurants." *Natural Health,* February 2004, 31

An interview with Nora Pouillon, the owner of Restaurant Nora, the first of many organic restaurants certified by the U.S. Department of Agriculture's National Organic Program.

Horovitz, B. "You want ambiance with that?" *USA Today,* 30 October 2003, 3B.

McDonald's, Boston Market, Cheesecake Factory, and Ruby's Dinner and other fast-food chains are undergoing new market segmentation. They discuss what they are planning and what they are offering.

Hoover, L.V., Ketchen, D.J., Jr., & Combs, G.J. "Why restaurant firms franchise: An analysis of two possible explanations." *The Cornell Hotel and Restaurant Administration Quarterly,* 44.1 (February 2003), 9–16.

This article uses data from 91 large restaurant chains to identify two reasons for franchising: It resolves some outlet-monitoring problem created by expansion, and it gives the firm access to inexpensive capital.

"Implementation Trends and Strategic Growth of Restaurant IT: 5th Annual Restaurant Industry Technology Study." *Hospitality Technology Magazine.* (2003)

<http://www.htmagazine.com/2003_RTS/index.html>.

For the fourth time in five years the Restaurant Industry Technology Study finds that restaurateurs are predicting growing investment in information technologies. Topics include: IT investment culture, considerations for IT investment, IT strategy, communicating with technology, and conclusion and recommendations.

Johnson, N. "Low-carb menus at area eateries a response to growing demand." *South Bend Tribune,* 13 January 2004, C1.

This article looks at how restaurants are doing in response. It considers TGI Friday's and their new Atkins menu selections, but also Don Pablos, Ruby Tuesday, and Subway, all of which either have or plan to roll out low-carb menus.

Kant, K.A., & Graubard, B.I. "Eating out in America, 1987–2000: Trends and nutritional correlates." *Preventive Medicine,* in press. 3 December 2003.

<http://www.sciencedirect.com/science?_ob=MImg&_imagekey=B6WPG -4B3NM86-5-1&_cdi=6990&_orig=search&_coverDate=12%2 F03%2F2003&_sk=999999999&view=c&wchp=dGLbVlz-zSkzk&_acct= C000015498&_version=1&_userid=260508&md5=022c78995706e228b 282e10896a66cfd&ie=f.pdf>.

This study examined the increasing popularity of restaurant dining and its possible contribution to increasing adiposity of the American population. The results confirm that in 1999–2000, more Americans ate out, and ate out more frequently than in 1987 and 1992. Higher eating-out frequency was associated with adverse nutritional consequences including higher caloric intake.

Kauffman, M. "Sauce is OK, but hold the pasta; Trendy Low-Carb Diets Change Restaurants' Ways." *Hartford Courant,* 3 January 2004, A1.

This article looks at the new trend of low-carb diets in the restaurants. Many restaurants, and even pizza parlors, are adding Atkins and South Beach diet food items to their menus. This "specialty diet"/preparation may soon become a major trend in the industry.

Kim, K. "National Restaurant Association commends HHS for focus on nutrition education as solution to address obesity." National Restaurant Association. 12 March 2004

<http://www.restaurant.org/pressroom/pressrelease.cfm?ID=834>.

The National Restaurant Association plans to combat obesity with an aggressive effort to educate consumers about the importance of living a healthy lifestyle.

Kotis, M. III. "New restaurant trends provide entree into local markets." *Commercial Investment Real Estate Journal*, 22.3 (May/June 2003), 8.

Increasing municipal restrictions on development are a growing concern in the restaurant industry. Therefore, restaurants look at the regulatory environment first when entering a new market. More stringent planning standards are a product of local governments' desire to encourage smart growth and improve quality of life.

Macarthur, K. "Fast-food rethinks marketing; the fat police are taking names, and quick-service alters ad message, menu." *Advertising Age*, 74.26 (30 June 2003), S2.

This article looks at what QSRs are doing to convince increasingly wary consumers that fast food does not equal bad food. It also shows that while many of these companies are trying to change their image, that may not be necessary.

McCarthy, T. "The Four-Bite Feast: A graze craze catches on, serving up mini-meals that are full of flavor and easy on the wallet." *Time*, 162.16 (11 August 2003), 56.

"Grazing"—eating small portions of many different foods—is, as the author states, "the newest trend in food."

Macdonald, D. "Hot, Hot, Hot in 2004." *Florida Times-Union*, 1 January 2004, E-1.

This article gives food and beverage trends for the upcoming season: champagne, low-carb menus, Cuban and Puerto Rican influences, reduced portion size, more popular pork, and seating outside.

"McDonald's Restaurants Gone Wireless in Manhattan: Eat In and Log On." *TEKLatino*. 22 March 2003.

<http://teklatino.com/news/ennews/archives/00000057.shtml>.

This article states that high-speed Internet access is now growing in the quick-service foodservice establishments. With the business and leisure travel in urban areas, you can almost not afford to not keep up with the changes in technology.

Mclaughlin, L. "Fondue: Now It's Hip to Dip." *Time*, 161.6 (10 February 2003), 83.

The low-carb diet is causing a resurgence in Fondue restaurants, because cheese is an increasingly popular replacement for high-carb foods.

"Make it convenient to come." *The Economist* (US), 369.8354 (13 December 2003), 11.

This article looks into the rapid growth of the convenience food market, what restaurants are doing, and how grocery stores are responding by stocking hot and cold premade foods.

Markels, A. "Gourmet chain gangs." *U.S. News & World Report,* 8 March 2004, 76.

This article looks at the new trend toward "polished-casual" chains such as Bonefish Grill and The Cheesecake Factory, which are a step above TGI Friday's and Olive Garden.

Meler, M., & Cerovic, Z. "Food marketing in the function of tourist product development." *British Food Journal,* 105.3 (2003), 175–192.

This article views tourist products as combinations of goods and services. In food marketing, a guest is offered not only food and beverages but also a variety of immaterial satisfactions. These immaterial "partial tourist products" eventually will be manifested in an increase in the room-and-board and secondary expenditures.

Much, M. "Restaurant Trends, Panera, Krispy Kreme Downplay Diet Impact." *Investor's Business Daily,* 3 March 2004.

This interesting article looks at the fast-casual trend and how Panera and Krispy Kreme are meeting the Atkins diet craze. It shows numbers for growth for Krispy Kreme, Panera, and California Pizza Kitchen.

Nwogugu, M. "Corporate governance, strategy and corporations law: The case of Jack in the Box Inc." *Managerial Auditing Journal,* 19.1 (2004), 29–67.

This article looks at the impact of a number of trends on the restaurant and food service industries. These include demographic changes, advances in technology, growing competition, changes in labor laws, changes in food sourcing/purchasing, increasing regulation, and many other developments.

"Outlook for Restaurant Industry Positive as Restaurant Performance Index Remained Steady in December." U.S. Newswire. 30 January 2004.

The Restaurant Performance Index is increasing, and the Expectation Index has risen by over 0.6 percent.

Panitz, B. "Food Trends: Tracking What's Hot and What's Not." *Restaurants USA.* March 2000.

This article describes the upcoming trends in the restaurant industry, from Nuevo Latino to tapas, with interviews of people who are heavily invested in the field. It also warns that these "fads" can disappear just as rapidly as they appeared.

Perlik-Senior, A. "Drivers Wanted; Perpetual drive-thru upgrades help QSRs keep up with life in the fast lane." *Restaurants & Institutions,* 15 February 2004, 73.

This article looks at what the fast food and QSR community is doing to help improve its biggest moneymaker, "the drive-thru." It goes into depth on what many of the big chains are doing, how they plan on implementing change, and how it will affect them.

Perry, C. "Before there was Hard Rock. . . ." *Los Angeles Times*, 7 January 2004, F.1.

This article looks at new restaurant theme concept trends, emphasizing that while the themes may be new, one thing has not changed at all: They serve exotic, cutting-edge food.

Pethokoukis, J.M. "Bye-Bye, Burgers." *U.S. News & World Report*, 2 December 2002, 36.

This article says that stagnation in the fast-food industry may get worse before growth returns. It also looks at a few of the "quick-casual" restaurants that are giving the major players a run for the profits. These include Chipotle Mexican Grill, Baja Fresh Mexican Grill, and Panera Bread.

"Quickservice Restaurant Trends." National Restaurant Association. 20 April 2004.

<http://www.restaurant.org/research/qsr.cfm>.

According to this article, quickservice restaurants have reported an increase in hiring.

Richler, J. "Next on the menu: Simplicity seems to be the future trend in restaurants." *National Post*, 7 January 2004, AL02.

Menus and décor are being simplified, while quality receives greater attention at upscale restaurants.

Ricketson, L. "Now it's 'fast casual' for your dining pleasure." *Providence Business News*, 17.42 (3 February 2003), 3.

Rhode Islanders are trading in their greasy fast foods and restaurant reservations for quickly prepared, nutritious meals. "Fast-casual" eateries are now catching on in New England, as they have elsewhere.

Roberts, W.A, Jr. "Lost in the Translation." *Prepared Foods*, 172.2 (February 2003), 11(3).

Restaurants such as TGI Friday's and California Pizza Kitchen are putting their brand names on a growing number of products offered to the consumer via grocery stores instead of at the branded store.

Rojas, M. "Learning the fats about life." *The Journal News* (White Plains, NY), 8 March 2004.

This article considers McDonald's announcement that it would phase out its Super Size servings by the end of the year.

Scarpa, J. (2003). "Best Western." *Restaurant Business,* 15 October 2003, 1.

The article talks about the trend toward Southwest cuisine, listing menu items from Lonesome Dove Western Bistro, James Beard House, Red Sage, and Tejas. Even chain restaurants are following the trend.

Sheridan, M. "European Union: Though no longer the sole source of American culinary inspiration, Europe continues to export food trends worth savoring." *Restaurants & Institutions,* 112.28 (15 December 2002), 18(6).

This article looks at the trend of chefs traveling the world for new restaurants and bringing back ideas, ingredients, and new dishes to spice up American cuisine. Many chefs are able to take old-world classics and finely tune them to be more health- and taste-conscious.

Sloan, E. "Bet your bacon on breakfast." *Food Technology,* 57.1 (January 2003), 16.

Food manufacturers are introducing nontraditional items into the early-morning meal. In-home breakfasts continue to lose share to eating out, but 77 percent of all breakfasts are still eaten at home. The biggest news is in grab-and-go products like the $2.4B bar category, but soy and juice combinations are becoming more important. Restaurants are serving bigger portion sizes and more spicy flavors.

Soriano, J.M., Font, G., Molto, J.C., & Manes, J. "Enterotoxigenic staphylococci and their toxins in restaurant foods." *Trends in Food Science and Technology,* 13.2 (February 2002), 60–67.

This article presents an overview of the increasing threat of bacterial toxins in restaurant foods. It also reviews food poisoning outbreaks, principal sources of contamination, and food safety measures that can be applied to eliminate enterotoxigenic staphylococci in restaurant foods. This is a critical issue for restaurants in light of diseases affecting the beef and poultry divisions.

Sparks, B., Bowen, J., & Klag, S. "Restaurants and the tourist market." *International Journal of Contemporary Hospitality Management,* 15.1 (2003), 6–13.

This study finds that restaurants are an important factor in the choice of a holiday destination for some tourists. It also provides insight into how tourists select restaurants. Both destination marketers and restaurant managers will benefit from this work.

Steven, K. "Salad fad latest and greatest, new menu items, new restaurant location coming." *Charleston Daily Mail* (West Virginia), 1 October 2003, P1D.

This article looks at salads and other new menu items that are appearing on many QSRs menus. It cautions that some salads are more dangerous than a full-size burger with all the fixings.

Thompson, M.G. "Optimizing Restaurant-table Configuration: Specifying Combinable Tables." *The Cornell Hotel and Restaurant Administration Quarterly,* 44 (1 February 2003), 53–60.

The author suggests that restaurant managers should know how best to combine tables to ensure service level and maximize revenue during peak hours. Knowing the number of different-sized combinable tables to have on hand is by far the most important determinant of capacity optimization. The article focuses on walk-in restaurants.

Turner, M. "'Waiter, Hold the Carbs, Please.'" *News & Record* (Greensboro, NC), 11 February 2004, D1.

This particular article looks at the low-carb trend from a different standpoint. It looks at what both chain and nonchain restaurants were and are doing to accommodate guests with low-carb requests.

Witkowski, T.H., Ma, Y., & Zheng, D. "Cross-cultural influences on brand identity impressions: KFC in China and the United States." *Asia Pacific Journal of Marketing and Logistics,* 15.1 (2003), 74–88.

This research measured and compared the brand identity of Kentucky Fried Chicken (KFC) in China and the United States. The Chinese had much more positive impressions of KFC than their U.S. counterparts. Brand identity impressions were correlated with overall customer satisfaction and future patronage intentions for both groups, but much more so for the Americans.

Wolf, B.D. "Catering To the Low-Carb Crowd." *Columbus Dispatch,* 25 January 2004, O1F.

This article talks about the low-carb craze. One consultant says that it may be essential for restaurants to offer low-carb items.

Wootan, M., & Berman, R. "Should chain restaurants be required to publish nutrition labels on their menus?" *CQ Researcher,* 13.4 (31 January 2003), 95(12).

This article is part of a series debating the issue of including nutritional information on menus. It concludes that legislation will require this in the near future. The authors look at the current obesity problem in the United States and the issue of liability as it relates to restaurants.

Yee, L. "The Invisible Chef." *Restaurants & Institutions,* 113.10 (1 May 2003), 14.

This article suggests that restaurants based on chef-driven concepts and style may not be able to survive. Because of high turnover, restaurants must focus more on their own definition and style rather than on a particular chef.

SECURITY

Caplan, H. "War and Terrorism Insurance: How to Promote Long-Term International Stability and Affordability." *Air and Space Law*, 29.1 (February 2004), 3–28.

This article suggests that leading economies can lay foundations for a comprehensive international structure of stable and affordable insurance for war and terrorism risks covering all classes of personal and commercial insurance business. A Draft Convention is submitted as a focus for discussion.

Hall, H.V. *Terrorism Strategies for Intervention*. New York. Haworth Press, 2004.

Written for threat-assessment professionals in the post-9/11 era, this timely book will help you understand the motivation to commit acts of terror, the thinking patterns common to many terrorists, the psychology of Muslim fundamentalists, methods for predicting the likelihood of chemical/biological attacks, and a great deal more.

Jürgensen, A. "Terrorism, Civil Liberties, and Preventive Approaches to Technology: The Difficult Choices Western Societies Face in the War on Terrorism." *Bulletin of Science, Technology & Society*, 24.1 (February 2004), 55–59.

Expanding the law enforcement and surveillance authority of governments to combat terrorism undermines the freedoms and civil liberties necessary to democratic institutions. An alternative might target high-risk technologies vulnerable to terrorism, such as civilian airlines and nuclear reactors, and protect civil liberties by reducing or eliminating their use.

Lepp, A., & Gibson, H. "Tourist roles, perceived risk and international tourism." Thesis, University of Florida.

International tourists can be classified according to the degree of novelty and familiarity sought. This study investigated the hypothesis that tourists seeking familiarity would perceive higher levels of risk associated with international tourism than those seeking novelty. Women perceived a greater degree of risk regarding health and food, while more experienced tourists downplayed the threat of terrorism. However, tourists' role was the most significant variable, with familiarity seekers being the most risk-adverse.

MacGeoch, A. "Terrorism: Who's Liable? The Legal Status of Hotel Owners and Management Companies." *Hotel Online*. <http://www.hotel-online.com/News/PR2003_4th/Oct03_Terrorism Liability.html>.

This article considers the liability of owners and operators for terrorist risks in a typical hotel-management contract. *Force majeure* provisions and "damage, destruction, and condemnation" clauses have become crucial in allocating the respective liabilities of an owner and an operator following a terrorist attack.

Mankin, L.D., & Perry, R.W. "Commentary: Terrorism Challenges for Human Resource Management." *Review of Public Personnel Administration,* 24.1 (March 2004), 3–17.

This article addresses changes in the U.S. government since 9/11 from the standpoint of human resource management. It covers both changes in the environment in which public organizations operate and how to cope with behaviors that can be reasonably expected from employees exposed to terrorist incidents.

Nunn, S. "Seeking tools for the war on terror: A critical assessment of emerging technologies in law enforcement." *Policing: An International Journal of Police Strategies and Management,* 26.3 (2003), 454.

As the war on terrorism escalates, police agencies are using technologies that electronically scan individuals, structures, and vehicles to identify things hidden from public scrutiny. Public policy gaps arise when new systems give police sensory capabilities that fall outside existing procedural standards such as probable cause and reasonable suspicion. As these new technologies diffuse among police agencies, policies should be guided by questions about whether technologies work as designed, whether they are effective, and whether they accomplish antiterrorist and crime control objectives. Traditional rules for wiretapping can offer models for operating policies for the new scanning and imaging technologies.

Perry, R.W. "Municipal terrorism management in the United States." *Disaster Prevention and Management: An International Journal,* 12.3 (2003), 190.

Many cities, building on a federal program begun in 1997, have developed metropolitan medical response systems (MMRS) to address the consequences of terrorist incidents. The basic system design has been tested both through drills and incidents, including the attacks on the World Trade Center, and appears to function well. This paper describes the philosophy and elements of the MMRS model.

Rathmell, A. "Controlling Computer Network Operations." *Studies in Conflict and Terrorism,* 26.3 (2003), 215–232.

Efforts to control military use of computer network operations (CNO) through arms control or multilateral behavioral norms are being undermined by the failure of the leading powers to decide whether it is more important to exploit their CNO advantage for national security or to protect the global information environment on which it depends. In resolving this dilemma, strategists need to consider global interdependency and the role of the private sector.

Ridder, R. "Jakarta Bombing Likely to Harm Thai Tourism and Slow Recovery from SARS Scare." *Bangkok Post*, 7 August 2003. Republished by *Hotel Online*.

<http://www.hotel-online.com/News/PR2003_3rd/Aug03
_ThaiTourism.html>.

The car bombing at the JW Marriott Hotel in Jakarta raised concerns across the region that renewed terrorism fears would hurt investor confidence and economic growth, but the impact of the bombing on hotel-industry stock prices has been limited.

Sacco, K., Galletto, V., & Blanzieri, E. "How has the 9/11 terrorist attack influenced decision making?" *Applied Cognitive Psychology*, 17.9 (November/December 2003), 1113–1127.

Prospect theory is used to examine decision-making behavior since the September 11, 2001, terrorist attacks. The results show the emergence of two tendencies not seen during "normal" historical periods: a strong, long-term, lasting search for security when the outcome of a decision is perceived as a gain, and medium-term, risk-avoiding behavior in the loss domain.

Szyliowicz, J.S. "Aviation Security: Promise or Reality?" *Studies in Conflict and Terrorism*, 27.1 (2004), 47–63.

This article analyzes the state of aviation security as it existed prior to the 9/11 terrorist attacks and then evaluates the changes that have occurred since. It concludes that no overall systematic program has yet been put in place to deal with the threats that terrorism poses to the various elements of aviation.

Tzannatos, E.S. "A decision support system for the promotion of security in shipping." *Disaster Prevention and Management: An International Journal*, 12.3 (2003), 222.

Despite efforts to address the issues of maritime security, the shipping industry still lags in implementing security measures. A decision support system (DSS) for the promotion of security in shipping is presented.

Whisenant, W.A. "Using biometrics for sport venue management in a post 9/11 era." *Facilities*, 21.5/6 (2003), 134.

This paper assess technologies that may be used to assist venue operators in preempting a terrorist act or some other organized act of violence. This forecast focuses on biometric technologies. It includes both interviews with industry experts and a review of published and unpublished materials about biometrics.

TRAVEL AND TOURISM

Barrett, R. "Travelers Ready to Open Wallets: More consumers will venture farther from home, spend more in 2004, survey finds." *Milwaukee Journal Sentinel,* 10 November 2003.

< http://www.jsonline.com/bym/news/nov03/184025.asp>.

This article states that the number of vacationers planning to spend more than $5,000 on a vacation in 2004 is up nearly double from 2003's numbers. On average, a vacationer is expected to "spend $2,962 in 2004 on airfare, accommodations, sightseeing, meals, souvenirs, and other vacation expenses. That's up 37 percent from $2,163 in 2003."

Barrett, D., Jr. "Tourists want nature, wildlife official says; Jean Lafitte urged to develop lures." *Times-Picayune* (New Orleans), 9 October 2003, 11.

This article talks about a growing segment of the tourism industry, nature-based tourism.

Bercovici, J. "Adventure Travel Comes in From the Cold." Folio, 1 February 2004, 2.

<http://foliomag.com/strategies/marketing_adventure_travel_comes /index.html>.

This article looks at the gradual resurgence of adventure tourism as consumers recover from September 11, the market crash, wars in Afghanistan and Iraq, and the rise in terrorism. Using such words as "secret" and "hideaways," as is common in this market, lures tourists in need of a break.

Bodeen, C. "China an engine of growth for world tourism industry battered by terrorism, war and epidemics." Associated Press Worldstream. 19 October 2003.

This article reports that in 2001 China came in fifth in the world for tourism markets. By 2020, China is predicted to be the top destination for tourists. It is predicted to surpass France with over 130 million tourists.

Cahill, D. "Consumers Highly Inclined To Purchase Vacation Packages Online, But Frustrated With Lack of Flexibility in Planning." Business Wire. 17 December 2003.

This article states that consumers are increasingly open to purchasing vacation packages online, but frustrations with the lack of flexibility in the planning process have kept completion of such transactions low. The majority of consumers (68 percent) feel that they can assemble a better package on their own, and often do so at multiple sites.

Carmichael, T. "Americans Pick Their Favorite Romantic Destinations; National Geographic Traveler and Yahoo! Travel Survey Reveals Romantic Travel is on the Rise." Business Wire. 5 February 2004.

This article reports that 80 percent of Americans surveyed said they were planning to take a romantic vacation in 2004, compared to the 50 percent who went on one last year. It lists both the most romantic domestic and international locations.

Chapman, B. "Ready for the rebound: Many planners are cautiously optimistic for a better year in 2004." *Successful Meetings,* 52.13 (December 2002), 33.

This article says that "2004 could actually be a good year for the meetings business, as long as SARS, terrorism, and Wall Street don't interfere." It goes on to say, "Planners are seeing signs of increasing demand for meetings, and increasing budgets to fund them. They're just hoping that nothing happens to derail this progress."

De Lollis, B. "Corporate travel accounts go online." *USA Today,* 9 February 2004, 1B.

This article looks at attempts by Internet booking agencies to gain corporate accounts. It states that "Expedia, Orbitz and Travelocity have gained more than 2,000 business clients since they began chasing corporate accounts in late 2002, based on interviews with the three companies' executives."

Dezember, R. "Surfside Retail Areas Are New Shopping Meccas." Newhouse News Service. 3 March 2004.

Many contemporary beach resorts are turning into year-round shopping destinations. After Hurricane Frederic, Baldwin County, Florida, went from being an agricultural and fishing economy to a thriving shopping mecca.

Doonar, J. "Special Report—Travel: A state of independence." *Brand Strategy,* 4 December 2003, 26.

"Greater accessibility, cheaper flights, and online purchasing have changed the way people go on holiday," Doonar reports.

Doyle, P. "Tourism industry gearing up for busy year." *St. John's Telegram* (Newfoundland), 10 January 2004, B10.

This article looks at the resurgence of tourism to Newfoundland, Labrador, and Canada in general. Tourism is expected to increase in 2004, due in part to the 500th anniversary of the French presence in the area.

Gilden, J. "As the traveler's world changes, the agent's role does too." *Los Angeles Times*, 7 March 2004, L3.

This article looks at the tough time travel agents are facing as a result of 9/11, the Internet, and the economic slowdown. It advises that for making complex travel arrangements consumers should still seek the help of a travel agent.

Goodrich, J.N. "September 11, 2001 attack on America: A record of the immediate impacts and reactions in the USA travel and tourism industry." *Tourism Management*, 23.6 (2002), 573–580.

<http://www.sciencedirect.com/science?_ob=MImg&_imagekey=B6V9R-46081GP-4-1&_cdi=5905&_orig=search&_coverDate=12%2F31%2F2002&_sk=999769993&view=c&wchp=dGLbVzb-zSkWb&_acct=C000015498&_version=1&_userid=260508&md5=39e63e6af4c6755145701e8306c9087a&ie=f.pdf>.

This article reviews published reports of the September 11 attacks and discusses the impact of the terrorist event on the travel and tourism industry in the United States.

Greene, K. "Agents: Americans will travel more in 2004." *Telegraph Herald* (Dubuque, IA), 28 December 2003, A1.

In early 2004, for the first time since 9/11, there is an increase in all travel categories. "Americans will take 213.4 million trips this winter, an increase of 2.3 percent over last winter," Greene notes.

Hammond, R. "Forget the outdated idea of 'ecotourism'." *The Observer*, 28 March 2004, Observer Special Supplement, 2.

This article talks about the new trend in "eco-tourism" and delves into the idea of responsible travel and tourism.

Herndon, D. "America Seen Lagging in Tourism Recovery." *Newsday*, 23 November 2003, E04.

This article states that "While the rest of the world appears to be learning to cope with times of crisis, America is not expected to share in a travel recovery until 2005 at the soonest, according to forecasts presented earlier this month at London's annual World Travel Market. Ever fewer Americans have been traveling abroad each year, and fewer foreigners are coming to America."

Jaakson, R. "Beyond The Tourist Bubble?, Cruiseship Passengers in Port." *Annals of Tourism Research*, 31.1 (January 2004), 44–60.

Passengers from four cruise ships on port visits to Zihuatanejo, Mexico, were observed. The study shows that passenger activities in port fit into four patterns. The area in port visited was identified as a tourist bubble consisting of a core and a periphery. Strong boundary cues define this space.

Jones, C. "Increase in tourism spending bodes well for LV, official says." *Las Vegas Review-Journal*, 23 March 2004, 1D.

While this article uses Las Vegas as its primary example, it has some very good numbers for tourism as a whole. It goes into depth on the 3.5 percent increase of tourism industries sales, as well as air transportation and restaurant and bar sales.

Marble, A. "National Business Travel Association Releases 6th Annual Business Travel Cost Forecast." *Business Wire*. 14 October 2003.

This article looks at a study recently released by the National Business Travel Association (NBTA). The study indicates that business airfares will increase 5 percent, hotel rates by 3 percent, and corporate car rentals by 2 percent in 2004.

Marble, A. "Positive Economic Trends Seen Fueling Business Travel Upturn." *Business Wire*. 30 January 2004.

This article looks at another study by the NBTA. In this one, 71 percent of respondents feel that business travel will "rebound significantly in 2004 and into 2005, with more than half (54%) predicting the recovery to occur sometime this year."

Maria, A. "Tourism Malaysia's aggressive promotion in Jakarta paying off." *Business Times* (Malaysia), 15 December 2003, 2.

This article details how Malaysia is working to pull more tourists in from Jakarta, Indonesia, and other surrounding areas. It cites attractions such as a Formula 1 race and predicts that because of this and several other factors, the number of tourists visiting Malaysia will increase from 750,000 to 1.5 million this year.

Marta, S. "Corporate travel may hamper travel industry recovery." *Dallas Morning News*, 7 October 2003.

This article is different in that it looks at the trend of tighter travel spending by corporations, which the author suggests is actually harming the major players in travel. This in turn is making the entry into the market much easier for new low-cost carriers, taking more and more business from the major carriers.

"Nigeria; Tourism: an 'Untapped' Goldmine." *Africa News*, 29 November 2003.
This article looks at the untapped "gold mine" of Nigeria. The author states that Nigeria "has clearly been left to us to exploit since the government has set the ball rolling."

Obenour, W.L. "Understanding the meaning of the 'journey' to budget travelers." *International Journal of Tourism Research*, 6.1 (Jan./Feb. 2004), 1–15.
<http://www3.interscience.wiley.com/cgi-bin/fulltext/107583835/PDFSTART>.
The purpose of this study was to construct a better understanding of the significance of the journey to budget travelers. This research confirms the complexity, holistic reflections, and personal travel history associated with the journey. The participants' narratives indicated the primacy of personal authenticity instead of cultural authenticity.

Olsen, M.D., & Connolly, D.J. "Experience-based Travel: How Technology Is Changing the Hospitality Industry." *The Cornell Hotel and Restaurant Administration Quarterly*, 41.1 (2000), 30–40.
<http://www.sciencedirect.com/science?_ob=MImg&_imagekey=B6V60-40JG1FD-3-1&_cdi=5800&_orig=browse&_coverDate=02%2F29%2F2000&_sk=999589998&view=c&wchp=dGLbVzb-zSkWA&_acct=C000015498&_version=1&_userid=260508&md5=b9c38197ef289bc9b3966bab1d3eb3f3&ie=f.pdf>.
Two think tanks sponsored by the International Hotel and Restaurant Association examine the use of information technology to build customer satisfaction in the hospitality industry.

Rawls, L. "Tourism Making Strong Revival." *Palm Beach Post*, 13 December 2003, 10B.
This article shows that although Palm Beach County has not fully recovered from 9/11, the numbers show a great increase in travel to the region. Bed taxes have increased, as have occupancy rates and the number of passengers coming through Palm Beach Airport.

Sakaguchi, S. "JTB Publishes Survey Results on Travel Trends and Prospects for 2004." JCN Newswire. 20 January 2004.
This report of study results shows many good numbers for domestic and overseas travel, average expenditures, total travel, and average number of journeys. It then discusses those topics in depth.

Shattuck, H. "Minority travel surge mirrors industry outreach." *Houston Chronicle*, 25 January 2004, 4.
This article looks at the travel industry's outreach to minority travelers. It shows that during the 2000–2002 travel years, Hispanic American

travel increased by 20 percent, Asian American travel by 10 percent, and African American travel by 4 percent.

Sims, S. "The Fido Friendly Travel Club—Traveling with Your Dog Just Got Easier for this Growing Trend." *Business Wire*. 28 October 2003.

Traveling with your pooch is a growing trend, with 14 percent of all U.S. adults saying that they have taken their dog(s) with them on a trip of 50 miles or more away from home.

Smith, R. "Travel study predicting higher room rates in 2004." *Las Vegas Review-Journal*, 23 October 2003, 1D.

This article looks at the possibility of hotel room rates climbing in 2004. The author states that low supply growth suggests a recovery may begin in 2004 and build gradually over the course of the year.

Satler, G. "New York City Restaurants: Vernaculars of Global Designing." *Journal of Architectural Education*, 56.3 (1 February 2003), 27–32.

This paper explores some of the unique characteristics that define globalization and global cities through an investigation of recent design trends in New York City restaurants over the past fifteen years.

Tedeschi, B. "E-Commerce; If you are looking on an Internet discount site for a bargain hotel rate, look fast. The hotels are striking back." *New York Times*, 15 March 2004, C6.

According to this article, hotel properties are fighting back against online booking agents. To combat the rise of the e-travel agencies, hoteliers last year began investing more heavily in their own websites and started guaranteeing consumers that their sites would offer the same prices available anywhere else.

Thornton, K. "Orbitz Survey Reveals That Cost-Savings Tops the List of Business Travel Priorities for 2004." *PR Newswire*. 29 March 29, 2004.

Orbitz's study shows that the most important factor for business travelers is cost savings for their companies. The study also revealed that respondents choose to use an online travel booking agency 2 to 1 over more traditional methods.

"Tourists flocking to Australia in record numbers, figures show." Agence France Presse. 16 March 2004.

This article shows that the tourism market in Australia is increasing rapidly, with 420,200 international arrivals in January, up 6 percent on the same month last year.

Wadula, P. "Tourism body to spend R468m marketing SA." *Business Day* (South Africa), 23 March 2004, 2.

This article looks at the large sum South Africa is spending to try to attract more tourists to their growing country. The country already has 2 percent of the global tourism market, and tourism marketers there want to raise that number.

White, A.A. "American Express study reveals improved prospects for business travel industry in 2004." *Canada NewsWire*. 6 October 2003.

This article looks at the results of a study conducted by American Express. The firm's Global Business Travel Trends and Forecast for 2003–2004 indicates that the travel industry is showing strong signs of recovery. It warns, however, that this may raise prices for the business traveler later in 2004.

Wilson, E. "China tourism to triple in size over next 10 years; challenges remain." *AFX–Asia*. 14 October 2003.

This article looks at the tourism market in China. It shows that the Chinese economy has overcome the SARS epidemic, and the number of tourists visiting the country is set to triple in the next 10 years.

"Why Tourism to Business Is a Vital Attraction and Rising Profits." *Daily Post* (Liverpool), 13 November 2003, 4–5.

This article looks at the growing travel and tourism market in North and Mid Wales. According to the North Wales Hoteliers Association, business was up 8 to 10 percent in 2003.

Index